BLUEGRASS GENERATION

D1602603

MUSIC IN AMERICAN LIFE

*A list of books in the series appears
at the end of this book.*

BLUE GRASS GENERATION

A MEMOIR

NEIL V. ROSENBERG

Foreword by Gregory N. Reish

UNIVERSITY OF ILLINOIS PRESS
Urbana, Chicago, and Springfield

Publication of this book is supported by grants from
the Manfred Bukofzer Endowment of the American
Musicological Society, funded in part by the National
Endowment for the Humanities and the Andrew W. Mellon
Foundation, and from Memorial University of Newfoundland.

Library of Congress Cataloging-in-Publication Data
Names: Rosenberg, Neil V., author.
Title: Bluegrass generation: a memoir / Neil V. Rosenberg;
    foreword by Gregory N. Reish.
Description: Urbana: University of Illinois Press, [2018] |
    Series: Music in American life | Includes bibliographical
    references and index.
Identifiers: LCCN 2017049202| ISBN 9780252041761 (cloth
    : alk. paper) | ISBN 9780252083396 (pbk. : alk. paper) |
    ISBN 9780252050442 (ebook)
Subjects: LCSH: Rosenberg, Neil V. | Banjoists—United
    States—Biography. | Bluegrass musicians—United States—
    Biography. | Bluegrass music—1961–1970—History and
    criticism.
Classification: LCC ML419.R672 A3 2018 | DDC 781.642092
    [B] —dc23
LC record available at https://lccn.loc.gov/2017049202

Contents

Foreword

I MET NEIL ROSENBERG in September 2005 during the Bluegrass Symposium held at Western Kentucky University in Bowling Green. This was my first foray into bluegrass and country music scholarship after some ten years of musicological focus on twentieth-century European classical music. Though confident about my presentation on the roots of bluegrass guitar styles in prewar "hillbilly" music work, I was unusually nervous, fearing that my analytical approach and heavy reliance on my own transcriptions of well-known recordings would meet resistance from an audience of folklorists and historians, many of whom relished the music's oral tradition. Adding to my anxiety, the chair of my session was the most distinguished bluegrass historian in the field, Neil Rosenberg. He seemed to enjoy my presentation, but not knowing Neil I wasn't sure whether his supportive response was genuine, merely polite, or obligatory in his role as chair. The next day, Rosenberg gave the symposium's keynote address and, in the follow-up, was asked to reflect on promising developments in the field of bluegrass scholarship. To my delight and astonishment, he cited my presentation as a new model, one in which "serious" musical scholars turn their attention to this music that had been largely ignored by the previous generation of musicologists. It is no exaggeration, therefore, to state that Neil Rosenberg helped to set me on my path as a country and bluegrass scholar, and he has continued to offer his generous support since that first encounter.

Neil's work had already been an inspiration to me, from his seminal early article on the emergence of bluegrass, to his Bill Monroe discography, to his magisterial *Bluegrass: A History*, first published in 1985 and still the definitive broad look at the music's evolution. What makes these writings particularly important is not just their insight and instructiveness but the deep understanding that comes only from someone who was there. In the present memoir, Neil writes about generations: the musicians who forged bluegrass from prewar string band styles and the young folklorists like himself who helped both to shape and to document the creation of a genre. To those in my generation, who came to bluegrass after the advent of newgrass and the sea change initiated by *J. D. Crowe and the New South* (Rounder 0044, 1975), Neil's work fusing careful scholarship with firsthand accounts of Bill Monroe and most of the genre's other key figures was as essential to our perspective as the music itself.

This memoir recounts, in marvelous and breathtaking detail, just how truly Neil Rosenberg was the right person in the right place at the right time. It focuses on the crucial period in the early- to mid-1960s during which the "story of bluegrass," a style by then some twenty years old, began to be understood and its narrative constructed. Arriving at Indiana University in Bloomington in 1961 for graduate studies in folklore, Neil had already discovered bluegrass by way of the folk revival, an awakening that would ultimately help to sustain the music itself. Up to that point, bluegrass had simply been considered a distinctive idiom within the spectrum of postwar country music, one that combined old-fashioned instrumentation, vocal styles, and repertory with a decidedly modern rhythmic drive and instrumental virtuosity. The late 1950s and early '60s were lean and challenging years for bluegrass musicians, despite the commercial success of an extraordinary group like Flatt & Scruggs. The discovery of bluegrass by young folkies like Neil, who had not been born into the culture, ultimately proved to be a godsend for the music, bringing thousands of new and eager fans hungry for something they perceived as more genuine than rock 'n' roll, folk-pop, or Nashville sound country.

But Neil Rosenberg was not just another kid from the coast with a banjo. He came to Indiana as a versatile and open-minded musician, deeply interested in roots music of all kinds and already well aware of the vital connections between bluegrass and folk traditions. His exposure to bluegrass at that point consisted largely of Flatt & Scruggs, The Stanley Brothers, the Osborne Brothers, and the Country Gentlemen, groups that had already begun to capitalize on the college market. That Neil knew very little at the time about Bill Monroe, the man whom Neil's friend Ralph Rinzler put forward as the "father of bluegrass," symbolizes the watershed moment at which Neil entered the scene. Suddenly he found himself at one of the music's epicenters, a place where it was thriving away from college campuses and folk festival stages. From this moment, bluegrass was not only coming to young urban folk music fans, but they were starting to come to bluegrass, where it lived.

The Brown County Jamboree in the tiny hamlet of Bean Blossom, Indiana—situated just twenty miles from Bloomington—had been a rural country music park since about 1939; Bill Monroe purchased it in 1952.[1] Nine years later, Neil eagerly and quickly inserted himself into Monroe's world, playing in the Bean Blossom house band and as a member of the Blue Grass Boys. He took on organizational and financial responsibility at the park. He brought to these endeavors the tools and mindset of a budding folklorist, making copious notes about every performance, every experience, every encounter, and honing the art of field recording under the tutelage of Brown County radio technician and Monroe confidant Marvin Hedrick.[2] All the while, Neil was developing as a professional folklorist through his studies at Indiana University, sharpening his research and writing skills, and cultivating a deeper understanding of bluegrass and hillbilly music as artifacts of folk culture.

He was, in other words, an outsider who became an insider while somehow maintaining the observational stance of the documentarian. Through Neil's unique lens we observe the creation of the genre and an awakening of its cultural significance. We also meet a colorful cast of characters, some already famous to readers and others much more obscure: regional musicians Shorty and Juanita Shehan, Roger Smith, and Denzel Ragsdale (aka "Silver Spur"), critical local fans and Bean Blossom documenters Marvin Hedrick and Jim Peva; professional musicians like John Duffey, Bobby Helms, and Bessie Lee Mauldin; and enterprising folklorists such as Judy McCulloh, Joe Hickerson, and Gus Meade. There are, of course, revealing portraits of Bill Monroe himself in these pages, as well as his brother Birch and members of the Blue Grass Boys. We learn about legendary performances in the Jamboree's "old barn," and visits from then little-known artists like Loretta Lynn and Jerry Garcia. This is a remarkable and vivid story of a genre's cultural transformation, at a crucial historical moment, in one of its most important locations, populated by memorable personalities, and all told by one of its central figures.

Gregory N. Reish

Acknowledgments

A MEMOIR IS A PRIVATE JOURNEY into the past. I'm grateful to many friends and acquaintances for help along the way in tracking down images, recordings, facts, memories, and other data. Thanks to Tom Adler, Tom Barton, David Blakney, Frank Davis, Tom Ewing, Daniel German, Frank Godbey, Scott Hambly, David Harris, Tom Hensley, Joe Hickerson, Charlie Leinenweber, Timothy Lloyd, Gary Reid, Art Rosenbaum, Lisa Rosenberg, Sandy Rothman, Scott Sanders, Walt Saunders, Rick Shubb, Mayne Smith, Otto Willwood, and others whom I may have overlooked in recalling the lengthy process of writing.

I was able to utilize my old tape recordings through the help of David Taylor, Michael Taft, and Todd Harvey at the Library of Congress' Archive of Folk Culture. Deadhead bluegrass historian Brian Miksis generously donated his time and expertise to make these recordings accessible for research and writing. Carl Fleischhauer, the photographer with whom I wrote *Bluegrass Odyssey*, gave valuable assistance with the illustrations. I'm much obliged to all.

Thanks to Blair Babcock, Carl Fleischhauer, David Hedrick, Gary Hedrick, Frank Hoffman, Erik Jacobsen, Charlie Leinenweber, Franklin Miller III, Ann Milovsoroff, Jim Peva, Lisa L. Piercey, Jeff Place and Jim Work for permission to use photos, recordings, and portions of letters in this narrative. Thanks also to Memorial University's Research Grant and Contract Services for a generous publication subvention.

I'm grateful for useful feedback from Ted Rowe and Terri Thomson Rosenberg, who read early drafts, and from Fred Bartenstein and Jim Rooney, who reviewed the final draft for the press.

University of Illinois Press editor Judith McCulloh, originator of the *Music in American Life* series, urged me to tell about my time at Bean Blossom. Support and direction from this distinguished folklorist and bluegrass fan set me to working on the book and, after her death in 2014, moved me toward its completion. I'm deeply grateful for her insistence, which led me to reexamine my life in American music.

I owe special thanks to Laurie Matheson, who took over when McCulloh retired in 2013, for substantial and essential editorial advice. Valuable assistance has been given by others at the Press as well, including Nancy Albright, Jennifer Clark, Kevin Cunningham, Dustin Hubbart, and Julie Laut. My thanks to them as well. Thanks are also in order to my old friend Charley Pennell for his good work in preparing the index.

Finally, I dedicate this work to my partner Terri Thomson Rosenberg, whose vision, patience, and love sustains me.

Introduction

THIS BOOK IS A MEMOIR of my life as a musician and student between 1961 and 1963. In June 1961, at the age of twenty-two, I moved to Bloomington, Indiana, to begin graduate studies in Folklore at Indiana University (IU). Soon after arriving, I went to the little town of Bean Blossom in nearby Brown County, met "Father of Bluegrass" Bill Monroe, and became involved in his music business, the Brown County Jamboree, starting in the house band. By December 1963, when this narrative closes, I'd worked several times in Monroe's band and just finished four months as manager of the Jamboree. Tom Adler's wonderful 2011 book *Bean Blossom* traces the history of this venue from its beginnings in the forties into the twenty-first century. Today the Jamboree site is known as the Bill Monroe Memorial Music Park and Campground. The annual bluegrass festival that Monroe established in 1967, still going today, is now the oldest of its kind.

Bean Blossom has become a synonym for bluegrass. I've written extensively about this music—I'm still in the business—but only briefly about the experiences that launched my career in it. That's what this book is— grassroots music business history. I have drawn as much as possible from contemporary documents, including personal correspondence, business records, photographs, and written tape transcriptions.

In 1959, I bought a tape recorder and began copying phonograph recordings and trading tapes. Back then if you wanted to learn bluegrass, you had to either see it in person or get it from recordings. Tape trading introduced me to live performances on radio and at concerts, but I had few opportunities to experience good professionally played bluegrass in person until 1961 when I moved to Indiana and began to study folklore and learn the art of field recording.

Early in 1962, I bought a mike stand and a Shure microphone at Marvin Hedrick's shop in Nashville, Indiana. I began recording at the Brown County Jamboree that summer. My tape collection started growing.

Bluegrass and country shows are musical theater. When I recorded a show, I kept the machine running to capture the whole stage event in its full aural context. Now, over a half-century later, I've listened once more to twenty-three different shows and two jam sessions that I preserved on thirty-one open-reel tapes. My descriptions of performances, particularly those of Bill Monroe, are based on these recordings (there's a list at the end of the book).

In some descriptions I quote the performers' dialogue between songs. Like scripts from spontaneous theater, this conveys the character of the performers and the rhythm of the shows.

Listening to events at which one was present fifty years ago is an uncanny experience. It evokes some memories, but it also refutes or denies others. Not a big surprise that a half a century lends new perspective! My narrative is built in part upon this aural trip, during which I aimed to recall and write about learning experiences during a time when my musical world and the world of bluegrass music were being reshaped.

The title of this book came to me only after I'd finished. Jim Rooney, who read the manuscript for the University of Illinois Press, wrote to them: "At the end of this account it is impossible to escape the fact that [Rosenberg] was describing the crucial shift which has resulted in 'Bluegrass' being considered an entire genre of music."

I realized that I had written not just about myself, but also about a generation of early activists supporting a then relatively unknown music. We were a nascent movement, a diverse but like-minded group at the beginnings of a process that has made bluegrass music a familiar name. There are metaphors—*generation* is one—which historians and other scholars use for such movements. I wasn't contemplating them as I wrote this, so I've put my thoughts concerning metaphors for movement into the Afterword.

BLUEGRASS GENERATION

Prologue

BORN IN 1939, I grew up in the American Far West, settling at twelve in Berkeley, California. By then I'd been playing violin for five years. By fifteen, with a growing interest in folk music, I quit the violin and moved to guitar. Our midcentury cohort of teen folk fans in Berkeley played, sang, partied, collected records, and went to concerts by nationally popular touring acts like Pete Seeger and the Weavers and by rising local stars like Odetta and Rolf Cahn.

In 1957, at eighteen, I went back east to begin four years at Oberlin College in Ohio, returning home each summer to work. Folk music was popular at Oberlin. Pete Seeger performed there every year. During my time there, I met many of the best-known folk artists of the time—people like Bob Gibson, Odetta, Theodore Bikel, Sonny Terry and Brownie Mc-Ghee, Guy Carawan, Ewan MacColl and Peggy Seeger, and The New Lost City Ramblers.

Discovering Bluegrass

An Oberlin classmate from New York City introduced me to bluegrass. I slowly fell in love with this music. The 5-string banjo playing of Earl Scruggs made bluegrass a hip thing for younger folk music fans. Pete Seeger's instrument of choice, the 5-string was just exotic enough to my generation to obscure its minstrel-show roots. Down-home virtuoso Scruggs had a way of playing it that fit in and moved with contemporary country music. He didn't strum or brush, he picked—fast, subtle, powerful.

I wanted to learn to play like that—but how? No reliable music—tablature or score—was in print. I collected recordings of bluegrass performances with notable banjo playing like that of Ralph Stanley, Don Reno, and above all Scruggs. I slowed records down and played along with them, and asked more experienced banjoists for guidance, gradually working at playing it like Earl.

The banjo was central to bluegrass as I first understood it, but that was just a start, for clearly bluegrass was an ensemble form—to use Alan Lomax's wonderfully overblown words, "the first clear-cut orchestral style to appear in the British-American folk tradition in five hundred years."[1]

Folk Music

At Berkeley High from 1954 to 1957, my classmates and I studied the guitar and learned about music that used it: folk, blues, jazz, flamenco. We hung out at each other's homes, record shops, and music stores. We listened to records, learned new songs, and acquired specialized roots musical skills.

African American music was popular in the region. San Francisco had a flourishing jazz scene; blues and R&B were big in the East Bay. Much of our early jam session music involved blues and jazz.

I was drawn deeply into African American folk music through the Folkways recordings of 12-string guitarist and singer Huddie Ledbetter ("Lead Belly"). Looking for others like him led me to the recordings of Jesse Fuller, who lived nearby in Oakland. A one-man band playing a self-invented foot bass, he wore a rack around his neck that held harmonica, kazoo, and microphone, and picked an enormous old electric 12-string guitar.[2] Fuller was a great singer and entertainer, the first really good finger-style folk guitarist I saw in person.

Immersed in folk music, we performed regularly for friends and family. In high school we began presenting our music to public audiences like school assemblies and the local FM radio station, KPFA. My closest Berkeley musical partner was Mayne Smith. We had met in junior high; he convinced me to try folk guitar and he began playing the 5-string banjo.

At Berkeley High, I met another musical friend, Scott Hambly, from south Berkeley. The low-ceilinged Hambly basement with its pool table, hi-fi, and purloined highway signs became our musical hangout room; Scott's pal John Thomas's cabin in Redwood Canyon, back in the hills behind Oakland, became our favorite site for parties or "blasts" as we called them. When Mayne and I went to Oberlin in the fall of 1957, Scott started at Cal (UC Berkeley).

Jesse Fuller at the Berkeley Folk Festival, June 1959. I'm sitting in front with new friend Tom Barton. (Courtesy of the Dave Harris Collection)

College Folk

Music was big at Oberlin. There was a school of music, a flourishing jazz scene, and a new folksong club. A campus group, The Folksmiths, had a new Folkways album.

Because Mayne and I both played, our room became a hangout site for folkniks. One classmate who became a musical friend was Franklin Miller III from Gambier, Ohio. He was just learning guitar when we met; he got good fast. We listened to records together and shared the joys of exploring new stuff on our instruments.

The Oberlin folk scene was centered at Gray Gables, a co-op dorm. Women roomed and boarded there; men boarded. All paid for room and/or board by working. A number of us left our instruments at this co-op in a small basement room called "Lower Siberia." We jammed there before and after meals. Mayne began learning bluegrass banjo Scruggs style. I taught myself mandolin on a banjo-mandolin that was in the room.

At these jams we met Chuck Crawford, one of the Folksmiths. From Mansfield, Ohio, he played the banjo and guitar, sang very well, and had a neat record collection that included jazz greats Django Reinhart and Fats Waller.

From the start of my four years at Oberlin, I stayed in touch with Scott Hambly back in Berkeley. We exchanged letters frequently as we both encountered new musical friends. Home at Christmas in 1957, I taught Scott mandolin chords. Over the following summer, we often got together to play and sing blues with two guitars.

That summer, Mayne, Scott, and I performed folk music around the Bay Area. In August, we recorded a custom LP, which included two bluegrass songs with Mayne on banjo, Scott on mandolin, and me on guitar: "Jesse James" and "Little Maggie."

In September 1958, I began a second year at Oberlin. In January 1959, I moved into an off-campus room with Franklin Miller and another classmate. By now we were deeply into bluegrass—listening to Wayne Raney on WCKY from Cincinnati, honing vocal harmonies, buying records by mail order from Jimmie Skinner Music (also in Cincinnati), and trying all the bluegrass instruments. I began practicing on a borrowed banjo.

In April, Franklin and I went into Cleveland with Chuck to visit his brother, who was working in the record section of a department store. He showed us a new Folkways album by The New Lost City Ramblers (NLCR)—Mike Seeger, Tom Paley, and John Cohen. We knew their names from earlier folk recordings; seeing this new album—their first—I imagined a bluegrass band. Instead, we heard an antiquarian project in which a folksong revival supergroup carefully reconstructed old recordings of southern string band music. The album had a lot of neat songs and tunes, with interesting textures and instrumentation. From its extensive notes, I learned about the idea of *old-timey*, a new word to me. The NLCR was following Alan Lomax's groundbreaking idea about treating style of performance as a marker of musical skill—authenticity, some would say—that was as important as repertoire. They not only sang hillbilly songs, they tried to sound, play, and look like hillbilly musicians.

First Bluegrass Band

In May, we created a band on the Oberlin campus—or a band name, at least: The Lorain County String Band. Mayne, Franklin, Chuck, and I, along with John Schuler, Ritchie Sharrett, and Phil Specht (all jammed with us in Lower Siberia), constituted the band, which played in public only a few times. We made a demo at WOBC, the Oberlin radio station.

Second Bluegrass Band

In the summer of '59, Mayne and I returned home and joined with Scott and Pete Berg, a new friend from LA he'd met at Cal, to form a band with a name that evoked the site of our high-school blasts, "The Redwood Canyon Ramblers." Pete took up the washtub bass. Mayne, Scott, and I played banjo, mandolin, and guitar. After a few weeks Mayne got sick and had to leave the band. Pete moved to guitar. Borrowing a Gibson Mastertone, I became the banjo picker. We hired country bassist Betty Aycrigg and closed a successful summer by recording a demo at KPFA.

Among my new musical friends that summer were two fellows from Bloomington, Indiana—Jim Work and Tom Barton. Both were sons of professors at Indiana University (IU) and shared our musical interests. My path would cross with theirs later in Indiana.

Neither demo that I was involved with in 1959 was sent to anyone. We'd been at this music just a short time, and were intimidated by the recordings from which we were learning. We knew little about the music business and had few connections in it. Our focus was on learning the musical craft. It was just dawning on us that a band was a musical theater troupe. At the end of the summer, I bought the 1954 Gibson banjo I'd borrowed. That was a big investment: $185 of my own meager savings.

Third Bluegrass Band

Fall 1959 was relatively quiet at Oberlin. My parents wouldn't let me take the banjo back to Oberlin—they were afraid it would lure me away from my schoolwork! I had dreams of that Mastertone—and told them so. In October, they shipped it to me, unannounced, and I was one happy boy. After reading about Gibson banjos in Mike Seeger's notes to his new Folkways anthology *Mountain Music Bluegrass* style, I knew that recent archtops like my 1954 model were considered inferior to the old prewar flatheads that Scruggs and Reno played. *Archtop* and *flathead* described the metal tone rings on the drumhead part of the banjo (called the *shell* or *pot*), rings over which the banjo head was stretched. My new archtop was the best banjo I'd ever played. I changed the head from skin to plastic that fall—my first invasive surgery on an instrument.

Bluegrass was getting popular on campus. Tom Allen's painting of Flatt & Scruggs from Alan Lomax's article, "Bluegrass Underground: Folk Music in Overdrive," in the latest *Esquire* was quickly torn out and tacked up in the main dining room at the co-op. We were listening to Lomax's album of Earl Taylor and Stoney Mountain Boys with ace banjo picker Walter Hensley and singing songs from *Mountain Music Bluegrass Style*. Tom Barton came over from IU for a weekend visit, bringing as a house gift a new bluegrass anthology on a label I'd never seen, Starday. He'd gotten it at a neat Bloomington music store, Rone's. He told me about the folk scene in IU and Bill Monroe's park at Bean Blossom where he and some friends had won a talent contest recently.

At the beginning of 1960, we started a new bluegrass band: The Plum Creek Boys. Franklin had a fiddle and was working on "Orange Blossom Special." Chuck got an old Gibson mandolin and took the role of tenor singer-mandolinist established in bluegrass by Monroe. I went back to guitar. We recruited banjoist John Schuler from our Lower Siberia jams and the Lorain County String Band.

In the previous two years, we'd regularly visited Antioch College, a couple hours' drive south of Oberlin in Yellow Springs, Ohio. There was a similar folk music scene there, plenty of places to crash and opportunities to jam. There we met a married student couple, old-timey and bluegrass musicians Alice Gerrard and Jeremy Foster. They had neat old instruments, tapes of live bluegrass and old-time music, and were friends of Mike Seeger.[3] Hanging in their apartment was a poster for a Stanley Brothers show at Sunset Park, a country music park near Washington, Jeremy's home. Alice was from the West Coast, a great singer and banjo picker. They had a bluegrass band, the Greene County Stump-Jumpers. In

February, we invited them up to Oberlin to perform at a Folksong Club concert in which we also performed.

In March, Jeremy and Alice organized an appearance by the Osborne Brothers at Antioch. These bluegrass pioneers, recording artists who'd been at it for over a decade, headlined this—the first college bluegrass concert.[4] The Plum Creek Boys followed the Greene County Stump-Jumpers as an opening band. Backstage, I became acquainted with the evening's stars: Bobby and Sonny Osborne and Benny Birchfield, a good banjo picker who was then their bassist and later their guitarist and singer of the third voice in their trio. We shared sips from the pint of Georgia Moon that I had in my guitar case. Onstage, they wowed us with elegant vocals and hot picking and entertained with comedy, reinforcing my growing perception of bluegrass as musical theater. In the next decade, they would go on to great success bringing bluegrass to country music fans with hits like "Rocky Top."

For spring vacation 1960, three of us Plum Creek Boys went down to Wheeling, West Virginia, to see the Osbornes at a live Saturday night broadcast of the World's Original Jamboree on WWVA at the Virginia Theater. We were blown away by another bluegrass band there, Jimmy Martin and his Sunny Mountain Boys—J. D. Crowe, Paul Williams, and Johnny Dacus. Driving home Sunday morning, we listened to live bluegrass gospel music on a local radio station. I began to realize that this music was all around us in Ohio.

Much of it existed in the world of country music. As a child I'd listened to country and western on radio, in movies, and on records. My favorite singers were cowboys like Gene Autry, but that interest ended by the time I was ten. Now, listening to country deejays like Wayne Raney, who always played some bluegrass on his WCKY broadcasts from Cincinnati, we also heard contemporary country music. For the first time, I began to dig the new pedal steel guitar sounds pioneered by musicians like Ralph Mooney, who played for new country star Buck Owens.

Chuck Crawford and I discovered a little record store on Broad Street in Elyria that carried lots of bluegrass and country. I listened to and bought Starday and King singles and LPs, the latest Flatt & Scruggs, and the new Harmony reissues of The Stanley Brothers, Bill Monroe, and the Carter Family. In May, the shop owner, noting my interest in bluegrass, sold me a brand new 45 from under the counter where he had it on consignment. The Wright Brothers' tabloid ballad, "The Island Creek Mine Fire," was about a disaster that had happened in West Virginia on March 8th—another reminder of bluegrass activity in the area.[5]

In the spring, Chuck met some musicians from Carter County, Kentucky, in his hometown of Mansfield. We spent an evening visiting them: playing music together, comparing instruments, getting acquainted. By the end of the semester, when the NLCR was featured at the Oberlin Folk Festival and I met Mike Seeger and John Cohen, we had firsthand experience—visual and cultural images to go with the music we'd been studying.

Fourth Bluegrass Band

In the summer of 1960, we regrouped into the Redwood Canyon Ramblers in Berkeley with Mayne on guitar and Scott on mandolin. Franklin and I joined on fiddle and banjo. A few weeks later, we found a jazz bass player, Tom Glass, who was with the band for the rest of a very successful season. We advertised ourselves as "the Bay Area's first and only genuine bluegrass band," had a good audition at a famous SF venue, the hungry i, and, by August, we were talking with North Beach club owner Jack Dupen about starting a bluegrass bar.

At a new music store in town, Lundberg's Fretted Instruments,[6] I met Jon Lundberg, an expert repairman with an encyclopedic knowledge of instrument history. Lundberg stoked my interest in antique instruments. The names and numbers assigned to elegantly crafted and ornamented old Martin guitars and Gibson banjos and mandolins evoked a mystique that grew as one learned their history. Visual and aural treats!

Working in Lundberg's shop was well-known local repairman Campbell Coe, who modified my banjo that June. Campbell and I made a swap—he took my '54 archtop shell and gave me a prewar flathead Mastertone shell, adapting the other parts of the '54 banjo—neck, resonator—to the new shell. Now, except for the postwar peghead, it looked just like Earl Scruggs's Gibson. This was the banjo I would play for the next three decades.

At KPFA that June, I ran into Alice Gerrard and Jeremy Foster. They told me that Mike Seeger and his wife were in town with the New Lost City Ramblers for Cal's Berkeley Folk Festival and needed a place to stay. I offered a space in our family home and began a friendship with Mike that lasted until his death in 2009. Seven years my senior, he was always willing to share his experiences and insights about music with me.

Mike and his NLCR bandmate John Cohen came to see the Redwood Canyon Ramblers at the Continental, a Berkeley restaurant hosting an after-hours "cabaret" during the festival. We had adopted the bluegrass dress code of the time: dark shoes and slacks, white shirts, clip-on string ties, and cowboy hats. After our set, John and I discussed dress and repertoire ideology. He told me the NLCR had decided against the country music image projected by string ties and hats, opting instead for a thirties documentary photo look with slacks, straight ties and vests, no hats. They also decided not to do religious songs, while we always included a few hymns on the show.

We worked music full-time that summer, expanding our repertoire of folk and old-time done bluegrass style with our own arrangements. We developed comedy routines and spent a lot of time listening to bluegrass recordings. The new Folkways album by the Country Gentlemen, their first, caught our attention that summer. Mike had produced it and John had done the cover photo. There was some radical stuff there!

At the end of the summer I rode with my parents to visit friends in Montana's Bitterroot Valley. On the way back home we stopped at my grandmother's place near Spokane. There, in a pawnshop, I found a Gibson mandolin from around 1904, an early 3-pointer "F" with a picture of Orville Gibson on the label. It had seen rough usage—the neck had been broken at the nut. It was repaired with a rough splice that reached from the 8th fret to the middle of the peghead. In the old fingerboard above the splice, were the original delicate mother-of-pearl inlays. The pick guard, with a fancy pearl fleur-de-lis, was inlaid on the body. The buttons on the tuners had delicate floral inlays. Its black finished top and dark stained back were, like the neck, battered but beautiful. It was in its original case, a flimsy cardboard and cloth contraption. I had to have it!

I dragged my dad to the shop. Failing to bargain the price down, he paid the full $35. I sat in the back seat playing and fondling my new old Gibson as we drove home to California through eastern Washington and Oregon.

How I Came to Bloomington

I returned to Oberlin in fall of 1960. Chuck Crawford had moved to Washington, D.C.; I visited him there at Thanksgiving. Alice Gerrard and Jeremy Foster had graduated from Antioch and were living nearby. One night Jeremy took Chuck and me to see the Country Gentlemen at the Crossroads Bar in Northern Virginia. The music was great! Since recording their Folkways album, they'd added a new bass player, a teen whiz named Tom Gray.

Between sets, I introduced myself to mandolinist-tenor singer John Duffey. He was six years my senior, but we shared some of the same suburban cultural style. I said I was from California and we started talking hot rods. I could keep up with him on that subject, but he knew a lot more about bluegrass than I did. He told me about old recordings and then we got into instruments. I mentioned I'd just found a Gibson 3-pointer in a pawnshop, and he immediately offered to swap me an old Paramount tenor banjo and a Dobro-mandolin for it. I wasn't interested. We carried on talking about instruments—he told me about a guy who was doing fancy inlay, repair work, and banjo neck building for them—a former member of their band named Tom Morgan.

Finally, I mentioned our Oberlin Folksong Club. I was now president, helping plan next spring's Oberlin Folk Festival and considering bringing in a bluegrass band. We'd liked the show the Osborne Brothers put on at Antioch and wanted something similar. Duffey told me they could put on a better show than the Osborne Brothers and gave me his address.

January 1961, as my final semester at Oberlin began, I was making plans for the future. I decided to go on for a graduate degree in folklore, which only IU, with its Folklore Institute, offered. I got advice from former Folksmith Joe Hickerson, a Folklore Institute graduate student since 1957 and sent in my application.

I was now engaged. I'd met my fiancée, Ann Milovsoroff, at the co-op in the fall of 1959. A new boarder, a year behind me at Oberlin, she took guitar lessons from me that fall. We struck up a friendship and began dating in early 1960. She was learning to use her new Japanese 35 millimeter single lens reflex camera. I introduced her to bluegrass and, during 1960, she photographed performers in action at Oberlin, Antioch, and Berkeley, including Jeremy and Alice, the Plum Creek Boys, the Osborne Brothers, and the Redwood Canyon Ramblers. Now, in 1961, we'd decided to marry. She was now learning to play the autoharp—she'd picked one up while home for Christmas in Vermont. We began building a repertoire of old-time and bluegrass songs. Our wedding was scheduled for June, right after my graduation.

In February, we rented a car and drove to Bloomington. I had an interview with Richard M. Dorson, Director of the Folklore Institute at IU. Joe Hickerson found accommodations and had a folksong party to introduce us to IU folklore students and Bloomington folk musicians.

In April, I learned that I'd been accepted into the IU graduate program with a three-year fellowship in American Studies and Folklore. In May, we returned to Bloomington, apartment-hunting. Tom Barton put us in touch with Charlie Leinenweber, a high-school buddy who played old-time and folk guitar. Charlie and his wife, Charlotte Bell, were living in an old house near the campus that had been divided into four apartments. One was coming free in June; we took it.

Back at Oberlin, jamming in Lower Siberia one afternoon, I watched as my neat old Gibson mandolin, which was leaning against the wall, slowly slid sideways. When the peghead hit the floor the neck splice came unglued. Suddenly, I had a nice old broken, unplayable mandolin.

The Country Gentlemen were headliners at the 5th annual Oberlin Folk Festival in May. As president of the Folksong Club, I was called upon to write a preview article for the student newspaper. The editor was the same classmate who'd introduced me to bluegrass in 1957. This was my first writing for print. Not much had been published about bluegrass. I focused on the connections bluegrass had with earlier forms of folk music and described it as a kind of theater.[7]

This concert was the first at a college for the Country Gentlemen, who up to that point had been playing bars and country music parks in the Washington, D.C. area. It was a great success. In the following decade they became the most popular bluegrass act at folk venues, gaining the label "progressive" for their melding of folk and bluegrass influences. By the end of the weekend, I'd gotten to know all of them better, especially Duffey. John offered to repair my broken mandolin, restore the missing original inlays, and refinish it.

Weeks later, just before I left Oberlin, I received a package with a tape Duffey had promised to send me of early bluegrass recordings. Also included was a two-page letter on Country Gentlemen stationary with, among other things, his first report on my mandolin. It was coming along slowly: "It is so humid down here that it is difficult to paint. . . . Let me remind you," he added, "of the big all-bluegrass show on the 4th of July at Oak Leaf Park in Luray, Va. Bill Monroe, the Stanley's, Jim & Jesse, Bill Clifton, Mac Wiseman, and us'uns will be there."[8]

Duffey also wrote of the band's second Folkways album, due out that week; described a fancy Gibson F2 mandolin he'd bought in Cleveland on the way home from Oberlin; and asked me about the chances of a date at Oberlin in October. I didn't keep a record of my answer; while I must have told him I no longer had a say in affairs at Oberlin, I also must have somehow encouraged him to think I might help him find college bookings.

In any event, in those days before there were bluegrass festivals, magazines, or websites, I felt myself growing in touch with the music through our correspondence. Looking back, I see now that my musical friendships had gradually been acquiring new dimensions, moving from casual socializing to doing business. I would not hear again from Duffey all summer, months when I was deeply immersed at Bean Blossom.

SUMMER 1961

Meeting Monroe

June–July 1961

AT THE END OF JUNE 1961, days after we newlyweds moved to Bloomington and I started graduate courses at IU, our neighbors Charlie Leinenweber and Charlotte Bell took us to the Brown County Jamboree in Bean Blossom, Indiana. They promised a musical adventure, said that the Jamboree presented afternoon and evening country music shows every Sunday from spring to fall. Bill Monroe's brother Birch, an old-time fiddler, managed the place, which Monroe owned. Bill appeared often, they said, although not as often as he was advertised to be there. He was advertised for this Sunday.

I was eager to experience the best in bluegrass. I'd seen the Osborne Brothers and Jimmy Martin live the year before, and the Country Gentlemen just a month ago. Mike Seeger's Folkways album *Mountain Music Bluegrass Style* with its encyclopedic notes was my bible. I owned new 45s by Flatt & Scruggs, the Stanley Brothers, the Country Gentlemen, and Bill Monroe.

Monroe was a distant icon. My introduction to bluegrass music had come in 1957. I heard Flatt & Scruggs and the Stanley Brothers before I heard Bill Monroe. I didn't rank his recordings at the top of my list when friends and I began listening to records and comparing favorites.

In 1959, when I started learning to pick the banjo in the style of Earl Scruggs, I began hunting for performances that spotlighted that instrument. My search was like that of the famous ballad scholar, Francis James Child, who described his search for authentic ballads among the popular music as digging for jewels in dungheaps.[1] To me, the banjo was the jewel;

I was moved by things like Scruggs's "Earl's Breakdown" and Don Stover's break on the Lilly Brothers' "Tragic Romance."

There was much about bluegrass I didn't understand or appreciate. Monroe's recordings were dominated by fiddles, which I didn't dig at first. Most of the singing was, to my ears, very twangy like the old country and western music I'd left behind when I became a teenager tuned into Oakland's R&B radio.

Many of Monroe's best recordings were not in print and difficult to find. Nevertheless, he was already "legendary." I'd heard much about him—even that he had a country music park in Bean Blossom, Indiana.

Though Monroe had been on the Grand Ole Opry since 1939, he was not the well-known American musical icon he would become. Today, over a century since his birth, he's in the Bluegrass, Country Music, Songwriters, and Rock and Roll halls of fame. In 1961, there was no bluegrass festival circuit. He was a mysterious and distant figure who'd never given an interview.

Within days of moving to southern Indiana that June of 1961, Charlie and Charlotte brought us to the evening show to see Monroe in person for the first time at the Brown County Jamboree, held in a low barn (I describe it in the next chapter) in the little hamlet of Bean Blossom.

There were only a few cars outside the barn. Before paying at the ticket booth, Charlie and I approached a blonde woman who was nearby; she stood next to a road-weary Olds station wagon with Tennessee plates. Charlie asked her if Bill Monroe was really there. She said he was, and soon we saw her—Bessie Lee Mauldin—playing bass with him, along with Bobby Smith on guitar, Tony Ellis on banjo, and Shorty Shehan on fiddle.

I recognized Shorty because he and his wife, singer-guitarist Juanita Shehan, and bassist Jim Bessire—the house band—had preceded Monroe's show. Bill pointedly introduced Shorty as "a fine old-time fiddler." I don't recall details of the music he played. I'd heard quite a few of his record hits, such as "Mule Skinner Blues," "Footprints in the Snow," "Blue Moon of Kentucky," and "Uncle Pen." He somehow sounded different here, doing the songs in person, weathered, like his mandolin.

I know much more now about Bill's mandolin than I did that night. It was a Gibson F5 Master Model that he'd bought in a Miami barbershop in 1945. Labels inside were signed by Gibson acoustic engineer Lloyd Loar and dated July 9, 1923.[2] Bill used it for the rest of his life, on the road and in the studio. It's now in the Country Music Hall of Fame in Nashville.

In 1961, I had only recently heard about the Gibson Master Model—the F5—because Scott Hambly had just gotten a new one. Its long neck and high bridge gave the instrument uncommon volume and versatility. My impression that night was that in Monroe's hands it was, to use a favorite term of his, "powerful."

Also striking to me was the banjo Tony Ellis was playing. I could tell it was an old Paramount (most people played Gibsons) with a skin head and a new neck with a completely unadorned fingerboard. Following the show, I introduced myself to Ellis and asked to look at his rare banjo. After showing it to me he asked if I played the banjo, and when I said I did he urged me to get my banjo so he could look at it.

I brought it in from the car, set it down in front of the stage where we'd been sitting, and opened the case for Tony. Shorty and Juanita Shehan, standing nearby, urged me to play a tune. I sat in the front row of the old barn and played "Weeping Willow," a version of "Bury Me beneath the Willow" that I'd seen Eddie Adcock of the Country Gentlemen play a month earlier.

Looking up from the fretboard as I finished, I noticed Monroe had come over to listen. Soon after this, I wrote to my folks about his words of encouragement: "That's pretty good pickin', boy."[3] And I've always remembered what Juanita told me later that summer—Bill had said to her that I would make a good banjo player some day—words that made me feel very good.

Following that modest audition, Shorty and Juanita invited me to come by the Jamboree any time and pick with them. I came out a week later and paid my fifty cents at the door. Admission price at that time was fifty cents if there was local talent and a dollar for a "star." Shorty saw me in the audience and, from the stage, asked me if I had my banjo. I nodded and he said, "Well go get it and come on up."

I wrote to my parents about this in early July, my first letter to them after leaving home. As in all of my letters to them, I spoke in a didactic voice, casting my exciting musical experiences as part of what I needed to do as a serious graduate student: "I have found that my prior knowledge in Folk Music is serving in good stead in my studies of Folklore—I have records and tapes of stuff which is new to many of the people that I've met. Also, I have gone out to the local hillbilly 'park' which holds a 'jamboree' each Sunday, and met several good old-time fiddlers. In fact, I took my banjo out there last week and they invited me up on stage to play five or six tunes. . . . I'm enjoying learning more about what has heretofore been a diversion."[4]

After I came off stage that day, Shorty asked me if I'd paid to get in. When I told him I had, he told me "don't you pay to get in any more." And after that day I never again paid to get into the Brown County Jamboree. At that point I wasn't paid to play, either, but I was happy to be able to come to the park whenever I wanted and, in exchange for playing, be able to get in free. I could afford to go to the weekly shows at that rate! I was a new apprentice on the way to becoming a regular.

Bean Blossom

1961

THE BEGINNING OF MY immersion into the Brown County Jamboree, my baptism into the bluegrass and country music business, came that summer of 1961 when, on almost every Sunday, I drove to Bean Blossom to play regularly with Shorty and Juanita. Ann sometimes came along.

I had never owned a car until that June when we received a new Rambler American two-door sedan as a wedding gift from my parents. Its only optional equipment: seat belts and a limited-slip differential. As a teen I'd hung out with hot-rodders, gone to sports car races, and followed Grand Prix racing in the auto sport monthly *Road & Track*. I loved driving, winding over the Hoosier back roads in our new car. I left behind the new stresses of graduate student life with each week's drive to Bean Blossom.

After lunch on Sunday afternoon, I headed east from Bloomington on State Highway 46, the main east-west road into Brown County. Passing Brown County State Park, the highway dropped down into Nashville, the county seat.

To its nineteenth-century pioneers, Brown County was a rough hilly backwater, a rustic home to Civil War copperheads and post–Civil War "whitecaps," Democratic in Indiana's Republican political landscape. It was remote, a frontier pocket. Its landscape was not friendly to farming. It was widely viewed by its neighbors as a place of poverty and illiteracy—stereotypes associated with Appalachia, from whence many of its first settlers had come.

In the early twentieth century, with the building of roads and the coming of automobiles, Brown County became a tourist attraction. *Indianapolis Star* humorist Kin Hubbard's daily column, "Abe Martin of Brown County"—Martin was a fictional humorous rustic pundit—helped to popularize the county. In the fall, people drove there from Indianapolis to see the beautiful foliage in its hills. By the 1920s, it had an art colony; summer homes were being built. Brown County State Park with its Abe Martin Lodge came in the 1930s—depression relief for a county that relied on tourist dollars.

By 1961, Nashville—with arts, crafts, and souvenir shops, and a restaurant famous for its apple butter—had become an upscale destination, like Cape Cod in Massachusetts, Taos in New Mexico, Fredericksburg in Texas, Carmel in California, Elora in Ontario. There was a lot of tourist traffic in Nashville on Sunday afternoons.

From Nashville, I took a smaller state highway, 135, north to Bean Blossom. Climbing out of town through wooded hills, it passed art galleries, apple orchards, and summer homes—some of them recently built log cabins—en route to its crossroads with State Road 45, an even smaller highway that meandered through the woods from Bloomington, coming out in Bean Blossom.

The Brown County Jamboree: A Log Cabin in a Barn

In *Bean Blossom: The Brown County Jamboree and Bill Monroe's Bluegrass Festivals*, Tom Adler gives the history of the Jamboree barn. In 1961, it had changed little since its beginnings in the forties. Situated on the east side of the highway just north of Bean Blossom's small cluster of homes and businesses, parallel longways to the road, was a long low building in the middle of a fenced field. A single-lane dirt driveway circled it. Patrons drove into the park, turned left, and parked in the field around the barn. They entered it by the ticket booth in the north end.

The building, with its high central ceiling and low-roofed sides, resembled a working barn. Much of the interior remained as it was built in 1943 with concrete and gravel floors, concession stands, bleachers, and old theater seats. Occupying the center of the building's final third before the stage was a large smooth concrete pad. A dance floor on Saturday nights, on Sundays it was covered with folding metal chairs facing the stage.

The stage had a rustic look. Barkwood slabs down to the floor at the front matched a log cabin exterior that intruded from the backstage wall, with doors and windows. Above it was a roof, and on it antique farm implements. On the wall hung two coonskins, dried gourds, and a garland of colored corn-on-the-cob. Along the back of the stage itself were chairs and a bench. At stage right sat a battered old piano. Along the front edge of the stage were electric fans, spotlights, an ancient amp, and a single mike on a stand.

The amp, covered with soot, had survived a fire in 1958. A few charred rafters near the stage testified to the event and to the minimalistic style of maintenance favored by Jamboree manager brother Birch Monroe.

Jamboree audiences sat on a dance floor in a barn, looking up at a stage in front of a cabin. Performers came onstage from the cabin doors, walking out, as it were, to play in the barn.

Backstage in the Cabin

Beginning with my third visit to the Jamboree, no longer obligated to pay at the door, I entered at the back. Driving in, I circled the barn to its south end, passing a small building just east of the barn that housed the restrooms. I parked near the door that led into the backstage area, nose in toward the horse barn on the south boundary of the park.

Unlike the Jamboree barn, the horse barn was the real thing. Bill and Birch kept horses and fighting chickens in it. During the week, the chickens sometimes ran free on the Jamboree property—you had to be careful about where you stepped, back there near the horse barn.

The back door to the Jamboree barn, technically a stage door, was at the rear of a boxlike room that extended from the end of the building. This door was always open during Sunday's Jamboree shows. Inside, walls of the room were covered with graffiti—the signatures and slogans of two decades of country music stars who'd played the Jamboree. Next, you walked into a second room with a small window, which abutted stage right.

Together these two rooms were known as "the back room." This is where performers tuned up, dressed, and left their instrument cases.

From these back rooms a hallway ran across the back of the building behind the stage. In it were steps up to the level of the cabin doors onto the stage, connected by a floor at stage level to another set of steps that led to the control room on stage left. In the control room's interior wall was a window onto the stage. Beneath it were shelves for portable broadcasting equipment. At the front of the room, a door opened out onto a set of steps into the audience area next to the chair-covered dance floor.

Going between the Cabin and the Barn

At stage left, a set of stairs ran down to the dance floor, just a few feet from the control room steps. The audience floor level from the side of stage left to the control room entrance was a meeting place for performers and audience members between shows, a friendship and power center.

The control room door was kept closed, limiting backstage access. If audience members wanted to visit backstage, they went out one of the side doors and walked around to the back of the barn where the door to the back room was, as noted earlier, always open. Musicians would often come into the backstage area via the control room. In my repeated visits to the Jamboree as a musician in 1961, I began to meet others more familiar than I with the etiquette of the backstage cabin.

House Band
July–August 1961

MY EDUCATION AT BEAN BLOSSOM began in the house band. When Shorty Shehan was filling in on fiddle with Monroe in June, Bill introduced him as "a fine old-time fiddler," which he was. I also got to know his wife and partner Juanita Doyle, who was a great singer and a fine rhythm guitarist. Also in the band was bass player Jim Phillips (Bessire).

At three we opened the afternoon show. We played material meant to be familiar to the audience—mainly country songs and tunes old and new. They sang duets, and Juanita did the latest and older country hits. Shorty leavened this mix with old-time dance tunes and showpieces on the fiddle, and I was called upon to do a banjo piece on each show. Sometimes Shorty would invite guest performers to join us for a song or two.

Throughout our performances Shorty and Juanita would do comedy. They didn't have fancy routines, just comic bits, like their banter during "Orange Blossom Special." Shorty often opened the show with this famous programmatic piece that begins with two instrumental parts imitating a train. The first part, in E, re-creates the train's wheels with a percussive shuffled bow, the train whistle with long bowed double stops, and the bell plucked on the high E string with the little finger.

Shorty made sure the audience knew the program of the piece—as he started slowly, he spoke of the train leaving the station and picking up speed, and told everyone to listen for the bell. Then he'd break into the second part, a fast hoedown in A with intricate shuffle bowing.

The rest of us played "backup"—Jim hitting the bass on the downbeats, Juanita playing guitar in jaunty western swing rhythms that used no open strings, just chords (at least two to a bar) damped to create a percussive "sock" sound that made the guitar into something like a drum. I played a fast roll on the banjo, trying my best to re-create Ralph's part in the Stanley Brothers' 1955 recording from which I'd learned the piece.

After the first two parts, Shorty and Juanita, returning to E, would sing the verse and chorus. It's best known today because of Johnny Cash's version, but that didn't exist in 1961. Twenty years before, "Orange Blossom Special" had been introduced on record and popularized in shows by Bill Monroe and the Blue Grass Boys.

On their second time through the tune, Shorty and Juanita followed Monroe's recording, with improvised comic banter over this musical texture of the first part. Shorty told how the train was now traveling through the countryside. "What do you see now?" Juanita would ask. "I see the bull coming out of the corn," Shorty would answer. A few more bell rings and some bow shuffling followed, and then Juanita asked: "What do you see now?" "I see the corn coming out of the bull!" The audience laughed and applauded as he broke into the second part of the tune.

Shorty had what seemed to be an inexhaustible supply of one-liners. His new coat was seersucker—Sears sold it, and a sucker bought it. He'd point to the spotlight in the front corner of stage left and ask Juanita if she knew what that reminded him of. "No, what?" she would reply, and he'd point to the identical unit at the corner of stage right and say, "That one, yonder."

The main fare in our shows consisted of Shorty and Juanita's renditions of country songs. That summer I learned how to play songs I'd heard infrequently, like "Heartaches by the Number," "I Fall to Pieces," and "Pick Me Up on Your Way Down," all recent country hits, love songs that the audience recognized viscerally with applause at the beginning of the song.

A regular comic piece in Juanita's repertoire was Jimmy Dickens's 1954 hit "Out behind the Barn." Juanita put conviction and humor into telling about how "I got my education out behind the barn" with Daddy's strappings, the first cigarette, and kissing and petting:

> You might think it ain't no fun
> To be a poor ole farmer's son
> You don't know what all I've done,
> Out behind the Barn.[1]

Shorty and Juanita rendered these songs with authority; like many in the audience, they had grown up on farms. Country music professionals for two decades, they'd been on television from Indianapolis and played extensively in the region. Shorty had worked at a famous Kentucky radio jamboree, Renfro Valley, and had been a member of Monroe's Blue Grass Boys in 1951. Indiana country music fans knew and loved them and their music.

I couldn't have picked a better couple to introduce me to the music, and to the Jamboree audience. Not only were they locally popular, but they were warm and welcoming to me. They introduced me as a student from California who was studying at IU. They liked my banjo playing, it added to their show. Many of the tunes I chose to play were old-time pieces, like "Weeping Willow" and "Little Maggie," that Shorty had grown up with.

The first time I took a banjo break, Shorty stood behind me and, fingers in my belt loops at either side of my waist, moved my pants back and forth in time to the music. I was startled but some how kept my musical concentration. The audience laughed and applauded.

Meeting the Audience
July 1961

ATTENDANCE AT BEAN BLOSSOM in 1961 was sparse. No more than twenty people were at that first show we attended in June. Each week, adults, often couples, made up most of the Jamboree's small audiences. Sometimes carloads of friends arrived; married couples occasionally brought children. Most traveled no more than an hour or two from their home to the Jamboree for an afternoon or evening of musical entertainment. Many attended regularly—maybe not every Sunday, but once or twice a month. These statistics are impressionistic, for at that point no one was doing surveys and I was just beginning to meet people.

Most in the audience lived and worked in industrial midwestern America—Indianapolis and its adjacent region, filled with factories, military bases, and agribusinesses. The small towns they lived in were gradually becoming part of an urban and suburban landscape connected by increasingly fancy road systems surrounded by strip malls. People came to the Brown County Jamboree because they liked the music and the shows in which it was presented. The rural landscape and the Jamboree's rustic setting appealed to people who enjoyed country music theater.

Many seemed to have relatives in, or were immigrants from, the upper south—particularly Kentucky. Often they had grown up on farms or in small farming communities. Indianapolis had a substantial African American population, but with one exception—a 1963 sit-in—no black people came to the Jamboree during the years when I was a regular. This was an all-white audience chiefly of native-born people of rural background, mostly Hoosiers and Kentuckians.

Most of the people I met there had only a few clues about my identity. Often Shorty and Juanita introduced me, the banjo player, simply as "Neil." My last name was, to most who heard it, German, and to some of those, German-Jewish. These were my identities: name, home, occupation, age, banjo player. How, I wondered, did these identities position me in the country music business?

Let's start with **Name**: My parents were from Washington State. My dad, Jess Rosenberg, was the youngest son of cloak maker and union organizer Meyer Rosenberg. He and his wife, Fannie Gould, were Russian-Polish Jews who had come to the United States as children with their families at the end of the nineteenth century. They'd moved to Seattle in 1919. Dad went to the University of Washington, became a lawyer, and started working as State Superintendent of Elections in the capital city of Olympia in 1934.

My first name came from my mother's father, Neil A. Smith. He and his wife Edna met and married in a small town near Ionia, Michigan. They moved west in 1907. At the time of the birth of my mother, Mildred, Neil had been working ten years for the Northern Pacific Railway and was station agent in Wilbur, a small town south of Grand Coolie in the wheat country of Eastern Washington's Lincoln County. Mom, known from childhood as Mitts and later Mitzi, went to Washington State College (it's now "University"). After graduation in 1934, she came to Olympia to work at the Department of Agriculture.

Mom and Dad met in Olympia and married in 1935. She broke an engagement with her college sweetheart and eloped with dad. The rabbi in Seattle married them after giving her a certificate of conversion. Her parents disowned her—for twenty-four hours. It was a happy and loving marriage. I was born in 1939, and my brother Donny was born the following year.

Home: Shorty and Juanita described me as being from California. When Jamboree patrons and other musicians spoke to me about this, they often mentioned their relatives in California, asking if I knew them or the town where they lived. Most often, such people seemed to live in southern California, and I would explain that I was from Berkeley, near San Francisco in northern California. Often this was heard as "Beverley" and connected to "Hills." Berkeley would become famous (or infamous, depending on your politics) in the midsixties, but it was not a familiar California place name to most people at the Jamboree in 1961–1963.

Our family left Olympia in 1949 when dad went to work as a lawyer for the Atomic Energy Commission in Los Alamos, New Mexico. We lived there a little under two years before he took a job with the Western Highway Institute, a trucking industry research foundation in San Francisco. We moved to Berkeley in 1951. My parents lived there for the rest of their lives. My brother died in an auto accident in 1959.

Occupation: Shorty often mentioned that I was a graduate student at IU. A full-time *occupation*, it was an apprenticeship.[1] I was working for my papers—degrees that would fetch me a day job. Although most of the other people who worked at the Jamboree also had occupations other than music, they were never identified on stage as plumbers, salespersons, factory workers, shop owners, or truck drivers.

I was identified as a student because it was an unusual aspect of my identity. I was the only IU student playing country music at the Jamboree. Most audience members were not college educated, and college students weren't usually fans of country music.

But of course everyone *knew* about IU. It was the biggest and oldest state school. I would be asked what I was studying, and when I said "folklore" it was an unfamiliar term that I was rarely asked to explain. Next came questions or comments about friends or relatives who were connected with the college (as it was generally described), and finally a discussion of the IU sports teams.

Talking sports came easy to me. I'd been raised in a sporting family. Grandpa Neil was an ace pitcher whose father, a doctor, had played professional baseball in the 1880s. Both parents played tennis throughout their lives. Mom captained the girl's field hockey team at Washington State. As player-coach, Dad led the Washington State National Guard Armory basketball team to the state AAU championship when I was about four. I'd managed the football team at Berkeley High, and my brother, at the time of his death, was on a football scholarship at Claremont Men's College. We'd attended professional football and baseball games; followed college basketball, football, and track; and gone to sports car and unlimited hydroplane races. Being able to chat about sports with people at Bean Blossom was much easier than talking about my interests in music as a folklorist. That helped me fit in.

Age: During that first season, 1961, at the Jamboree, I was twenty-two, identified and perceived as a young man. I was also a newlywed. Ann came with me several times that summer and fall. At various times, she photographed the barn and the house band on stage. Once she joined us onstage to play autoharp; Shorty introduced her to the audience as my new bride.

Banjo Player: Just performing on stage playing the banjo made everyone at the Jamboree aware of the fact that I was an apprentice professional musician. For many, that was all they knew about me.

Then and now, I was happy with that. I've been a musician since the age of seven. The music flowed from my parents' interest in the arts. Since the age of nine, I've been involved in the performing arts as musician and actor. A decade later, I embraced the banjo, or, as Bobby Osborne taught me in 1960, the banjer.[2]

Playing the Five
1953–June 1961

AS A CHILD I HEARD and saw the 5-string banjo through records, radio, and the movies. But I wasn't aware of it until Mayne Smith introduced me to Pete Seeger's banjo in 1953. We were 14.

Created by Africans in the new world, the banjo (or banjar, as Thomas Jefferson called it) differed from all other stringed instruments I knew of because of its fifth string. The first four strings of this instrument are in a headstock or peghead at the top of the neck, just as with a uke or violin. But another, shorter, string runs from a tuning peg mounted on the side of the neck. The neck widens at this point, so that when looking at a 5-string banjo neck, you notice its asymmetry.

With its skin head and the odd fifth "drone" or "thumb" string, as it was sometimes called, it was an exotic instrument when, in the nineteenth century, it was introduced to American and international audiences via the minstrel show. By the beginning of the twentieth century, there were factory-made banjos of many designs. Its association with the stereotypes of minstrelsy and the invention of the electric guitar drove the banjo out of popular music by midcentury. When I first heard Pete Seeger, the 5-string banjo was once again an exotic instrument.

Between fall 1955, when Mayne got a banjo and I saw Pete Seeger in concert for the first time, and the summer of 1959, when I got my first 5-string, I'd become acquainted with banjo music. Pete Seeger was a virtuoso who showed the versatility of the instrument and demonstrated how banjo and voice fit together. Pete pushed us to explore: if you like this, he said, check out my sources. We listened to old-time banjo on albums by Tom Paley, Obray Ramsey, and others. I began noticing young folk musicians playing 5-strings.

Lots of Oberlin students had guitars and 5-strings. Many also had portable record players. A classmate from New York played us the new Folkways album, *American Banjo: Scruggs Style*. On it we heard Eric Weissberg use Scruggs tuners to play Woody Guthrie's "Hard, Ain't It Hard." This was my introduction to bluegrass—the word, the music, and its technology, especially the Scruggs tuners.

With its fifth string, the banjo was already an unusual instrument. But Earl Scruggs had taken banjo construction a step further when he invented his Scruggs tuners. In an early chapter of his book, *Earl Scruggs and the 5-String Banjo*, Earl explained his invention: "My brother, Horace, and I used to sit around home working with ideas. One idea was to attempt to retune the banjo while playing a melody. I would retune my banjo, perhaps from a G into an open D."[1]

In 1951 he recorded and composed "Earl's Breakdown," an instrumental that included a section in which he tuned the second string down and back, producing a distinctive slurred sound. "I began receiving requests for this number on almost all of our performances," he recalled. To alleviate the challenge of retuning accurately so frequently, he drilled a hole in the peghead between the first and second string and installed a tuning peg with a cam that pushed the second string in and out. At the same time, he installed a similar peg between the third and fourth string pegs enabling him to retune the third string in the same way. He used this in 1952 along with the first peg when he recorded "Flint Hill Special," another instrumental that featured the slurred sound of strings plucked while being retuned.

By 1954, the year my Mastertone was manufactured, Gibson was installing Scruggs tuners at the factory, and my banjo had them. Bluegrass banjoists embraced the technology and began using them to play and record old songs like "Home Sweet Home."

When I became The Redwood Canyon Ramblers' banjo player, I was already focusing on the bluegrass banjo recordings. At the beginning of the summer, in Seattle for a family wedding, I'd discovered a music store, The Folklore Center, within walking distance of my grandmother's apartment. I bought a Reno & Smiley album there, spoke with a local bluegrass musician, and met Irwin Nash, a tape collector with whom I exchanged addresses. When I got home, I bought a Wollensak tape recorder.

That fall of 1959 when Tom Barton came to visit me, he brought some of his records. I taped one, a 45 by The Lilly Brothers and Don Stover, "Tragic Romance," which introduced me to Stover's marvelous banjo playing.

Around the same time, I got a tape from Irwin Nash. It had come to him from a friend stationed in Pensacola who'd recorded television broadcasts by a band I'd never heard: Jim & Jesse and the Virginia Boys. He'd taped only instrumentals—no songs. I later learned that Jesse McReynolds's mandolin playing was a big part of their instrumental sound, but these recordings highlighted the amazing playing of others in the band: fiddler Vassar Clements and banjoist Bobby Thompson.

By this time, I'd heard a lot of the early bluegrass banjo pioneers: Earl Scruggs and Ralph Stanley and Don Reno. Now I was discovering others, younger musicians like Eddie Adcock, Don Stover, and Bobby Thompson who were advancing the art. By the time I got to Bean Blossom, I was following bluegrass banjo closely. There was always something new to learn and try.

When I arrived at IU, I found that the tape recorder was an important part of the professional folklorist's tool kit. A personal library of recordings was also an asset. I collected recordings of music—often old and/or obscure—that seemed significant, especially if they included the 5-string.

Whenever Shorty and Juanita introduced me, everyone's focus, including mine, was on the banjo. I was ready to go with familiar tunes like "Weeping Willow" and, with the Scruggs tuners, "Home Sweet Home." I practiced at least an hour a day. Working on the 5-string was a good way to unwind after a morning in the library stacks or at a seminar. Playing the banjo in public or at parties was a great way of meeting new musical friends. That first summer in Indiana, it happened a lot.

Letters to Home
August 1961

I WROTE HOME EVERY WEEK. This was the main way of giving my folks our news. About once a month I'd put in something about my extensive musical activities. I didn't want them to think I was neglecting work as a grad student.

On Wednesday, August 16, 1961, just after my first graduate summer school courses had finished, I wrote with the news that I'd passed with "A's" and was on vacation until the week after Labor Day. In an earlier letter, I'd told of meeting Monroe at Bean Blossom. Now I began to introduce my new musical friends, telling first about "a very good bluegrass guitar player" with whom I'd entered last Sunday's talent contest.

We met in the back room just after the house band had finished playing for the afternoon show. Pat Burton, a smiling, enthusiastic, red-haired boy from Illinois, introduced himself to me. We talked banjo. He brought out a guitar. We jammed.

Pat had studied the singing of Mac Wiseman, who'd sung lead to Bill Monroe's tenor on the 1949 classic "Can't You Hear Me Calling?" near the start of a substantial career in country music. Wiseman's early '50s Dot records—songs like "Homestead on the Farm"—had become part of the bluegrass jam and cover repertoire. Wiseman's much emulated vocal style—he sang high but not quite so lonesome as mellow, sort of like Hank Snow on helium, and he played a mean backup guitar. Pat was into all this and did it well.

We decided to enter the contest. I don't recall who the other contestants were, but typically these events drew male and female country singers, bluegrass combos, rockabillies, and teenage rock and rollers. I reported the results in my letter: "We won first place in the afternoon and third place in the evening. Our prize was two-fifty [$2.50] apiece and two tickets to the Grand Ole Opry in Nashville."

This prize sounds typical of Bill's older brother Birch Monroe, whose minimalistic style I've already mentioned. Birch, ten years older than Bill, had moved to the region after Bill purchased Bean Blossom. He lived in nearby Martinsville and worked at a factory there. At Bean Blossom on the weekend, he managed the Saturday night dances and the Sunday Jamboree. He was an old-time fiddler, leading the band on Saturday nights and occasionally performing as Bill's guest at the Jamboree.

Birch ran the contests at the Jamboree in the style of radio quiz shows where the audience voted with applause. He selected two of his friends—regular Jamboree patrons—and the three of them would rank the applause. Winners were paid cash. Opry tickets would have been a stretch for his operating style. I don't recall actually getting them.

I told my folks that my new musical friend also played the banjo and we were entering another contest at Bean Blossom the following Sunday—a banjo contest. We decided to enter playing two banjos in harmony, a sound that the Osborne Brothers had pioneered on their early MGM recordings four or five years ago. You didn't hear people doing it that much back then. We drove up to Crawfordsville to practice. Pat was living there with his married older sister, Ann Williams; she would play rhythm guitar for us.

Pat told me about his friends from high school days in Urbana, the three Bray Brothers. They all had been playing bluegrass since 1954. In 1958, they'd teamed up with Red Cravens, a guitarist they'd met at Bean Blossom, to become "Red Cravens and the Bray Brothers." Last year, right after two of the Brays got out of the Army, they had the house band job at the Jamboree. In May of this year, they'd played the first concert held by the new Campus Folksong Club at the University of Illinois.

Pat spoke a lot about this band, but I didn't get to hear them play because they had just signed with a major label, Liberty Records, and that month they were driving west to an LA recording date. They would be recording as "The Bluegrass Gentlemen," a name concocted by their new Nashville agents at the Jim Denny Bureau.

Harley Bray was Pat's banjo hero. When we practiced our banjo duets, Pat gave me a little seminar on backup techniques—how Earl does it, as interpreted and explained to him by Harley.

Finally, my letter came around to telling my parents that I'd been working Sundays all summer, playing in the house band at Bean Blossom, "gaining lots of experience." I didn't mention that I was gaining no money. I was saving the cost of admission each week in exchange for working onstage for no more than a half-hour each show. The "experience" included meeting people and learning about the life surrounding the music. And there was an added bonus for Shorty and Juanita—I was a new young picker who didn't have stage fright and did have pretty good chops, given that I'd only been picking for a couple of years. That appealed to audiences and drew to the audience new faces from IU where I was starting to become known as a musician at folk venues. Placing in the talent contest reflected this.

Because of my contributions, friendship and trust with Shorty and Juanita grew. I wanted to learn more about the music; they were pleased in my interest. We socialized between shows, and so I introduced these musical friends to my parents, mentioning that we'd shared dinner with them on the grounds last week. They had spoken of old ballads they recalled from childhood, and we had made plans to visit them for supper and a recording session this week. "They are both from Kentucky," I explained, "and know a large number of old ballads from tradition."

That was what I thought I knew. Gradually, I learned that Shorty Shehan was from Tennessee and Juanita Doyle from Indiana. Her parents were from Kentucky. I was excited about the connection between these contemporary performers and the traditional music I was now studying as a folklorist-in-training. I'd heard a lot about field recordings in my first graduate folklore course at IU's summer school.

That evening at Shorty and Juanita's Franklin home after supper, I turned on the recorder. For them it was part of a social visit; for me it was a first attempt at fieldwork. I didn't know quite what to say so I just expressed my interest in old songs. Juanita sang a variety ranging from the old Indiana ballad "Pearl Bryan" to "I'll Take You Home Again, Kathleen." Soon they urged me to get out my banjo, and Ann her autoharp. Another musician was visiting them that night too, an electric guitarist, and he joined in when we did.

After about a dozen pieces, I convinced Shorty to play the banjo, an instrument he'd played in his youth. He played ten tunes, including a rough version of "Coal Creek March" that I coaxed out of him. He and Juanita closed the evening with a genuine Child Ballad, "Late Last Night When I Came Home" ("Our Goodman"). After I brought the tape home, I listened

August 1961 banjo contest. Pat Burton, me, and Pat's sister Ann Williams.
(Courtesy of Ann Milovsoroff)

to it and wrote a table of contents. I didn't think it was a particularly well-
done example of field recording. I laid it aside to practice for the contest.

Five days after the contest, I wrote my parents that Pat and I had won
second place. We'd worked out our parts carefully and dressed up in white
shirts, string ties, and cowboy hats. But Art Rosenbaum, a fine old-time
banjo player, backed by Shorty and Juanita, beat us with a medley of Uncle

Dave Macon comedy pieces that wowed the audience. Afterward, Shorty told me I would have won if I'd soloed—it's not what you play, but how you play it, he told me.

Art had met Shorty and Juanita in June, at the afternoon Jamboree show on the same Sunday when I met Monroe at the evening show. Art was a virtuoso, soon to have his own banjo album on Elektra, a leading folk label.

He was from Indianapolis but now lived in New York City. A professional artist, he was studying at Columbia University. He had been into folk music for a long time—we had mutual acquaintances from that. In the following years when Art came home to see his folks, he'd visit us in Bloomington. He introduced me to people in the Indianapolis and New York folk music scenes. He was a dedicated field recordist and researcher and would later record Shorty and Juanita doing some of the same songs they'd sung for me.

Some of my new musical friends visited our apartment that summer. One evening, Mitchell Land, a mandolin player I'd met at Bean Blossom who was then working as a fireman in Brazil, Indiana, came down. We hosted a little musical get-together. Among the guests was a local bluegrass guitarist and singer, Jim Neawedde, an IU student I'd met through our next-door neighbor, Charlie. They'd been musical friends at University High in Bloomington, first into jazz, then folk, and now bluegrass.

After we'd played a few pieces I decided to record what we were doing. The only tape I had handy was the one I'd recorded a few days earlier at Shorty and Juanita's. There was a bit of unused space on the second side and I turned on the recorder as we explored our repertoires looking for familiar bluegrass jam tunes—like "Old Joe Clark," "John Henry," "I'm Using My Bible for a Roadmap," and "Lonesome Road Blues."

Meeting the Regulars
August 1961

BY THE END OF AUGUST, I'd played enough—six or seven Sundays—at the Jamboree to describe the scene to my parents as: "the 'house band'; Shorty, his wife Juanita, who plays guitar, Jim Phillips the bass player, whose father owns an apple orchard and provides us with big jugs of excellent apple cider."[1]

Jim was using "Phillips" for his stage name that summer; most people knew him by his father and grandfather's surname, Bessire. Apple farmer Dale Philip Bessire had come to Brown County in 1914 as "one of the original impressionists that made Brown County an historic art colony."[2] Jim, who was my age, was one of the backstage regulars at Bean Blossom. When a visiting band needed a bass, he was there.

As Jim and I became acquainted he told me about a local man, Marvin Hedrick, who owned a radio-TV shop just outside of Nashville. Marvin held weekly jam sessions at his shop; Jim usually attended. He urged me to come by Marvin's and join them for a jam. I didn't meet Hedrick until that fall.

Jim and I talked about such things backstage and out on the Jamboree grounds where we shared meals between shows. He had been to Grand Ole Opry and knew more about the music than I did. I began asking questions of him and Shorty and Juanita about their musical experiences.

I was eager to know more about Bill Monroe. Shorty had played with and knew Monroe. Now, spending Sundays playing at the Jamboree with Shorty and Juanita and hanging out with them before and after shows, I began hearing stories about Monroe.

The Brown County Jamboree House band, late summer 1961—Shorty and Juanita Shehan; I'm standing behind Juanita. (Courtesy of Ann Milovsoroff)

Shorty had worked as a Blue Grass Boy playing bass for a couple of seasons in 1951, right before Bill bought the Jamboree. He was proud to have participated in one of Bill's Decca recording sessions that October. Bill's band then included West Texan Edd Mayfield on guitar, North Carolinian Gar Bowers on banjo, and young Alabama fiddler Gordon Terry. One of the two songs they recorded, "Christmas Time's A-Comin'," had become a much-played seasonal classic.

Fiddler Tex Logan, who had just finished an undergraduate degree at MIT and was working at WWVA with Wilma Lee and Stoney Cooper, composed the song. Bill and the Boys learned it from Logan, who sang it with his fiddle in an unusual tuning. Monroe asked Logan to play at the recording session but that didn't work out, and Gordon Terry was faced with a challenge: Logan's tuning was new to him.

Shorty spoke proudly about how he showed Terry the special tuning for his break on the song. Terry fiddled on the recording, but, Shorty said: "I composed the break." And he backed up this story with performance. He and Juanita always did "Christmas Time" at late fall shows.

Juanita also had stories from these times. She described the costumes that the Blue Grass Boys wore—jodhpurs with high riding boots. Monroe followed a rigorous road schedule those days, playing every night. Often the Boys wouldn't undress for days at a time, sleeping in the car. They'd have to be back in Nashville for the Grand Ole Opry each weekend. She told of Shorty coming home late one night after a long road trip with his feet so swollen from traveling that she had to cut the high tops of his boots open so he could get them off.

They left this rugged life at the end of 1951, returning to Indianapolis to resume a career on radio and television. During the midfifties Shorty put together a western swing band that included the cream of central Indiana's country musicians—people like fiddler and guitarist Joe Edwards, who later was the leader of the Grand Opry's staff band.

In 1957, he took this band to Cincinnati to audition for Capitol Records. It was a great band, he told me, but this was the beginning of the rock-and-roll era, and their music was going out of fashion. The band set up and auditioned in a studio for Capitol producer Ken Nelson. Afterward Nelson told Shorty that he had a good band, but (referring to a current teen favorite) said, "I need a new Ricky Nelson."

Shorty said he answered in disgust—if that was what Capitol wanted, he could make it happen: "Just give me the money and I'll buy a bed for the studio and fly in Ozzie and Harriet!"

Rock and roll had impacted their career, as it did for many country musicians at that time. In 1961, the memory of this crash was still fresh but he still had enthusiasm for his music. That summer he talked about Starday, a company in Nashville that was interested in recording bluegrass. He spoke about us going to Nashville for a recording session. I eagerly wrote about this to friends in California, but ultimately it was only talk. Shorty was always working on deals.

He and Juanita had been performing at the Jamboree off and on for the past decade and had gotten to know Monroe better than most. Bill was very private, not an easy man to know well. Everyone was curious about the relationship between him and Bessie Lee, the woman I'd seen playing bass with the band in June. Juanita said that she'd heard but didn't believe a rumor that Bill and Bessie had gotten married on the stage of the Opry. A few years earlier, she recalled, a talented local musician had played a show with Bill, auditioning for a spot in the Blue Grass Boys. After the show when a group of them were chatting backstage this musician started questioning Bill about Bessie. "Say, Bill, are you and Bessie married, or what?"

According to Juanita, Bill just looked at him. That was the end of his audition; he never played with Bill again. He'd asked a foolish question, and Bill had not appreciated it. Bessie remained a mystery.

Shorty spoke of old-time and country musicians he'd worked with growing up in East Tennessee and later in Kentucky at the Renfro Valley Barn Dance. He was proud to have met Leslie Keith, the fiddler who'd helped put "Black Mountain Rag" on its road to fame, and he had seen and worked with many other greats of the music.

He told me that he'd learned, by working with top country performers like Monroe, that you never know who's out there in the audience. He'd met people backstage after the show who could play rings around him on the fiddle—great musicians. Shorty's point was that your job on stage is to create a show, not show off. Good music is important but the audience comes to be entertained.

Roger Smith and Bryant Wilson

My experience with good pickers in the audience began that summer when I first saw two other Jamboree stage regulars, Roger Smith and Bryant Wilson. The afternoon show had finished; the evening show didn't start until eight. I was out on the Jamboree grounds somewhere—having a meal with the band at one of the picnic tables.

Afterward, as I headed to the backstage door to get ready for the evening show I passed a dump truck parked in an odd place. People didn't usually park on the edge of the road beside the southeast corner of the barn near the backstage door, facing north. The driver had come off the highway through the Jamboree park gate, turned right, and driven around the end of the barn counterclockwise and stopped. I had two thoughts: I'd never seen a dump truck at Bean Blossom; surely Birch wouldn't allow someone to drive in the wrong direction like that and park that way. I didn't know it was Roger's truck.

Inside the dressing room was a crowd—all the small room could hold— and at its center were two men playing guitar and banjo. Dressed casually, they were tall, lean, serious, and totally absorbed in their music. The guitarist had a Martin D-28, the banjo picker had an old Gibson archtop. They were singing and playing "Toy Heart," a song Bill Monroe had recorded on Columbia in 1946 when Flatt & Scruggs were Blue Grass Boys.

Today, Monroe's recordings from that period are available in digital form, but in 1961, only a few of those old 78s were on LP. I'd recently gotten a tape of "Toy Heart" and, being a banjo student, had marveled over Earl Scruggs's break. I'd tried to figure it out, but it wasn't easy—there was a little rhythmic catch at the end that I couldn't get just right.

So while I enjoyed the whole performance—the banjo picker sang Monroe's harmony part to the guitarist's powerful vocal on the choruses—it was the banjo break that impressed me the most. He nailed it, putting in all the subtle touches Scruggs had used. His picking had great intensity and drive. Relaxed and natural, he gave no impression that he was working hard to make this music. His art flowed easily. I'd heard several local banjo pickers at Bean Blossom that summer—he was by far the best.

The banjo player was Roger Smith; the guitarist was Bryant Wilson. I think that was the only song I heard them play. My first impression of them, from afar, was that they looked a bit scary, like tough guys, and that their music was really great. Afterward, Roger put his banjo in the case and said goodbye to those in the crowd (I may have been the only one who didn't know him), saying he had a load to deliver.

So who was this musician? I would get to know Roger well over the next few years; much of what I tell now he related to me in 1967 when we drove together from Columbus, Indiana, to Connersville, Indiana en route to a recording session in Ohio.[3]

He was born in Amelia, Virginia, in 1926 and grew up on the family farm in eastern Appalachia near Mount Airy, North Carolina. Old-time, hillbilly, and country music were in his life early with local musicians and, by the midthirties, radio. He started playing the fiddle at twelve and was playing for square dances at thirteen. He never stopped playing his music, but he had TB and spent several years in a state sanitarium.

By the time he was twenty-five, realizing that he'd never be able to do heavy manual labor, Roger chose music. His professional career began at WPAQ in Mount Airy, already a center for the new bluegrass music. He made his first recordings in 1952 fiddling with the driving bluegrass/old-time two-banjo band of Larry Richardson and Happy Smith, and he was still at the station in 1954 when he began working in the band of Decca artist Jim Eanes.

Eanes, a country crooner with a flair for bluegrass, had worked with Bill Monroe in the late forties. Many good bluegrass musicians worked in his bands. Roger was with Eanes only a short time when Bill Monroe's manager, Carlton Haney, offered him a job in the house band at the Jamboree. He took it, and moved to Bean Blossom.

At that time, there were some cabins out east of the barn (by 1961, only a few ruins were visible). Roger moved into one of the cabins in April 1955. By that time, while still fiddling, he'd developed into a good banjo picker. He performed and broadcast at Bean Blossom that season, living there until the Jamboree closed. By then he'd met Rose Logston, daughter of the couple who ran the food and drink concessions at the Jamboree, whom he would later marry. He stayed in Indiana that winter, playing in clubs and giving lessons. The following year, he worked as a Blue Grass Boy with Monroe. I don't know how long Roger was with Bill, but this was the beginning of a relationship that lasted many years.

Bill was on the road constantly and in those days band turnover was frequent. If Monroe had a gig within driving distance of Roger's home and he needed a fiddler or a banjo player, he'd call. Roger was working as a truck driver. He moved permanently to Indiana in 1958 and settled in Columbus in 1960.

When I saw him this day the following summer, he was taking a break while driving a dump truck for a Columbus contractor. Then and for many years after, he always carried an instrument in the cab of his truck.

Bryant Wilson was born in the town of Columbia in Adair County, Kentucky, on the western edge of Appalachia in 1924.[4] His mother died at his birth. Raised by his aunt, he grew up with Christian singing in and out of church, got his first guitar at eleven, and, like Roger, began listening to records (Roy Acuff, Bill Monroe) and the Grand Ole Opry as a teen.

In the early 1940s, he began working in Edinburgh, Indiana, a small town north of Columbus close to Camp Atterbury.

By 1945, when he first performed at the Brown County Jamboree, his aunt and cousin had joined him in Edinburgh and he was playing with various local and regional hillbilly bands. His favorite singer was Hank Williams, but unlike Williams he was a lifelong abstainer who disliked the drinking of fellow band members. He would later write a song about this, "Stepping in Daddy's Tracks."

In 1948, he bought a home recording machine (a disc cutter) and by 1951, when he married, he was writing songs. The following summer he made his first record, a 78 for the Arrow label by the Johnson County Ramblers. In 1953, he created his own record label, Comet, making recordings in an Indianapolis studio and sending them to be pressed in Cincinnati.

After Hank Williams's death, Bryant stopped singing his songs. The following year, he teamed up with an Adair County banjo player who'd moved to Columbus, Leonard Burton, and his wife to form a trio that made a 45 pairing his song, "You Better Quit Your Stepping," with gospel standard "My Main Trial Is Yet to Come" in 1956. In 1958, he made his first bluegrass record, pairing a gospel tune, "Meet Me Up Yonder," with an instrumental, "James L. Special," and started a new band, the Kentucky Ramblers. From then on, he recorded only religious music.

Bryant, whose day job was in a Columbus factory, always had records to sell when he performed. He played churches, and dances. He was a regular at the Jamboree and at Mocking Bird Hill Park up in Anderson. His records were heard on the radio in Indianapolis and Louisville. By the time I saw him he had gotten to know Carl Story, the "Father of Bluegrass Gospel,"[5] a North Carolina singer-guitarist who would later record one of Bryant's songs, "My Time Will Come Some Day."

In the next few years Roger, Bryant, and I would become acquainted. Great musicians who were Jamboree regulars, they'd been playing there for years. It took me a while to get to know them; I'm pretty certain they had watched me in action from the audience. I was the new guy, the apprentice; still being scoped out by the regulars.

Freddie and Jack

Over the years, Roger and Bryant brought bluegrass on stage; but there were other regulars who sang straight country, and even a couple of died-in-the-wool rockabillies—Freddy and Jack Dotson. I thought these brothers were from Martinsville, but recently Gary Hedrick told me he's pretty sure they were from Edinburgh. They sang to their own accompaniment. One played guitar; the other wore a snare drum on a strap from his neck, which he beat with his hands like bongos. They did the usual rockabilly fare—Everly Brothers, Buddy Holly, Elvis, that kind of stuff—in an animated style that amused Jamboree audiences. Although they were regulars, I don't have any recordings of them. Recorders were not turned on for them like they were for Monroe or the other stars. But for a musical variety show, they provided guaranteed comic relief and were always welcomed by the management.

Birch Monroe

During the 1961 season, Shorty ran things onstage during the shows and was the Jamboree's public face. Behind the scenes was Jamboree manager brother, Birch. I didn't get to know him well that year because he wasn't around backstage much. He took care of things out front, collecting admission, overseeing the food concessions and directing traffic.

At each show near the end of our introductory portion, Shorty would invite Birch on stage and introduce him as the manager of the Jamboree. Birch would talk about forthcoming shows and dances, urging people to attend. He had a stack of 22-by-14-inch show cards—two-color posters printed usually at Hatch Show Print in Nashville, Tennessee, on heavy cardboard—advertising next week's Brown County Jamboree show. He invited audience members—"neighbors" was his favorite word—to take one or two along after the show. He told them to take them to a store they do business with, like the gas station or the local grocery, and ask to put it in their window.

I followed his instructions and took several each week. I'd usually keep one. I had seen posters like them, from Sunset Park, at Jeremy Foster and Alice Gerrard's apartment in Yellow Springs—and quickly became a collector.

On Monday I'd bring the other new poster to Rone Music in downtown Bloomington.

Bloomington
July–August 1961

RONE MUSIC WAS AT 314 North Walnut Street, on one of two busy north-south highways that bisected Bloomington, a few blocks north of the courthouse square, the town's center. A complete music store, it sold new and used instruments, sheet music, and records. It rented and repaired instruments. You could listen to recordings in playback booths. I dropped in regularly to look at new instruments and hear records.

By bringing in Birch's Jamboree posters, I got to know two men working there, the younger Mr. Rone, and a salesman, Louis, a friendly, garrulous, silver-haired, middle-aged man who liked talking about instruments and records, and enjoyed getting my news about the Jamboree and the folk scene at IU. When he found out I was studying folklore at IU, that became a topic of interest. Students often came in to buy records and instruments; I was familiar with that scene and found myself answering Louis's questions about new artists and musical fashions.

He was au courant with the instrument business—Rone was a Gibson dealer. The Gibson rep, Julius Bellson, came to the store regularly with new models, electric and acoustic, news of which Louis would pass on to me when I visited. He also noted my interest in new bluegrass recordings and began telling me about new releases—LPs and 45s.

This was the store where Tom Barton had gotten some of the records he'd shown me in 1959. Tom had also connected me with former high school classmates who shared his interests, like Charlie and Charlotte, the neighbors who introduced us to the Jamboree in June 1961. Through Charlie and Tom, I'd met Jim Neawedde. I had been jamming with these

Pigeon Hill Boys and friends, Bloomington, summer 1961. Me, Charles Leinen-webber, Tom Hensley, Bob Patterson, Jim Neawedde. (Courtesy of the Charlie Leinenwebber Collection)

new friends that summer. Soon Jim told me of another classmate who was a jazz pianist, Tom Hensley.

In July 1961, *Downbeat* published Pete Welding's review of the new Flatt & Scruggs album, *Foggy Mountain Banjo*, giving it five stars. This venerable jazz magazine generally sneered at country, and, in any case, five stars were rare in their reviews. The unusually positive review piqued Tom's interest. When he heard about this newcomer on the local folk scene who played Scruggs-style, he got Jim to introduce us. Most of the jazz guys I knew then were wiry, serious types. Tom was jolly and rotund, and although piano was his main ax, he also played the bass.

Tom was not only a fan of jazz greats like Bill Evans but also of musical comics like Spike Jones. Engaged with contemporary transgressive popular culture, he had edited an undergraduate humor magazine at IU. He was a lot of fun to hang out with, always had good new jokes. Jim and Tom and I got better acquainted jamming together at parties.

During my first summer in Indiana, the leading figure in Bloomington's IU campus folk music scene was Joe Hickerson. He organized and led regular folksong events, often called "folksings," at dormitory recreation centers, and had a weekly show, "Our Singing Heritage," on the campus radio station, WFIU-FM. He also ran a flourishing mail-order folksong record album sales business—the campus rep for Folkways, Elektra, Prestige, and other hard-to-find labels.

The scene was similar to those on big campuses everywhere at that time. Just off campus on Kirkwood a new coffeehouse, The Phase III, hosted a cadre of local performers—mainly students and others from the youth community adjacent to the campus. The emergent off-campus counterculture was, at this point, post-beat and proto-hippie. Shops on Kirkwood catered to hip new tastes. Tom Pickett's music store was pushing folk instruments and recordings. The big bookstore carried magazines like *Sing Out!*

During the summer, Ann and I sang together a few times at Hickerson's events; she played autoharp, I played guitar. I also had a few folk event gigs with Jim and Tom.

Meanwhile I kept everyone up to date on what was happening at Bean Blossom and my experiences with Shorty and Juanita. Jim and his friends knew who they were, and they also knew about Bill Monroe's brother, Birch. But Monroe himself was a distant figure. You could never be certain when he would be playing at Bean Blossom—sometimes he'd appear unannounced, sometimes he'd be advertised and then not show.

Jim's friend Dave Mercer—Merce—was a Monroe fan who worked at a liquor store near us. Chuck Crawford had told me about using wooden Cutty Sark Scotch boxes as bookcases. They were perfect for tapes and paperbacks. I asked Merce to save the empties. Whenever I'd drop in to collect one he would ask me when Bill would be at the Jamboree. If there were posters out, he'd want to know if Bill was *really* going to be there. He, like others, had grown tired of driving out to Bean Blossom only to discover Bill Monroe wasn't there as advertised.

A few of my new classmates in the Folklore Program, like Hickerson, knew about Monroe and had visited the Jamboree. One was Frank Hoffman, who'd come to IU from Pennsylvania, where he played a leading role in the state folklore society. He was not a musician but was an avid follower of folk music. He had been to the Jamboree, had even done some field research in Brown County, part of a fieldwork seminar project led by Professor Dorson in the summer of 1960. Over the summer I told him about coming shows—when I knew.

Summer Vacation

We left Bloomington on Monday the 28th for a two-week vacation with Ann's folks in Norwich, Vermont. This had been an intense musical summer, in which I made many new musical friends.

In Vermont, only a few miles down the road from Norwich, I discovered a tiny music store. Its owner, Mr. Goodyear, had been a Gibson dealer since 1914! He showed me his personal mandolin, an F4 that the company had given him when he started the business. My mandolin, another old Gibson, was broken and away with John Duffey being fixed—I was missing it. I asked if he had any mandolins for sale. He had two old oval-holed Gibsons, $35 each: an H2 mandola, and an A-Century mandolin. I could only afford one so I bought the mandolin.

In 1933, Gibson introduced two Century of Progress models for their exhibition at the 1933–1934 Chicago World's Fair—a guitar and a mandolin. They had similar fingerboards and pegheads covered in "pearloid," a celluloid plastic that had the look of mother-of-pearl. Inlaid into this were sections of rosewood, and in the rosewood were genuine mother-of-pearl pieces—the Gibson logo, and diamond and snowflake fret markers. Ornate or gaudy? Hard to say, but I liked it.

It had other unusual features for a Gibson mandolin: a pickguard glued to (rather than suspended over) the top, and a flat back (usually they were carved). It was in the original hard-shell case. It showed signs of being played, broken in but in excellent condition. The fingerboard was easy to play, and it sounded good. It was a little treasure I brought with me when we returned to Bloomington after Labor Day. I was eager to show it to my musical friends.

FALL 1961

Monroe Again

September 1961

ON SUNDAY SEPTEMBER 10TH, I went to Bean Blossom to work the afternoon show with the house band. Shorty told me that the previous Sunday while we were away Bill had played the Jamboree. A Folklore Institute mixer kept me from the Jamboree the following Sunday, so I didn't get a poster for the next week's show, on the 24th.

On the day before, I got a progress report on my mandolin repairs from John Duffey. He mentioned that they had recently shared the stage with Pete Seeger at Carnegie Hall and reported that they'd "sold well" to the audience but that the Folkways people thought them "too slick"—"they still want this music in the raw."[1] Bluegrass was beginning to appear more frequently in folksong revival venues, but Carnegie Hall was far from my mind when I arrived at the Jamboree for the next day's afternoon show and saw the poster facing the highway at the gate:

Bill Monroe
Blue Grass Boys
Special Added Attraction
—Vassar Clemonts—
Old Time Fiddler
Shenandoah Valley Trio

The poster's first two lines and the last were standard stock. But that "Special Added Attraction" was unique. I hadn't yet learned the names of Bill's influential fiddle players, but I knew who Vassar Clements was. Since 1959, I'd been listening to his virtuoso performances with banjo picker Bobby Thompson on a tape of TV show instrumentals by Jim & Jesse and the Virginia Boys.

Excited to see a hot young bluegrass fiddler I knew about, *today*, playing with Bill Monroe, I drove around to the back of the barn and went in to warm up with Shorty and Juanita for our part of the show. Monroe wasn't there, but several Blue Grass Boys were. With Clements was Bobby Smith, the guitarist and lead singer I'd seen with Bill in June. New to me was a second guitarist-singer, Jimmy Maynard.

Where, I wondered, was the banjo player? They said he was sick, they didn't have a banjo player with them. That was disappointing. I'd hoped to see, hear, and meet a good picker like Tony Ellis that I could watch closely and learn from.

Shorty and Juanita went out first with Jim and me to open the show—our usual twenty minutes. Afterward, as we came off the stage into the back room, Vassar took me aside. He said "Bill wants to know if you'll play banjo with us." "Us" was The Shenandoah Valley Trio—The Blue Grass Boys without Bill Monroe. Surprised, I said yes.

I may have also said that I didn't know the music as well as I'd like to but that I'd do my best to keep up and help out, etc., but most likely these were my thoughts rather than what I spoke. I was flattered to be asked and eager to help but also afraid of messing up the music through lack of knowledge and skill.

So, along with Birch who was playing bass, I went on stage as part of the Shenandoah Valley Trio. We did a mixture of old-time tunes and country, bluegrass and gospel covers. Sometimes unfamiliar with the material, I asked Bobby Smith to let me know the key before we started each piece. Even when I knew the song, I didn't always know it in their key.

My concern with keys was simple. Bill ran a tight show: he expected the band to know arrangements and keys. His musicians were like building trades workers, and success in this line of work requires good tools and the knowledge to use them properly.

As a tool for this line of work, my banjo presented special challenges. While Bill and Vassar and Birch played their instruments in the same open tuning throughout the show, I often had to change tuning using a capo, a device that clamps over the fingerboard, shortening the strings so that the instrument can be played easily to produce the characteristic open-string banjo ring in any key.

In later years, I worked to be able to play as little as possible without capoing and tuning. But in 1961, for me, having my banjo ready for the right key meant often putting a capo on the four main strings and retuning the fifth string using the simple friction peg and a single 7th fret capo, a slotted bone nut in the fingerboard.

When the banjo was uncapoed it was in the key of G, which worked for a lot of songs. Next up the neck was A. I could move from G to A and back without too much trouble, because there I could put the fifth string into that 7th fret bone nut capo and not worry about tuning.

But if we went up to a higher key, like B or C, I had to retune the fifth string, making it tighter. That pushed down on the bridge, which pushed down the head and tended to put the other strings out of tune. It could take me a while to get in tune between songs! Electronic tuners didn't exist then.

I had to work hard and fast to keep up, especially since I didn't always know the music. I was nervous! I had gotten comfortable playing with Shorty and Juanita, but I was new to these men and their music. They expected me to know what to do.

After we'd played six or seven songs, Bobby introduced Bill Monroe and we became The Blue Grass Boys. I can't recall what we played that afternoon. I wish I'd kept a diary, or at least gotten a complete tape recording. When I went home for supper, I called Frank Hoffman to tell him Monroe was there. He got his tape recorder, came out, and caught the end of the evening show.

What I do recall strongly from the first was how Bill related to me in terms of musical communication. During several songs he came and stood next to me and loudly beat mandolin chords in rhythmic variation to the song being played. This was very obvious to friends in the audience, who commented on it after the show. I thought he was trying to throw me off. Later, I decided it was part of how he trained musicians—beating the rhythm into me. Finally, I concluded it was both of these things—he was testing me, and he was teaching me. He didn't speak to me, didn't try to tell me what to do. He was throwing hardballs—could I catch them?

It was appropriate that the Shenandoah Valley Trio became the Blue Grass Boys. Monroe brought the music to life the moment he stepped on stage. Much of this came from his mandolin. His offbeat chord "chops" are often described as central to the bluegrass sound. But he shaped the rhythm even when he was doing other things. When he stood next to me and beat the chords out on that mandolin I began to get the message. Trying to throw me off the path, he pushed me to work at my timing.

It was good to have this diversion because what I also recall was a lot of frustrated tuning. My requests for keys must have started to bug Bobby Smith because at one point he purposely told me the wrong key. I didn't yet know that Bill communicated this information to the band musically rather than verbally—he'd play the chord of the key on the mandolin before he began the next song: if he chopped an A chord, that was your cue the song would be in A.

There were a few tunes on which I was expected to take a banjo break, but for the most part I stayed in the background playing rhythm and backup as best I could, given my lack of knowledge of the repertoire and the tuning challenges. Vassar had only recently rejoined Bill after years with Jim & Jesse. Bill was so impressed with Clements's fiddle solo that, after it was finished, he turned to him, accused him of practicing, and asked him to play another. With a hot fiddler and two lead singers, the banjo player was far from the center of attention that afternoon.

As we came off stage after that first show, Monroe and I spoke for the first time. I apologized for all my clunkers. He said, "You done your best," an oblique but sincere thank-you.

Pat Burton was there that afternoon. He told me later that he'd auditioned as guitarist and singer for Monroe. Bill had told him that he was a good singer but he needed to work on developing his own vocal style—he sounded too much like Mac Wiseman. Of course on that Sunday, Bill, with two guitar players in the band, could afford to be choosy.

That evening had the same lineup on stage except that Shorty replaced Birch on bass. Frank Hoffman came in toward the end of the show and set up his recorder. He got it running in the middle of my only banjo instrumental solo. Bill had asked me to play a tune. I volunteered "Little Maggie," a popular mountain folksong I'd learned in my teens long before I knew about bluegrass. My parents often requested it; it was one of the first Redwood Canyon Ramblers songs; I'd been doing it with Shorty and Juanita. It was a surprise for Bill—I never heard anyone else do it as an instrumental with him. But he knew it, and Frank's recording began just as Bill was taking his break, after which I ended it.

Six weeks later, Bill recorded his vocal version of "Little Maggie" for Decca. But today he was suffering from a cold and singing as little as he could. After my solo, Bobby Smith did three songs for which Vassar, playing brilliantly, provided most of the instrumental breaks and tenor vocal harmonies. Then he led the way on the old-time fiddle tune Bill had put on record in 1940, "Katy Hill." Bill took a break on it, something he didn't always do on this tune.

Time for comedy—Bill asked Bobby to sing "White Lightnin'," the popular George Jones hit. Next, he suggested some trios, on which he sang tenor: "On and On" and "Uncle Pen." The show ended as always with Bill's set speech urging people to buy his records and come to the Jamboree next week, followed by a brief rendition of "Y'All Come" with everyone on stage singing.

Aside from "Little Maggie" I took no banjo breaks on anything Frank recorded. I may have been offered an opportunity—a look, a nod—by Bobby or Bill for some, but I didn't know most of those songs well enough to do so. I concentrated on learning the tune and playing backup.

"Uncle Pen" was the one song whose arrangement and key I knew, but it had no banjo break. This was another song I'd heard before I knew about bluegrass. The final line of the chorus, in a cappella, "You could hear it talk, you could hear it sing," followed by the guitar's famous bluegrass "G run," made it a memorable piece from the moment it was published in 1951.

Five years later, Missouri country singer Porter Wagoner had recorded a cover of it. Where Bill's single had one fiddle, Porter's had three. It opened with the G run, which was done throughout by an electric guitar. Porter had added an extra verse, refashioned from "Old Dan Tucker." After Wagoner joined the Opry in 1957, he came to know the song as Bill did it in person. Only three days before this show, Wagoner had rerecorded it, this time without the extra verse and with an acoustic sound closer to Monroe's. Bill spoke proudly of this when he introduced "Uncle Pen" that night at Bean Blossom: "Right here's an old-timer that a lot of folks enjoy and we'd like to say that, ah, Porter Church has recorded this number in the last few days again and he's made a second recording of it, it's called 'Uncle Pen.'"

Who was Porter Church? Later I came to understand that Bill had unconsciously misspoken, using the name of another Porter, a bluegrass banjo picker active in the Washington, D.C., scene who had briefly worked for him. But on this day, most of Bill's introduction to "Uncle Pen" went over my head! I didn't even know Bill had written it about his own uncle and wasn't yet familiar with Porter Wagoner.

I came home with stars in my eyes. I'd made it through two shows playing with Bill Monroe and the Blue Grass Boys. The next day, I excitedly broke the news to a couple of fellow graduate students just before class. One knew only vaguely who Monroe was, and the other, who'd grown up in Southern Illinois loving jazz and hating country, recognized the name but found my news not exciting but amusing if not appalling. A week later, I wrote home to my folks: "Last Sunday, Bill Monroe was at Bean Blossom, and since his regular banjo player was sick, he asked me to play banjo with him. This was quite an experience and somewhat of an honor, since Monroe is the person who started Bluegrass."

Today, with all that has been said and written about Monroe, my second sentence needs explanation. The fact is I knew little about Bill Monroe. Flatt & Scruggs and the Stanley Brothers had drawn me into this music, opening the doors for discovering the great local bands in the D.C. area, Earl Taylor and the Country Gentlemen, and the popular regional bands like Reno & Smiley and Jim & Jesse.

Most of the details about "who started Bluegrass" were unknown to me. What little had been written about this music was chiefly in the liner notes of those four bands' LP albums and Mike Seeger's Folkways albums. Monroe was a distant figure in this literature, and beyond that I knew only what I'd heard in stories about him told at Bean Blossom.

My experience was "somewhat of an honor" because I just happened to be at the Jamboree when there was no better-qualified worker available for the job. Bill was like a building contractor with a tight budget and a close deadline. If he couldn't hire a finish carpenter, he'd make do with a jackleg apprentice. I had much to learn about this music.

Autumn Work

September–October 1961

WHEN I WROTE HOME and told of playing with Monroe, I first reported about my graduate studies in folklore at IU: "My work is starting to pick up—mostly research papers and collecting."

Folklore research then, as now, was based on data "collected" in fieldwork or ethnography—seeking people to explain and perform folklore. I'd begun to realize that my experience on Sundays at Bean Blossom offered me contacts for the musical side of such research—experts like Shorty and Juanita.

My courses covered genres other than music, but even here Bean Blossom would prove useful. One of my fall courses was Professor Warren Roberts's new seminar, "Folk Arts, Crafts and Architecture." Until now, the Folklore Institute had offered only courses in what is now called "intangible cultural heritage." This covered a broad swath of oral genres: tales, legends, jokes, proverbs, beliefs, customs, and so on.

Roberts's folktale research in Scandinavia, where some called their subject "folklife" rather than "folklore," had awakened his interest in the tangible traditions of material culture. He taught us about the work of European Folklife scholars and the great folk museums of Scandinavia.

As in most folklore courses, we were expected to do original research. I decided to study local fiddle-making traditions. The topic intrigued me and meshed with my personal fascination with instruments. Now, how to find someone to interview about this?

Such questions were part of graduate student life. I looked forward to leaving them behind to perform. In this context, music was a safety valve rather than a thing of study. A few days later, I wrote home again: "We are going to a concert (featuring Frank, Chuck and Myself) at Oberlin this Saturday, with all expenses paid by Oberlin."[1]

Franklin Miller had spent the summer in Columbus working at the Motion Picture Division of the Ohio State University. Among their projects was an experimental film to which he'd added a bluegrass sound track. In the process, he discovered Columbus's vibrant local bluegrass scene. He was full of interesting stories about musicians and instruments.

Franklin was in his final semester at Oberlin. He'd revived the Plum Creek Boys with younger musicians and then arranged for a Plum Creek Boys reunion, bringing Chuck Crawford from Ann Arbor and me from Bloomington for a night of local bluegrass at Oberlin.

I marvel now at our energy and stamina in taking trips to Oberlin and elsewhere on weekends in the midst of the semester. Perhaps we should have been hitting the books that weekend, but as I wrote my folks: "We've been getting all our work done ahead of time."

I was back at the Jamboree the following Sunday; the visiting performer was singer and fiddler from Nashville, Benny Martin, who featured an electric 8-string fiddle in his act. At the end of the show on this beautiful fall day, Birch announced that Bill and the Blue Grass Boys would be back next Sunday.

Stepping Up
October 1961

ON OCTOBER 22ND, Bill returned with the same band as last month, again without a regular banjo picker. Arriving at the Jamboree barn that afternoon, I was surprised to discover that Shorty and Juanita were also absent. Birch, who was backstage organizing the show, announced they were sick.

Jim Bessire and I were expecting to play in the house band. Instead, we were recruited to help the Shenandoah Valley Trio—Bobby Smith, Jimmy Maynard and Vassar Clements—open the show. Smith took over Shorty's emcee job.

Frank Hoffman was back with his tape recorder and his camera, so I have a record of that afternoon. I was somewhat better prepared this time when I was recruited to help out with the five, even though I owned only a handful of Monroe's recordings and a few things on tape. I was in practice and looking forward to playing.

The Shenandoah Trio did seven bluegrass, old-time, gospel and country pieces. Bobby Smith dedicated several of the pieces he sang to friends and relations in the audience. Jimmy, Vassar and I all were featured on solos.

For mine, I chose "Cripple Creek," an old banjo tune I'd learned before I knew about bluegrass. I played it once; Vassar took over with a series of hot and swing variations for his break. He was in fine form, and the audience appreciated it. I closed it with rough variations and a clumsy ending. Throughout, the audience applauded and cheered at the beginning of each break.

Bassist Jim Bessire and I sit in with the Shenandoah Valley Trio (Vassar Clements, Jimmy Maynard, and Bobby Smith), October 1961. (Courtesy of Frank A. Hoffman)

This was not applause for the performance as at jazz and classical concerts where you signal aesthetic appreciation of the performance by clapping at the end. This kind of applause—familiar in pop, country, blues, and rock—is an emotional response to the performer in action: appreciative recognition. At the Jamboree that fall, I was a new face becoming familiar. I got applause of this kind every time I went up to the mike for a banjo break that afternoon.

Now it was fiddle time. Bobby introduced a familiar tune: "What do you say we get Vassar up here to do 'The Orange Blossom Special'? I know you folks have been wanting to hear that. It's one of the most popular fiddle tunes."

Indeed it was. Shorty did it every week. Vassar's version was considerably fancier. There was no singing in his version. He played it straight the first time through; the second time around he poured on the coal. Like everything we did that day, it went by fast—two times and out. He was brilliant, mercurial.

Jimmy Maynard chose his own "Having Myself a Ball," a fast rockabilly-flavored number that was a lot of fun to play.

At the end of our stint, Bobby announced another act: "We've got some boys back here in the back, ah, they come with their names a while ago but

I've forgot 'em already. And they, I believe if we give 'em a great big hand, we can get 'em out here. I know they're mighty fine entertainers, what do you say?"

I'd seen these "boys" arrive that afternoon. Before the show started, we had been standing outside the back of the barn when a yellow 1950 Studebaker coupe slowly pulled up and parked. Two old men in fancy western duds got out and spoke with Birch. Was there room for them to do a guest set on the afternoon show, they wondered? Birch, looking to fill in for the missing Shehans, was happy to say yes.

They opened the trunk and took out a guitar and a mandolin. One man was diminutive, wiry, and nervous; this was guitarist-singer Jocko Keithly. The other, older and of a medium build, was mandolinist Jesse Fender.

They'd driven up from Bedford. Guitarist Hubert Ratliff joined them; I don't know where he was from. After a long pause, they came on stage. Jocko opened with an old cowboy song, Hubert did a fancy yodeling piece, Fender played his own mandolin tune, which Jocko identified afterward as "Don't You Want to Go Back to Old Terre Haute," and they closed with a spiritual, "When I Lay My Burdens Down." Jocko introduced it as "Burden Down."

I don't think I ever saw an old-time act like these guys again at Bean Blossom. Their fancy dress and old-time repertoire had an antique feeling. I resolved to meet them after the show.

Following a twenty-minute intermission, Bill Monroe and the Blue Grass Boys came on stage. Bill opened the show with his usual greetings: "Howdy folks, we're glad to be with you today. And I hope you've enjoyed the shows that's gone along here. We're gonna kindly open this part up with a little fiddle music."

He turned to Vassar: "Do you play a number called, ah, 'Bill Cheatham'? Have you played that yet?"

"No," said Vassar.

"All right, let's get with that."

And get with it we did. The performance followed the same pattern they used for all the fiddle tunes they did that afternoon—Vassar played one break, Bill the next, and back to Vassar, who ended it after playing just the first half. I had a recording of Vassar playing "Bill Cheatham" with Jim & Jesse but I'd never tried to play it. I stood back, listened, and played rhythmic backup like I'd been doing behind Shorty that summer. The only fiddle tunes I knew well at that point were "Orange Blossom

Special" and "Cripple Creek." I was beginning to recognize others, but many were new to me.

Bill followed his usual program. After the opening fiddle tune he did several solos, beginning with "Footprints in the Snow," the late forties hit he performed at virtually every show. Next was a fairly recent recording, "Lonesome Wind Blues," that caught the guitarists and me off guard. As we were changing capos, Vassar and Bill kicked it off; the rest of us caught up in the middle of the first chorus. This was typical of Bill's on-stage pacing: he moved quickly from one piece to the next and expected the band to be ready.

After the applause died down, Bill said, "All right, let's see here. Let's get one here where we can do some good banjo-picking in this number here." Turning to me, he asked: "Can you pick something that I sing?" I should have been prepared to answer but I wasn't. "Yes," I said, trying to think of one of his songs. "Molly and Tenbrooks" came to mind—I knew that. "What'd you like to do?" he asked, and then before I could reply, he said "How about 'Little Georgia Rose,' can you do that one?" I nodded meekly, even though I didn't know it. "About B natural there?" he said. I quickly retuned.

Vassar kicked it off with the music for the verse, Bill sang the chorus, and I stepped up to the mike and played as much as I could for having heard it just once—helped along by the audience's reassuring applause at the start of my break. It felt like I'd passed a test. After this point in the show, I took breaks on all his pieces in which a banjo break was expected.

Bill was in good spirits that day—he and Bobby told jokes and he did many of his standards. "Raw Hide" followed "Little Georgia Rose," and then "Uncle Pen." After, Bill explained: "Now that, that number was wrote about a uncle of mine and Birch's here, Uncle Pen Vandiver, and one of the finest old gentlemans ever been in the country. And played an old-time fiddle. And I, if it hadn't been for Uncle Pen that we could learn from, there probably wouldn't have never been no bluegrass music today. Because I know that's kindly where that we got our start. And, ah, could really keep time, that old gentleman could, and, ah, he's helped us a lot on down through the years."

Uncle Pen was Bill's real uncle! This was news to me. It strengthened my feeling that to understand bluegrass you really needed to understand old-time fiddling.

Then came the portion of the show where he called for requests. Many in the Jamboree audience knew Bill's repertoire from previous shows, Opry performances, and records. "Mule Skinner" was shouted first—"That's a new one, but we'll try it" Bill joked. Jimmy Rodgers's "Mule Skinner Blues" was his first hit, another one he did at every show.

Other requests followed—Bill passed on "Satisfied Mind" (Porter Wagoner's first hit), but he took on his own "I'm on My Way to the Old Home," shouted from the front row by Pat Burton. Then someone asked for "Wait a Little Longer Please Jesus," a song he had recorded a few years ago. "We'll try that for you," he said; "I believe it's just time right now, we'll do some hymns for you, and we'll start with that one there."

Elsewhere I've described the difficult "hymn time" show segment that followed.[1] At its end, Bill apologized for not rehearsing and then said: "Now we're gonna turn loose on an old-time fiddle number here with Vassar. He wants to do 'Panhandle Country.'" In the wake of that 1958 Monroe recording came requests for three old-time fiddle tunes: "Down Yonder," "Bile Them Cabbage Down," and "Raggedy Ann." This was an educated audience—these tunes were well known to fiddle music fans in the audience. They appreciated Vassar's take on them.

A request for "The Waltz You Saved for Me" led Bill, who didn't know it, to ask wryly: "Anyone can sing that?" and then quickly turning to his brother asked: "Birch, can you sing that?" He continued, laughing: "I'd like to hear Birch sing that, 'The Waltz You Saved for Me,' now. You lead, if you sing lead I'll sing tenor to it."

Birch, who only sang bass on hymns, demurred. Bill laughed more then and continued: "I tell you we got a feller here that hasn't got to be on stage yet and he drove a long way, this boy setting right here and he sings a awful good song. What's his name?"

"Pat Burton" said Birch.

"Pat Burton. Now Pat I think you should come up here and do a number." The audience applauded, seconding Bill's invitation.

"And we'd like to have little Carol Logston come up and do a number for us too. We still got two more to get on the stage here. Everybody's always welcome here at Bean Blossom, and we're glad to have you to pick and sing with us."

Carol Logston was a daughter of the couple who operated the food and beverage concessions at the Jamboree; she was Roger Smith's sister-in-law. She was a very good singer, often performing as a guest vocalist at the Jamboree doing contemporary country "girl singer" hits.

Bill and Bobby went into a long comedy routine followed by a short gospel duet, and then Birch spoke up.

"Bill, let's call this young fellow up here, Pat Burton."

Bill agreed: "Yeah, I think he should come on up. If he'd like to sing one, be glad to have him."

"He plays here with us on Saturday night and we'd like to have him sing one here," Birch explained. This was Bill's cue to plug Birch's Saturday night dances.

"Yeah, I know, boy. They do have an old-time round and square dance here every Saturday night and they're having good crowds now, so you folks come over some Saturday if you'd like to round and square dance and enjoy yourself on Saturday night right here at Bean Blossom."

Pat was now on stage. "We're gonna call on Pat now and see what he'd like to sing. . . . Pat, pick out a good one here. And sing good and loud." Pat chose "When the Roses Bloom Again," a song from Mac Wiseman's first album. Bill thanked Pat when he'd finished: "That's mighty fine there. Pat has really got the making of a fine singer, he's got a good voice, got a good toned voice, if he'll just a-cultivate it and stay right in there he'll make a wonderful singer."

Then he introduced "a little lady here that can really rear back and sing like nobody's business, little Carol Logston." She sang Opry star Jeanne Shepherd's midfifties single, "Act Like a Married Man." Afterward, Bill kidded Bobby about this song—Bobby's in-laws were in the audience.

One more request—another hymn—and it was time to end the show. Bill began by promising that he'd be "back next Sunday for another show. Tell your neighbors that we'll be here. You folks come back too if you can. Don't forget us on the Grand Ole Opry, let's hear from you some time."

Like these last words, much of what Bill said in closing was formulaic. But what he said next reflected the existential situation that bugged Merce and others: "And then we're gonna have some other shows following that show [next week] up, ah, finish up the fall here that we believe you will enjoy. Ah, Rusty Adams is gonna be back here on the 18th of November along with Bill Dudley and we will have some good shows for you, so, ah, I was talking to Lonzo and Oscar and they want to come back, so we will have some good shows for you. Kindly watch the advertisements and everything."

Bill and Birch—the Jamboree's owner and manager—were competing with other similar venues that had their whole season booked and, if not printed up on fliers, at least announced and postered several weeks in advance. Here he was with next week, one date some weeks ahead, and a "maybe." No wonder the Jamboree was sometimes sparsely attended!

Bill closed saying, "We'll look forward to seeing Shorty Shehan here next Sunday," inviting the audience back, and to "drop around to the Grand Ole Opry" when in Nashville; then, hitting a chord on the mandolin, said: "Right now, speaking for all the gang it's time we were saying, 'Y'All Come.'" And the show ended musically, with one chorus of that song.

This afternoon, when I wasn't busy on stage, I had been looking into the research question that preoccupied me—does anyone know any fiddle makers? Although Birch had told me that someone who came to the dances had built fiddles, a trip to the dance the night before hadn't turned up that fiddle maker.

After the show, Frank and I spoke with Jesse Fender. He told us that he and Jocko lived in Bedford. He collected old instruments, owned a couple of locally built fiddles, and had made a guitar himself. He said he'd written more mandolin tunes, too. We got his address and arranged to visit him to record his tunes and look at his instruments.

Connections
October 1961

I RODE WITH FRANK HOFFMAN to visit Jocko Keithly and Jesse Fender. I'd never been to Bedford; Frank had. His dissertation research on obscene folktales had led him to IU's Kinsey Institute. He'd been collecting stag films for their library and archives. As we drove south from Bloomington, he pointed out several roadside stores where these 16mm porn films could be obtained, contact points on an underground network.

Jocko and Jesse lived in an old two-front-door house on the outskirts of Bedford. Those two-front-door homes, found all over southern Indiana, were a subject of discussion in our Folk Arts, Crafts, and Architecture seminar—a paragon of regional folk architecture.

The design worked well for these men—each had a side of the house. Enter the left door from the porch, and you were in Jocko's sparsely furnished side. His D28 Martin guitar in its case was underneath the bed. A paint-by-numbers oil of Jesus Christ hung on the inside wall, next to a 1930s clipping from the local paper telling how Jocko, who worked at the Bedford Hotel, had applied for his present job of busboy thinking he'd be driving a bus. It was a story he liked to tell, it tickled him.

The door on the right opened into Jesse's bedroom. Clothes hung on nails from the walls. The several dressers in this crowded space were filled with bits and pieces of old instruments.

Frank recorded Jesse playing and talking about his mandolin tunes. After the interview I asked Jesse about locally made fiddles and he showed me two, made by friends in the vicinity. He enjoyed talking about instruments. He spoke again of the guitar he'd made and told me he thought the people out in California who made the Fender electric guitars were distant kinfolks.

In the following weeks, I visited him frequently. He took me to meet fiddle makers and people who owned old locally built instruments. This was another underground network, one I soon became involved in, for most also owned factory-made, store-bought instruments. I began buying old banjos, guitars, and mandolins out in the country there and selling them in Bloomington to dealers and students.

By the time we visited Jocko and Jesse, I'd already made my first visit to the Saturday night dance at the Brown County Jamboree, hoping in vain to meet a fiddle maker. That was October 21st, the night before the show I described in the last chapter.

For Saturday night's dance all the chairs had been folded up, clearing the smooth cement floor in front of the stage. Birch was front and center, fiddling from the stage into its single mike. Pat and I joined the other musicians there (like Birch's friend, guitarist Kyle Wells, and Bryant Wilson) to support Birch's lead.

I was keen to learn fiddle tunes. Birch wasn't a show fiddler like Shorty and Vassar. Like many old-time fiddlers I've met since then, Birch started his tunes bowing quietly. He gradually turned up the heat, emphasizing rhythmic structure. He knew lots of old-time tunes and he knew the right rhythms for the dancers. Each dance lasted many times longer than the brief performances on stage. Playing square dances with Birch was a good way to learn those old tunes.

Here, too, I was introduced to local traditions I didn't know about. I'd done square dancing at school in Los Alamos when I was ten years old and had enjoyed it as a teen in Berkeley. At Bean Blossom, I encountered something new: there was no caller.

Instead, the head couple in each square led and called the dance. Most who came to this dance were regulars. They knew each other and all were familiar with the dances. This was an old local dance tradition, one that, as I later learned from Brown County fiddler Thurman Percifield, had been carried on in earlier decades at local homes. Through such contacts at Bean Blossom, my knowledge of local networks of tradition began to grow, often in unexpected ways.

I also had begun to meet others who were interested in what was perceived as the new music—bluegrass. Jim Peva discovered the Jamboree at about the same time as I did. Jim was a young Indiana State Police sergeant who'd come to a Monroe show at the Jamboree that summer, looking to hire Monroe to play the Police Department banquet in Terre Haute that fall.

This was the beginning of his lifelong involvement with Bean Blossom; he began coming to shows with his family. We first met and spoke after one of them. Jim was not a musician—he was a fan and soon a friend of Monroe's. He'd grown up with the Opry and country music but was just discovering the world of bluegrass.

Another was Mike Trimble, a young man from Bloomington who asked me for banjo lessons. His family was from Kentucky; he worked in the junkyard they owned. Older relatives played the 5-string banjo in the old brushing style (he called it "framming"), but he wasn't interested in that; he wanted to learn the Scruggs style like I played.

I met people like Mike and Jim near the stage in the main part of the barn or backstage when they introduced themselves and spoke to me between shows. I also started to get to know some of the accomplished musicians who showed up unannounced to play. Most important of these was Roger Smith, whom I'd seen from a distance in the summer playing with Bryant Wilson in the back room.

That fall, Roger had played the old fiddle tune, "Sally Goodin," on the banjo in an afternoon show. His old archtop banjo, a gold-plated Grenada from the twenties, sounded great. His playing was authoritative. It didn't sound like he was trying to play "Sally Goodin" someone else's way, even though what he did was very similar to Scruggs. He made it his tune.

After the show I complimented Roger on his playing. He asked to look at my banjo, the 1954 Gibson with a prewar flathead shell. He played it a bit and allowed as to how he preferred archtops to flatheads because it was easier to keep the head tight. He pressed down on my banjo head with his thumb, and the head gave—sank down—just a tad under it. He recommended that I tighten it.

The next morning at home I took the resonator off, got out the hex key, and started turning the screws on the hooks that pull down the tension hoop around the head. The procedure was simple: a quarter of a turn on each of 24 screws, around and around. I did this until the head broke! It was some time later that I heard the bluegrass banjo players' joke:

Beginner: "How tight should I have my banjo head?"

Veteran: "Tighten it until it breaks and then back her off a quarter turn."

Roger not only played with authority, he spoke with authority. Although I never took lessons from him (many did) he was my informal mentor in banjo and bluegrass for the next six years.

With Roger that day was Marvin Hedrick. Jim Bessire had been telling me all summer that I ought to meet Marvin, who had a radio/TV sales and repair shop in Nashville and held weekly jam sessions in the back room. He introduced himself and invited me to drop in.

White House Blues
October 1961

I PLAYED ONCE MORE with Monroe later that fall—probably on the last Sunday in October. The week before, Bill had promised that he, Shorty, and Juanita would be there.

And they were. But this time Bill was by himself. Shorty, Juanita, and I, with Birch on bass, became The Blue Grass Boys for that Sunday. I don't have a recording of that show, but I still recall how, on "Uncle Pen," Juanita, who played powerful rhythm on the guitar and knew plenty of chords but no lead runs, asked me to play the "G run" usually done by the guitarist. I enjoyed this show.

This time I'd brought along the Gibson Century mandolin I'd gotten in Vermont. After the show I asked Bill if he was interested in looking at it. He said he was, so I went to the car and brought it into the back room. I opened the case and showed it to him. He picked it up, looked at the flat back and the fancy fingerboard, got a pick, and began playing it. I don't recall a tune, just some runs and a few chord chops. I noticed the way his fingers seemed to float over the fingerboard, seeming to barely push the strings down even though they created perfect tones: a subtle strength. He told me that it was a nice mandolin, he liked it. I was glad to have his opinion.

Not long after that, I borrowed and copied Frank Hoffman's tapes of the two shows I'd played with Bill in September and October. To copy, I borrowed a second open-reel tape recorder, connected it to mine, and ran both simultaneously, one on "play," the other on "record." It was time-consuming work. I made only two copies—one for me and the other to send to Scott Hambly in Berkeley.

We were both into collecting bluegrass recordings—buying records and trading tapes. Just as the study of fiddle making flowed from and broadened my already keen interest in the instruments I played and collected, my graduate studies dovetailed with record and tape collection.

That summer I'd taken "Ballads and Folk Poetry," taught by ballad specialist Edson W. Richmond. I had been reading about ballad scholarship in liner notes and owned American folksong books like those of Carl Sandberg and Alan Lomax. But until I took this course, I didn't really know the scholarly lay of the land—the who's who, the issues.

One of our textbooks was a newly published history, *Anglo-American Folksong Scholarship since 1898*, by D. K. Wilgus, a professor of English at Western Kentucky University. Here, I learned about the work and ideas of great scholars like Francis James Child and Cecil Sharp. Wilgus also showed how hillbilly music—the roots of country and bluegrass, the stuff the NLCR called old-timey—could be seen as a kind of folk music.

Wilgus was the first folksong scholar fully conversant with phonograph recordings. Record review editor of the *Journal of American Folklore*, he knew about the hundreds of folk albums published in the past decade, especially those with "more authentic" field recordings. Students "are no longer limited by the printed page," he argued. "The sound of folkmusic can generally be heard."[1]

When time came to choose a term paper project, I decided to study a hillbilly recording, "White House Blues." It had interested me since 1958 when I encountered it on a Folkways album, Volume One of Harry Smith's *Anthology of American Folk Music*, "Ballads." Here, I heard Charlie Poole and the North Carolina Ramblers' version of this song about the 1901 assassination of President McKinley. Mayne, his father Henry, and I were listening to it at their home. At first I could not understand a word of it. But Henry's emotional response to this recording as a familiar sound from his youth moved me to learn as much of the words as I could. Chuck Crawford and I rearranged the verse order and made up some words to fill the gaps we couldn't understand. We often sang it as a brother duet and included it in our Lorain County String Band demo recordings.

Then I discovered that Bill Monroe had recorded "White House Blues," too, in a version quite different from Poole's. In my term paper, I compared the two. Professor Richmond gave me an A and suggested it would make a good MA thesis. I was excited about that idea and began doing research.

Harry Smith's notes were a great help to me. For each song he provided four sets of information: the record label contents, a brief tabloid headline summary ("McKINLEY SWEARS, MOURNS, DIES. ROOSEVELT GETS WHITE HOUSE AND SILVER CUP"), a discography, and a bibliography.

What made "White House Blues" interesting to me as a folklorist was that if you looked for it in books, Smith's bibliography based on published folksong canons showed it had been collected from oral tradition only once. Records told a different story: his discography listed four records. And that list didn't include Monroe's—Bill had recorded it after *The Anthology* was published. In this case, commercial records documented tradition more fully than the scholars.

Up to this point, I'd understood *discography* as a noun—the name for a list of records. Now I saw that it was also a verb, describing the type of research needed to compile a list of records. My mentor in this was Guthrie T. "Gus" Meade, a helpful older graduate student who'd come from Kentucky to IU in 1955 to study anthropology and folklore.

Gus was studying folksong on old hillbilly records. Even then he was compiling the data that constitutes his monumental *Country Music Sources*, a 1,000-page "Biblio-Discography of Commercially Recorded Traditional Music," published in 2002, eleven years after his unexpected death at the age of 58.

Joe Hickerson introduced me to Gus as a fellow musician. Gus was a sweet guy who sang, played the guitar, and fiddled. We soon fell to talking about old records and I asked him for advice in finding the old out-of-print records listed in Smith's "White House Blues" discography. He helped put me in touch with record collectors.

That fall I discovered *Disc Collector*, a mimeographed magazine by and for hillbilly record collectors, on the shelves of the IU Folklore library. Reading it cover to cover I began to learn something of the history of hillbilly record collection and study. I subscribed and bought back issues. Here I learned that bluegrass was part of what was being studied, for *Disc Collector* had published discographies of Flatt & Scruggs, The Stanley Brothers, and Bill Monroe. All were written by Pete Kuykendall, whom I'd heard of because he had played banjo for a while as a member of the Country Gentlemen!

End of the Season
November 1961

ON THANKSGIVING DAY (November 23) Scott Hambly wrote about the tape I'd sent of my performances with Bill that fall: "I got your tape and gave it close consideration as how you measure up to being a 'Bluegrass Boy.' It seems to me that you've made it. . . . If you can play for Monroe, you can play with anybody."[1]

His letter arrived that Saturday. I wrote back late the next night, having worked the Jamboree that afternoon and then written a ten-page term paper. I mentioned I'd be going to Indianapolis tomorrow for my preinduction Army physical. Happy to be thinking about bluegrass, I responded in detail about my experiences with Monroe.

> Glad you enjoyed the tape—naturally I did not put in the "Rawhide" where I f—up (Monroe surprised me—on purpose, as he likes to test his banjo pickers) on the last G chord bit, and "Panhandle Co.," where the banjo was horribly out of tune. However Shorty Sheehan said that Monroe was watching me the first two times (the third time: Shorty on fiddle, Juanita on Guitar, Birch on bass) playing wild off-beat rhythms to confuse me (and the guitar-picker), and that I came off quite well. You can't pick fancy Dan stuff with Monroe—what you have to do is change keys at the drop of a hat and pick fast as hell. I think a month or two on the road with him and I could pick most anything. But my work on the 5-string since I started playing with Shorty & Juanita in July (today was the last show of the season) has been on slow to medium stuff—even the fiddle tunes are slower than when Shorty does them with Monroe, although they are at a respectable pace. I don't do too much single-string backing yet but playing all the pop hits has led me to use Reno's backing (and solo) technique of no capo.[2]

I told him about that afternoon's show, which was the only end-of-season show during my years at the Jamboree where Monroe did not appear. Instead, there was a bluegrass band from Colon, Michigan: Mel Yoder and the Country Cutups. I said their banjo "picker . . . was J.D. Crowe all the way but they had to play pretty slow to get all the notes in on the instrumentals." Their singing was impressive: "fine 3-part, tho."

I then turned to a topic I'd mentioned in an earlier letter. At the end of the summer, Shorty mentioned that he had heard that Starday Records in Nashville was interested in acts such as ours and spoke of us making a record there. Now I reported: "The recording bit with Shorty & Juanita is very nebulous, although we plan to get together and work up some stuff on Sundays. Shorty is going to teach me how to sing 3rd part so we can do some spirituals & etc." Like most of Shorty's projects, this one never panned out.

Most of Scott's letter to me was about happenings in Berkeley, where the Redwood Canyon Ramblers were still active: "Out here we are going to give one of the best Bluegrass shows ever when we team up with Vern & Ray (the Carroll County Country Boys) from Stockton. These boys are really DAMN good!"

The show was set for December 2nd at Washington School, where we'd given a show the year before. He promised to send a poster.[3] He also listed a bunch of new bluegrass recordings he'd been listening to, wondering if I'd heard this new stuff. I hadn't—I could only afford to buy albums I considered important for my work. Following my appearances with Monroe, I was now collecting his records in order to study up on his discography. I had just gotten his latest album, *Mr. Bluegrass*. I'd also gotten Bill Clifton's new Carter Family Memorial album because it included a song related to "White House Blues."

In the middle of the following week, I was talking about my "White House Blues" research with Lynwood Montell, a folklore graduate student from Kentucky, who knew of my interest in an old Carter Family song listed in Harry Smith's "White House Blues" discography: "Cannon Ball Blues." Montell said a new record of that song by a bluegrass singer named Bill Clifton was being played on an Indianapolis country music radio station. The station was advertising that Clifton would be appearing next Sunday at an arena in Franklin, the town where the Shehans lived, about 25 miles northeast of Bean Blossom. I made plans to attend.

Cannonball Blues
December 1961

IN 1985, I wrote about Bill Clifton in *Bluegrass: A History*, describing him as "the first 'citybilly' in bluegrass,"[1] but when I met him in December 1961 I knew little about him except for his early recordings on Starday and Blue Ridge and his wonderful 1958 songbook, *150 Old-Time Folk and Gospel Songs*. It had a signed Foreword by A. P. Carter.[2]

The Carter Family, who recorded between 1927 and 1941, breaking up in 1943, was the hillbilly music act best known to the folksong revival. Favorites of Woody Guthrie, more of their records were included on Harry Smith's *Anthology of American Folk Music* than anyone else's. In October 1960, Joan Baez covered their "Little Moses" in her hit debut album.

A. P. Carter's death the following month was widely reported. In January 1961, Columbia records released the first Carter Family reissue on LP, and several groups began recording Carter Family tribute albums.

That fall at Rone Music, Louis showed me a new Starday album he thought I'd like—Bill Clifton's *Carter Family Memorial*. I bought it. It had "Cannonball Blues" on it—just Clifton singing and playing rhythm guitar with a second guitar fingerpicking the lead.

I realized at that point that I already knew this song by a different title. Maybelle Carter of the original Carter Family had continued on in the business after 1943 with her three daughters. I'd bought a 45 by the Carter Sisters and Mother Maybelle in 1959, because I recognized the title on one side, "Wildwood Flower"—the Carter Family's most famous song. On the other side was "He's Solid Gone," a version of "Cannonball Blues" with driving fingerpicking on the guitar by Mother Maybelle.

It was similar in many ways to the folk guitar fingerpicking warhorses in C like "Railroad Bill" and "Freight Train," both of which I already knew. I learned it quickly and kept it in my "singing with guitar" repertoire.

On a cold Sunday in December 1961, a week after the Jamboree had closed for the season, I drove up to Franklin to see Clifton, who was promoting the new Starday single from his Carter Family album. I had my guitar and banjo in the trunk. This was my only visit to this venue, a fairly modern building with a large stage at one end and a dressing room at the other.

When I walked into this room to meet Clifton, whom I'd never seen, I was surprised to discover that the Country Gentlemen—John Duffey, Charlie Waller, and Tom Gray—were his backup band. Only a few months earlier, in May, I'd booked them at their first college concert. I had been in touch with Duffey about his work on my mandolin, but he hadn't mentioned that he was headed this way.

A further surprise: banjoist Eddie Adcock wasn't with them. "What happened to Eddie?" I asked Duffey. "Oh, he's always been like that," John joked evasively. Over in a corner was his replacement, Walter Hensley, fingers wrapped around a Styrofoam cup of steaming hot coffee in an attempt to get them warm enough to pick. He seemed very shy.

Hensley had played with a Baltimore band, Earl Taylor and the Stoney Mountain Boys, in 1958–1959. Mike Seeger introduced them to Alan Lomax, who included them in his Carnegie Hall production, *Folk Song '59*. I first heard Hensley's playing with Taylor on a Seeger-produced Folkways album.

His playing blew me away. He was one of the best at using Scruggs tuners. He was picking an old Gibson archtop, from which he worked a Telecasterlike tone—sharp, high, ringing. I wanted to hear as much of him as I could. In the fall of 1959, United Artists released an album by the band: *Alan Lomax Presents . . . Folk Songs from the Bluegrass*. Lomax's copious and enthusiastic liner notes included descriptions of each band member. His paragraph on Hensley began: "Walter Hensley, lean, intense, randy, ironic and 23 years old" and went on to describe a mountain banjo boy with "true folk magic in every note" he played.

Duffey introduced me to Hensley and Clifton. There was a pressing matter to be resolved. John told me that Bill wanted to feature his new recording on the show. But Eddie had been doing the guitar break and Walter, Eddie's replacement, didn't play guitar. He asked if I had a guitar,

I nodded; Clifton asked me if I knew "Cannonball Blues" and could play Mother Maybelle's break; I said yes. I brought my guitar in, we practiced the arrangement, and I was now part of the show.

When Clifton heard I was doing graduate studies in folklore at IU his eyes lit up. He said he was gathering material for an album of war songs and would love to include some old folksongs. Did I know of any? I told him the IU Folklore Library had virtually every published folksong collection and promised to take a look.

When I got my guitar, I'd also brought in my banjo, the prewar Gibson flathead with a 1954 Mastertone neck and resonator. Walter asked to look at it. His prewar archtop, the one on his records with Earl Taylor, had a similar neck. He asked if he could try mine. Sure, I said, happy to be talking shop with one of my banjo heroes. He spent some time picking it.

After the show, Charlie Waller took me aside and told me Walter wanted to swap banjos with me. He offered, in addition to his archtop, two hundred dollars. Walter didn't have the money, Charlie said, but I do. That was a fair offer and I was flattered, but I didn't want an archtop. I don't think I even tried Walter's banjo.

At Oberlin the previous May, Charlie had told me that he really liked Hensley's banjo playing and hoped he'd be able to work with the Gentlemen some time. At that show in Franklin, I stayed on stage playing along with the band after doing "Cannon Ball Blues," soaking up Walter's interpretations of the classic Country Gentlemen and Bill Clifton repertoires. I regretted not having the tape recorder along.

I did take home from that day, in my own banjo repertoire, a tune he played backstage before the show: "Grandfather's Clock." I knew the tune, but I'd never heard it done on the banjo, and as far as I know no 5-string recordings of it existed then. It was a great idea that quickly became a staple in my repertoire.

My backstage conversation with Duffey ranged widely. I'd helped him get their first college folk club booking, and now they were beginning to get bookings elsewhere in the folk world. I told him of my adventures at Bean Blossom playing with Monroe, and Shorty and Juanita. He filled me in on the progress he'd made with my mandolin, which was presently in the workshop of inlay master Tom Morgan. He also spoke of recent recording session work.

In addition to their Country Gentlemen work—an album was due out on Starday soon—they had been helping out Clifton in the studio, along with Mike Seeger, who played autoharp, clawhammer banjo, and guitar. In fact, it was Seeger playing the Mother Maybelle guitar break on Clifton's "Cannonball Blues."

I recalled and mentioned my friendship with Seeger, who'd stayed at our family home in Berkeley the previous year. Duffey told me that, at a recent session, Seeger had told him that he was singing the tenor part to one song wrong. "Who the hell does he think he is, telling me how to sing?" he said angrily. I was taken aback by John's intensity, but it did seem a logical question. He'd told me in his September letter about their reception at Carnegie Hall—liked by the crowd, snubbed by the critics. This kind of summary judgment irked Duffey. Indeed, the *New York Times,* whose entertainment writer Robert Shelton, an enthusiastic fan of Scruggs and the Greenbriar Boys and the first to write about Bob Dylan, had called their Carnegie Hall set "lackluster."[3]

The folk music revival gatekeepers in New York City were beginning to recognize bluegrass, but their knowledge was spotty and their esthetics provincial. Though they'd brought Flatt & Scruggs and the Stanley Brothers to the Newport Folk Festival, most had never seen Bill Monroe and the Blue Grass Boys. The Country Gentlemen were off the radar in New York, but the undergrads in the Oberlin Folksong Club had already booked them for a return engagement at their spring Folk Festival.

We spent the Christmas holiday in Berkeley. The bluegrass scene was growing there. I joined Redwood Canyon Ramblers Mayne Smith and Scott Hambly in a jam session with Vern Williams, the mandolinist with Vern and Ray, who would soon have a new EP on Starday. Scott also played me some new bluegrass recordings from his collection, including one by the New York group that Franklin Miller had told me about in 1960—the Greenbriar Boys. Their new mandolinist, Ralph Rinzler, was an accomplished exponent of Monroe's style. I spent another afternoon giving a young high school student named Rick Shubb a banjo lesson—the only one he every got. Shubb would later make a name for himself as the inventor of a widely used capo.

SPRING 1962

Meeting Marvin Hedrick
January–June 1962

AS THE NEW YEAR BEGAN, I was learning about discography. Sparked by my experience as a substitute Blue Grass Boy at Bean Blossom, where I suffered from not knowing Bill's repertoire, I was working on a Monroe discography, collecting all of his recordings, mainly on tape.

I got assistance on this from Scott, who sent me tapes of old Monroe singles from his extensive collection. He'd just bought a 1924 Gibson F5 Master Model mandolin—one like Monroe's—from Mike Seeger. He wrote about playing all over California, sitting in with big-name bluegrass bands in LA, and sent me tapes from those experiences. He was also trading tapes with Pete Kuykendall, the Washington bluegrass discographer, and sharing those tracks with me.

I was sending him new stuff from my tape collection, which grew by leaps and bounds after I started attending Marvin Hedrick's jam sessions at his shop in Brown County. Last fall at Bean Blossom, he'd told me of these Wednesday night affairs and invited me to drop in. Soon after returning from Berkeley in January 1962, I called him to get details and directions. Hedrick Radio Service was in a roadside building on the outskirts of Nashville, Indiana, with a big radio-television antenna behind it and a service van parked beside. Next to it was the Hedrick family home.

Marvin was thirty-seven years old. A Brown County native, he'd gotten into electronics and hillbilly music in his teens. He was an RCA dealer; the front of his shop was filled with new radios, televisions, and tape recorders. There were records for sale, too, and a soft drink machine.

"We Service after We Sell" was his business slogan. In the middle of the back wall of the shop room, Dutch doors with a counter on the bottom half opened into the big repair shop at the back of the store. Marvin held his weekly jams here; they started around 7:00. The workspace was cleared; a tape recorder sat on a workbench at the side of the room. In front of it was a microphone on a stand and, directly in front of that, a music stand on which sat a big ring binder filled with sheets—mainly the Hedrick Service letterhead—with typewritten words to songs. We played and sang facing the microphone and workbench as if it was the front of the stage at the Jamboree.[1]

Several musicians were jam regulars. Charlie Percifield, from an old Nashville family, worked in the shop. He played the mandolin and was a bit younger than Marvin. Bernard Lee, at 41 the oldest of the regulars, was a fiddler from Avalon, Mississippi, who'd moved to work in Bloomington after the war. Jim Bessire, the bass player who'd first told me about Marvin, was usually there.

Marvin played the guitar—an old Gibson Southern Jumbo—with a thumb pick and sang lead on most of the songs. He had grown up on a farm in Van Buren township, in the southeast corner of the county in a section that later became part of Brown County State Park, hearing local musicians like fiddlers Louis Henderson and Thurman Percifield. As a teen, he'd been attracted to hillbilly music on the radio. At that time, most of Brown County outside of Nashville was without electricity. Marvin described listening to the Opry on a car radio, and nursing radio batteries and aerials for this and other special broadcasts. His favorites were Mainer's Mountaineers and Bill Monroe. All of this was, as he grew up, part of "old-time music."

Tom Adler has written of Marvin's early days at the Jamboree,[2] telling how he began attending in the early 1940s. During the forties, he studied electronics at a college in Chicago. He worked for a while at the RCA plant in Bloomington and then returned to Nashville, married, and opened his shop. That was around 1949.

By the time I met him, Marvin had built a record collection, mainly of bluegrass recordings. He'd also started a tape collection. Many of the songs in his songbook came from these recordings.

Running a tape recorder sales and repair business, Marvin learned about the new machines by using them to record off the radio and at the Jamboree. After Monroe bought the park in 1951, he'd gotten to know Birch,

September 1959. Blue Grass Boys and Brown Countians hanging out after a jam. Joe Stuart checks out Marvin Hedrick's new Gibson tenor guitar while Jack Cook (guitar), Ed Taggart (banjo), and Marvin Hedrick watch. (Courtesy of Jim Work)

and as a regular audience member, made his wishes known. He wanted to hear "bluegrass"—a new word then—by bands like the Stanley Brothers and Mac Wiseman.

He started taking the new RCA tape recorders to these shows in 1954. That year, he recorded Monroe—twice—and Mac Wiseman. The next year, he recorded the Stanley Brothers, and in the summer of 1956 taped a show by Bill, brother Charlie, the two of them together with Birch, and The Kelley Brothers, a bluegrass act from Kentucky with a recent single. One memorable afternoon! That fall, he got Monroe again and, on the same day, recorded a jam session in the back room. In '58 Reno & Smiley came; he recorded them and Monroe again. The following year, he captured another backroom jam session with a mix of local musicians and Blue Grass Boys.

Each time Hedrick recorded him, Monroe had different band members—fiddlers, banjo pickers, guitarist-singers—whose names were new to me then but are now familiar from my study of Monroe's music.

Marvin introduced me to songs he sang regularly that had been featured by Monroe's lead singers. At the beginning of each show, Bill called upon his guitarist to introduce himself by singing a solo, usually a recent country hit. Marvin had taped a couple of Monroe's shows at the Jamboree in the fifties when Texan singer-guitarist Edd Mayfield was with the band. Unlike most younger bluegrass guitarists, Edd played with a thumb pick, and he could do some very fancy lead work. Marvin admired and emulated Mayfield (a tragic figure, he'd died of leukemia while on the road with Monroe) and sang songs he'd taped Mayfield doing with Bill like "I Ain't Broke but I'm Badly Bent." Another favorite was Joe Stuart's "Alcatraz Blues" from a backroom jam tape.

These were easy songs for me to learn, and, with many other bluegrass standards that I already knew, were part of the fare at Marvin's jams.

This was my first experience in attending an organized weekly jam. Marvin, with guitar strapped on, would page through the songbook to find a good one to start with, something we all knew but that was not too familiar. "Truck Driving Man," which Jimmy Martin later recorded, was a favorite. He recorded each piece and would listen to them at work during the week.

Most of the talk between songs was about music. Marvin recalled thirties radio shows by Mainer's Mountaineers; Bernard Lee reminisced about Shell Smith and Willie Narmour, old-time musicians he'd grown up hearing in Avalon. These names were familiar to me from the NLCR's Folkways album notes.

We talked about new recordings, about musical goings-on at the Jamboree, elsewhere in Indiana, and the Opry (Marvin was a faithful listener). We shared news about other musical activities—Marvin, Bernard, and Charlie played for square dances up at the Abe Martin Lodge in Brown County State Park; I was picking a lot with Jim Neawedde and Tom Hensley—shows we had seen, and so on. We talked about instruments. We rarely discussed politics or sports.

I didn't come to every jam, probably once or twice a month at best. Others, like Roger Smith, also visited occasionally. Marvin's boys were taking lessons from Roger—Gary (age twelve) played the mandolin, and David (age nine), the banjo. They were often there.

We'd play for a couple of hours, with Marvin asking each musician in turn for a solo or a suggestion. I heard a lot of music and music history at these sessions. It was here that I began to learn how to play old-time fiddle tunes on the banjo; Bernard was always present and happy to play favorite standards like "Ragtime Annie" and "Soldier's Joy."

At the end of the jam, we'd pack away our instruments and move out to the front of the shop. Marvin would unlock the pop machine and treat all to a Coke or a Dr. Pepper. Talk about music continued; Marvin often spoke of his records and tapes.

Soon after I began going to the jams, I returned to Marvin's on a couple of afternoons when I didn't have classes to make tape copies of his bluegrass records—78 and 45 rpm singles that hadn't been reissued on LPs. I brought my recorder to his shop, attached alligator clips to his record player's speaker leads, and taped about sixty early classics and lesser-known pieces by Monroe, Flatt & Scruggs, Mac Wiseman, Jim Eanes, Bill Clifton, Charlie Monroe, Red Allen, and Sonny Osborne, and a record I'd read about but never seen or heard: "New Camptown Races" by mandolin wizard Frank Wakefield. A side benefit of this exercise was being able to copy master numbers, the building blocks of discography, from the original record labels.

During my visits to record, and at our after-session visits, Marvin would often mention tapes he had with this or that song or musician on them. I would ask to borrow them, and he generously began loaning them to me a few at a time.

He had recorded radio broadcasts, mainly the Old and New Dominion Barn Dances from WRVA in Richmond, WDBJ in Roanoke, WWVA in Wheeling, and the Grand Ole Opry from WSM in Nashville. I dubbed his tapes as I'd done with my copies for Scott the previous fall. I got 107 separate tracks. Performers included familiar early bluegrass stars like Monroe, Flatt & Scruggs, Mac Wiseman, and Reno & Smiley, as well as fifties country stars like Wilma Lee and Stoney Cooper, Charlie Monroe, and J. E. Mainer. New to me were the regional bluegrass bands of Hack Johnson and Toby Stroud. Hedrick identified gifted sidemen on certain cuts like Buck Graves with Stroud and the Coopers, and Blue Grass Boys Jackie Phelps and Jim Smoak.

Most prized were Marvin's live tapes from the Jamboree. I copied three Monroe shows and one backroom jam session. Unlike some who recorded shows, Marvin kept the tape running between songs. I heard musicians introduced and speaking on stage—Edd Mayfield, Kenny Baker, Bob Johnson, Joe Stuart, Gordon Terry, and Charlie Cline. Marvin had met these men and enjoyed talking about their character and their music. I would later meet some of these legendary Blue Grass Boys. The 1959 backstage jam included Stuart, fiddler Joe Meadows, Marvin himself, and another local bluegrass fan, Harold Lowry.

My time at the jams and listening to the recordings was the beginning of a period of deep learning. I was listening to a lot of bluegrass! Today, you can download such stuff and watch YouTubes of them. Back then, acquiring old recordings of the music was a challenge. I'm still grateful to Marvin for his generosity.

Marvin hadn't heard of the NLCR, the New York band that was re-creating the old recordings of groups like the Mainers, so I lent him my copy of their first Folkways LP. "Piss-poor fiddling," he said, as he returned it the next time I came to the shop. He liked the idea of what they were doing, though.

I was in irregular contact with Marvin for the rest of my years in Bloomington. If I didn't get to a jam session in a while we talked on the phone. I would drop in to buy something or just to visit while in Nashville on other business. Sometimes he'd have an old tape he wanted me to hear—I'd borrow it and return it later. We met at the Jamboree, too. Sometimes we'd both be there with our recorders. We shared bluegrass, folk, and old-time news; talked instruments; and just visited. He became a good friend.

College Kids
March–May 1962

MY INVOLVEMENT IN BLUEGRASS was deepening. Jim Neawedde, Tom Hensley, and I had formed a bluegrass band, The Pigeon Hill Boys—named after the westside Bloomington neighborhood where Jim was living. I continued regular trips downtown to hear the new bluegrass singles and check out the instruments at Rone's. The big bookstore just down Kirkwood from the IU Campus carried the New York folksong magazine *Sing Out!* Usually I browsed it at the newsstand, but when the February issue appeared with Earl Scruggs on the cover, I began buying it. Not only was folk music popular, but bluegrass was now considered an exciting new part of it.

That semester I was taking a seminar on the ballad. For my term project, I chose to study commercial recordings of "Pretty Polly," an American descendant of an eighteenth-century English broadside ballad. Broadsides were sheets of paper imprinted with song texts, news, and many other things, which were sold in the streets of big cities like London. At the center of the eighteenth-century music business, they were precursors of sheet music and, ultimately, of twentieth-century records and twenty-first-century YouTubes.

I found that the Stanley Brothers' 1950 recording of "Pretty Polly," with Ralph Stanley's moving singing and driving banjo picking, had been the model for many subsequent bluegrass recordings. The copyright notice on the label credited B. F. Shelton (who recorded it in 1927), but Ralph's words were different. I wanted to know where Ralph actually learned the song.

An opportunity to find out came in mid-March, when we took a weekend trip to Oberlin for a Stanley Brothers concert. This was my first time to see these bluegrass pioneers. It was a stripped-down version of the group I'd heard on records—just Carter and Ralph Stanley on guitar and banjo, with George Shuffler on lead guitar and Chick Stripling on bass. I was familiar with most of their repertoire, but in person their musical dynamics really struck me—a combination of intensity and restraint that gave depth to both singing and playing. Stripling, an old-time country comedian who worked with Monroe in the '40s, laid down his bass for an elaborate routine that included comic dialogue, song, fiddle, and dance. It was a stripped-down show, too. The Oberlin Folksong Club had heard they were appearing in Cleveland (forty miles to the northeast) that night, and offered them $100 for an afternoon show. The crowd raised the roof trying for an encore at the end, but to no avail. The band had a date in Cleveland.

After the show, several of us went backstage to meet and speak with them. Erik "Jake" Jacobsen, the new banjoist in the Plum Creek Boys (he later became a rock producer) broke the ice, asking Carter to explain how Ralph had learned three-finger banjo. He reported that Carter told him of a lesson from Earl Scruggs. I'd never heard that before—it raised my interest in bluegrass history.

I was hoping to ask Ralph about "Pretty Polly" but only Carter was there, so I asked him. He told me they had learned that song from their father; the record company had gleaned the copyright notice from the Library of Congress. A footnote for my term paper!

My accounts of grad work in folklore caught the attention of my old friend Mayne, who was finishing his degree at Cal. He would be coming to Bloomington this summer to begin an MA in Folklore at IU.

In March, another old friend, Chuck Crawford, called from Ann Arbor, where he was a grad student. The University of Michigan Folk Festival was being held during spring vacation weekend of April 20–22, and they'd asked him if the Plum Creek Boys, the bluegrass band he'd been in with Franklin Miller and me at Oberlin, was interested in performing. Chuck told them we'd be glad to play but there was a new Plum Creek Boys now, so the old band would need a new name.

We decided to use the name of our nascent Bloomington band, the Pigeon Hill Boys. Guitarist Jim Neawedde couldn't come so Chuck took his place. Bass player Tom Hensley was available, as was mandolinist Franklin Miller, who had recently moved to Columbus, Ohio, to continue his

Oberlin College, March 1962. After the show, Carter and Ralph Stanley posed outside Wilder Hall with me, Erik Jacobsen, and Franklin Miller III. (Courtesy of the Erik Jacobsen Collection)

work at the OSU Motion Picture Division. The film he'd been working on there last summer, "Football As It Is Played Today," with its bluegrass soundtrack, had just won a first prize at the big American Film Festival in New York. He'd applied to begin graduate school in Fine Arts at OSU the coming fall.

The Festival had concerts by two headline acts: Jesse Fuller from Oakland with his one-man band on Friday night and a new singer from New York billed on the posters as "Bob Dillon" (his proper name was Bob Dylan, of course) on Sunday afternoon. On Saturday night, everyone, including the headliners, played brief sets at a Hootenanny.

Three college bluegrass bands were on the show. Ours closed the Hootenanny after midnight, following "Dillon" who put on a well received set. As we sang "Angel Band," the night watchman strolled by down in front of the stage and stopped in the middle to punch his clock, evoking laughter from the audience.

"Dillon" gave a nice concert the next afternoon, full of humor and new music. I returned from Ann Arbor and told my neighbor, a graduate student who was writing about the folksong revival, that this guy would soon eclipse the current favorite, Joan Baez. Not long after that, playing Monopoly with the same neighbor on a Saturday night, we heard the Greenbriar Boys with

Ralph Rinzler do a guest spot on the Grand Ole Opry. The emcee made much of the fact that the band was from New York City. They were on the road in Nashville as Joan Baez's opening act. Yankee bluegrass was coming south!

And southern bluegrass was coming north! I learned that next month Flatt & Scruggs would be giving a concert at the University of Illinois. Jim Work wrote me about it. I'd met Jim in Berkeley in 1959. He was a good blues and boogie pianist who'd grown up in Bloomington and hung out with the jazz crowd at University High—Tom Barton, Tom Hensley, Jim Neawedde, and others. He'd seen Monroe at Bean Blossom and, now living in Lafayette, Indiana, studying engineering at Purdue, was newly into bluegrass and learning the guitar. We began corresponding and visiting.

In April, I heard at Marvin's that the Jamboree had opened under new management. Birch was still operating the Saturday night dances. Shorty and Juanita were not involved. It would be several months before I got out to Bean Blossom.

At the beginning of May, Shorty hired Ann and me to perform with him and Juanita in support of a local political hopeful. I described the experience in a letter to my parents:

> It's primary time in the Hoosier State, and although we haven't paid poll tax and registered, we are plunged into the political world via Shorty Sheehan, my fiddle friend from Bean Blossom. A staunch Tennessee Democrat, he is supporting a fellow who's attempting to get on the ticket (primarys are impending) as Senatorial Candidate. And so, this Saturday we (Ann & I), at 8 bucks a head, join Shorty and Juanita for a two hour job a-pickin' and a-singin' on the back of said hopeful's sound truck. Shorty is in charge of a precinct for this guy, and if all goes well, he hopes to be able to swing some deals whereby he will be able to buy Bean Blossom Park from Bill Monroe, etc., etc. (He is always working on one deal or another . . . as long as I'm not asked to invest, it's fun.)[1]

Around the same time I heard more about the Flatt & Scruggs concert at Illinois from Judy McCulloh. A fellow folklore graduate student, one of the few who knew of Bill Monroe, she was working as an assistant at the Archives of Folk and Primitive Music (AFPM), an IU institution I was just beginning to explore.

Judy's husband, Leon, was a professor at the University of Illinois in Champaign-Urbana. Judy visited him on weekends. On May 12, she went to the Flatt & Scruggs concert presented by Archie Green's Campus Folk-song Club. She came back with tapes of the show. She knew of my interest in bluegrass and asked me to come into the AFPM and help her write up a table of contents for the recording, which she was depositing in the Archives. I obliged and was able to identify it all correctly except for one or two of Paul Warren's fiddle tunes. Everything else was on Flatt & Scruggs records in my collection. This may have been the first time anyone gave a recording of a bluegrass show to a folk music archive. In exchange for my help, she let me copy her tapes and gave me a poster from the show, adding to my growing collection.

About the same time I received a long letter from Jim Work describing the concert, and soon he sent prints of the photos he'd taken. I regretted missing it and hoped I'd get a chance to see the leading band in the business soon.

SUMMER 1962

Back to the Jamboree
July–August 1962

VERY EARLY ON A HOT June morning, I was awakened by the sound of a guitar playing "Wildwood Flower" from the porch into our open front room window. Mayne Smith had arrived—he'd driven nonstop from Berkeley (Cambridge folkie Bobby Neuwirth was with him), coming to begin his MA in folklore at IU.

Mayne immediately became part of the Pigeon Hill Boys, and we began practicing with Jim Neawedde and Tom Hensley. Mayne was playing his new favorite instrument, the Dobro. Both Jim and Mayne sang lead or tenor, and Mayne also sang baritone. I sang some lead and played banjo and mandolin.

One of our first gigs was the theme for Joe Hickerson's IU-based WTTV television series "Folklore around the World." We were on-screen playing our cover of the Country Gentlemen's "Country Concert (John Hardy)" for eight weeks that

summer. Mayne and I also guested on the show once, along with Shorty and Juanita.

On Sunday July 8th, I went to the Jamboree. This was my first visit of the year. Hedrick had told me that Bill and Birch had leased it for the season to a man named Harry Weger. A singer and guitarist, Weger had toured with Roy Acuff in the late forties, returning home to the Wabash Valley where he became a fixture on local radio and television. He and his wife, Docie, ran a record store in Terre Haute. He continued to perform and had his biggest record hit in 1961 with "The Ballad of Jimmy Bryan," a memorial to a recently killed race car driver he'd gotten to know while working as a volunteer at the Indianapolis Speedway.

Weger, then thirty-five, had a good modern country band and show. They were the house band for that season. Docie ran the food concession, and next to it Harry set up racks of records from their store—the first and only time I saw records being sold that way at the Jamboree.

Headlining the show that Sunday was the Barrier Brothers. They were a bluegrass cover band, the first I'd encountered. The Philips label had recently released their album, *Golden Bluegrass Hits*, which featured their versions of earlier recordings by Monroe, Flatt & Scruggs, and Reno & Smiley. I set up my microphone and recorded their show.

The three Barrier brothers belonged to a family from a small community in Hardin County, southwest of Nashville near the Alabama border. They had moved to South Bend, Indiana, in 1953. At that time, when oldest brother Herman was thirty-three, Ernie twenty-eight, and Ray thirteen, Ernie began teaching Ray guitar. By the midfifties they were playing on a local radio station. Ray, playing guitar, did the lead singing. Ernie on banjo sang tenor harmony, and Herman on bass provided a third harmony voice and comedy. They'd been playing bluegrass in the region ever since. Like most such bands they had "day jobs." Herman was a cabinet maker, Ernie a welder, and Ray worked for a lumber company.

Early in their career, they'd been "The Ozark Mountain Boys" when Missouri fiddler Gene Dykes was in the band, and using that band name they made a few singles on Armoneer, a label owned by Ray Earle, a friend from Tennessee living nearby. Their albums came when, with the help of their Nashville agents, the Wilburn Brothers, they caught the attention of Philips, an international record label seeking a folk group. The burgeoning popularity of bluegrass—especially Flatt & Scruggs—with folk fans persuaded the company that they, too, could reach that market with the Barriers: bluegrass LPs were selling well to urban buyers in 1962–1963.

Although they always recorded with a fiddler, just the three brothers were playing today. At the center of their show was their superb singing, highlighted by Ernie's hard-edged banjo work. He was the only bluegrass picker I'd ever seen who used plastic Dobro brand fingerpicks instead of the metal Nationals that all others—following Scruggs—used. Herman was introduced as "Uncle Herman," wore a comedian's costume, and was featured with his comedy instruments—a guitar with a toilet seat on its front (he opened the cover to play it) and the kazoo. Toward the end of the show, Ernie's daughter Carolyn came out and sang three recent country hits. I enjoyed the entire show with its good singing and picking. Ray even played some lead guitar, very unusual at that time in bluegrass. And there was lots of comedy.

The Barriers were representative of bluegrass bands in the region that performed on weekends and evenings while holding down "day jobs." Most were immigrants from the southeast. They often had records, usually self-produced. I saw many such regional bluegrass troupers at Bean Blossom over the years.

I returned to Bean Blossom twice in August. On the fifth, the old-time banjoist and comedian "Stringbean" (David Akeman) was the headliner. During the war, Stringbean had been the first banjo player in Monroe's Blue Grass Boys. Deep into discography, I hoped to speak with him about Bill's first Columbia session that he'd played on in 1945.

I brought along my tape recorder; it malfunctioned during the afternoon show so I came back and got a slightly better recording that evening. At both shows, Stringbean's backup was provided by Birch on fiddle and Harry Weger on bass; in the afternoon, Birch's friend Kyle Wells joined them on guitar and they used the name of their old Jamboree band, the Brown County Fox Hunters.

At the evening show, Wells was replaced by Bryant Wilson, the singer-guitarist from Edinburgh that I'd first seen in action jamming in the back room with Roger Smith a year ago. Wilson had renamed his record company after his home county in Kentucky: Adair Records. In 1960, he released Harry Weger's first single on Adair.

This evening, at Harry's request, Bryant re-created his most popular recording, "Stepping in Daddy's Tracks," a recited sermon against drinking that depicted a little boy following his father to the tavern. After that and again after his next song, another of his compositions, he plugged his records—for sale today on Harry's record racks at the back near the food concessions. Then Harry sang and talked about his big hit, "The Ballad of Jimmy Bryan." He was proud of the recording, not just for the song, but also because it had been done in a top studio using the same "Nashville sound" studio musicians heard on such big country hits as Marty Robbins's "El Paso."

When Stringbean joined Birch, Bryant, and Harry we heard not only his comic repertoire, but a wonderful old-time sound, especially on the folksongs he sang like "John Henry" where Birch's bluesy fiddle, Bryant's solid guitar, and his frailed banjo put the NLCR in the shade.

Between shows, I approached Stringbean outside the backstage door where he was selling records. I told him the truth—I wanted to get his new Starday album but I didn't have any money. He gave me an album, signed it, and told me to pay him when I could. I thanked him and asked about that recording session. I knew from a listing that I'd seen in *Disc Collector* that six songs had been released from that session and another two were unissued. So I first asked him how many songs he'd recorded with Monroe.

"Eighteen," he told me. I could have asked many other questions about that session but I didn't know enough to think of asking the basics about who, what, where, and when. That high number he gave put me off. I figured he'd probably been asked that question many times and just pulled a figure out of the air. So I didn't follow up. Many years later, in 2002, when I was working on the update of my Monroe discography using new data found at Columbia by Bear Family Records owner Richard Weize, I discovered that in fact there were, counting multiple takes, false starts, and so on, a total of twenty-one separate tracks recorded at that session, so even if it was a guess, Stringbean was close to the mark.

Monroe made his first visit of the season at the end of the summer, on August 26, 1962. The Pigeon Hill Boys came out to see if we could play during the interval before Monroe went on.

Our band that Sunday at Bean Blossom consisted of Mayne, Jim and me. We went backstage before the show and asked Weger if we could play a few tunes on the afternoon's show. I think Birch was there, and I know Roger Smith was there, and in any case Weger, a friendly and easygoing guy, was happy to have another act, especially a band of college kids from IU, for the show. He was particularly impressed that we had Mayne's Do-

Roger Smith, fiddle, with the Pigeon Hill Boys at the Brown County Jamboree, August 1962. Mayne Smith, Jim Neawedde, me. (Courtesy of Ann Milovsoroff)

bro in the band—that was rare and had special meaning to him because of his tours years earlier with Roy Acuff, who always featured a Dobro.

I asked Roger if he would fiddle with us, and he agreed. We ran through our material with him quickly, establishing keys and showing him the songs we thought he might not know. This was not difficult material for Roger; he knew most of it. He did some great fiddling and, of course, the audience already knew him and me, so we were well received. Later, I wrote home and mentioned that we "received some words of praise from Bill Monroe," who was waiting backstage to follow us on.[1]

Bill had a completely different group of Blue Grass Boys from the last time I'd seen him. Frank Buchanan was playing guitar and singing lead, Benny Williams was on the fiddle, and David Deese was playing banjo.

There was a good-sized audience and Bill did all of his standards plus many requests. This band had been working with Monroe all summer. They were polished and professional.

Frank Buchanan was a good singer. He had been recording duets with Monroe that would show up on Bill's albums in the following years. Frank had left the band by then and never did get proper credit for all of his good singing on record with Monroe.

This was my first time seeing Benny Williams with Bill. Benny was the consummate Nashville sideman. He'd played lead electric with Grandpa Jones, bass with Flatt & Scruggs, mandolin with Reno & Smiley, and fiddle with Monroe. He also did comedy—imitations of Nashville stars singing their biggest hits—and played the 5-string. I would see him at the Jamboree with Bill many times in the coming years.

After the show I spoke with Deese. He was playing a new Gibson RB-100 banjo, the cheapest model (the number stood for the instrument's price): plain neck and wood, minimal binding, and no Mastertone tone ring under the head on which his name was painted in big black letters. I asked him why he was using that banjo. He told me he thought the park at Bean Blossom was outdoors, and this was the banjo he used for outdoor shows. Deese would later play with Red Smiley and other prominent acts.

Several days after that, a package arrived from Washington: my freshly repaired 3-pointer Gibson mandolin. It looked neat—the top was now blonde instead of black, and facsimiles of the original inlays made the fingerboard look complete and ornate.

I'd swapped the Century series mandolin I'd gotten in Vermont last year for a stereo. Then I bought a used '30s F2 Gibson down in Bedford; it wasn't that great and I soon sold it to Roger Smith. Now I was glad to have a mandolin again.

Duffey included an 8-item list of his repairs. Number 2 was "Install steel truss rod in neck." He told me later that the steel piece was a push-rod from the inside of an Oldsmobile engine. The list closed with a P.S.: "Taught mandolin several hot licks. *No charge*."[2] He'd probably jammed with it somewhere, or maybe tried it for a set at the club, for in addition to the pretty stuff, he'd also added a more modern adjustable bridge. Duffey liked to set his action high by raising the bridge up. He thought the additional string tension created more pressure on the top, and thus more volume.

Hot-rod thinking, I call it. Everyone was experimenting with instrument mechanics, looking for more volume from their music machine. We all played publicly into a single microphone, set high enough for the vocalist to reach comfortably. Instruments had to reach farther than voices.

Duffey, like Monroe, kept his bridges high. For me, that was too much action! I was only a part-time mandolinist with banjo player's fingers on the fretting hand. Twice as many strings to mash down meant those fingers got sore too fast so I lowered the adjustable bridge. It sounded good, was pretty easy to play, and fun to look at. Looking forward to using it at Pigeon Hill Boys gigs, I built a case for it.

Folk in Bloomington
July–September 1962

IN JULY, we moved to a new apartment in Bloomington on East 2nd street—the first floor of an old house, with enough room for our soon-to-arrive child. It had more space for coursework studies and jam sessions.

That summer, Sandy Paton, a folksinger I'd known since 1956, came to visit. He was at IU consulting with folktale specialist Warren Roberts about an album of traditional storytelling that his new company, Folk-Legacy, had in the works. Folk-Legacy was issuing material for folk enthusiasts who wanted the "real thing."

He was curious about what I was doing as a folklore student, so on August 21st, soon after he left, I sent him the tape I'd made the previous year at Shorty and Juanita's. In a long covering letter, I explained: "The recording and performances on it were not made with an eye to release, so this tape should be regarded as an audition tape. However, I am in contact with these friends and if you are interested a recording of record quality could be made."[1]

I told him, "the importance of Shorty and Juanita Sheehan lies in the fact that they represent not one but many traditions," and went on to describe their professional and traditional musical lives. Finally I wrote: "I am very interested in your opinion of these performers and the possibility of making a record of them."

Not long after I sent the tape to Paton, Art Rosenbaum, the banjo picker who'd beaten me in the contest at the Jamboree last year, dropped in. Since then, we'd become better acquainted during his visits home. He was in the midst of a quest to make field recordings of traditional music in Indiana. With him was Pat Dunford, an Indianapolis teenager and old-time enthusiast who shared his interest in recording.

A few weeks later, I got a long letter from Sandy Paton. He said he enjoyed the tape and thought the Shehans "deserve to be recorded." But, he added, "unfortunately, we are not in a position to handle it. . . . We can only produce so many records under our present capitalization and feel that the real *need* in the folk music recording field is for a company willing to release traditional songs performed in the 'older' style—i.e., a style less influenced by the commercial recording industry."

He urged me to continue recording: "If you can put together an album that truly represents the current state of traditional music in the southern Indiana area, including people like the Sheehans doing true folk material along with fiddle tunes, country dance groups, and a few of the old songs and ballads sung in an older traditional style, we would definitely be interested in producing the record."[2]

That's a pretty good summary of what Rosenbaum and Dunford were already doing. In fact, on the same day that Sandy wrote rejecting the Shehans, Art was in Franklin recording them! One song was included on Art and Pat's 1964 Folkways documentary of traditional music from Indiana, *Fine Times at Our House.*

The audition tape I'd sent to Folk-Legacy had been done on personal initiative. I was disappointed they weren't interested, but at this point, graduate work took precedence. I needed to move ahead with my master's thesis on "White House Blues." In order to do this I needed to hear obscure old recordings. So, on the same day I sent the tape, I wrote to Mike Seeger about an NLCR recording:

> I am currently attempting to gather enough versions of White House Blues to do a master's thesis on it. I have a copy of your recording of this (Songs from the Depression, Folkways FH 5264) in which you credit that particular version to Bob Baker. While I do not wish to cast aspersions about your fine performance of the song I would very much like to have a tape of Baker singing it, in the interest of accuracy. Also, since you know Baker, I wonder if you remember his stating how popular the song (E.G., [his] . . . version) was, and where he learned it—from family, country music shows of the time, or whatever.[3]

I enclosed my list—a discography—for the song: "If you have any versions which I do not have, I would appreciate you adding these and any stray info you might have to said tape. Also, if you have any show performances (other than by Monroe, of whom I have plenty), I would likewise appreciate getting them."

I offered to trade tapes, mentioned the three Monroe shows and other recordings I'd gotten from Marvin, and closed by mentioning the NLCR's forthcoming concert at Illinois. I'd read that his trio had a new member and told him: "I am anxious to hear the new NLCR." Joe Hickerson, Mayne Smith, and I had been talking that summer about starting a folksong club at IU, hoping to bring the NLCR to campus.

The Pigeon Hill Boys had now been together for most of the year. Since Mayne's arrival, we'd done a lot of broadcasts and personal appearances. At the end of the summer we were contacted through the I.U. School of Music's Musical Attractions office to perform "'country style' band dinner music" on Friday, September 8th, for the annual convention of the Indiana Motor Truck Association at the Sheraton Hotel in the spa town of French Lick, south of Bloomington near the Ohio River.

The director of the Association, Jimmy Nicholas, was a business acquaintance of my father. This year, their convention had a country-western theme and he knew that I played some kind of country music—hence the booking. The band consisted of Jim Neawedde, Mayne Smith, and me. We were all eager to see this regionally famous posh resort; I reported the experience to my parents soon after:

> French Lick: We got there about six and made connections with Jimmy Nicholas, who was quite busy, dressed in elaborate western clothes, but also quite congenial. He was off running a cocktail party, so we had dinner, which was paid for by the convention, in the Hoosier room. My god, what a snooty place. . . . Thus nourished, we retired to the convention hall, where well-lubricated truckers, disguised as cowboys and farmers (we looked a bit ivy league, despite our string ties and boots) were queuing up for a country dinner. We played for forty minutes—just instrumentals—while everyone talked and ate. The PA system wasn't functioning right and poor Jimmy was running back and forth trying to get everything adjusted. After dinner, Jimmy introduced us and mentioned that I was Jess Rosenberg's son. Then we played two songs and introduced five students (2 boys and 3 girls) from the I.U. music school who sang Broadway show songs quite well, and who were amazingly successful in capturing and holding audience attention.

After we finished, I visited Mr. Nicholas's table. Several of my father's friends dropped over to introduce themselves: "We talked for a while and then there was another function about to start, to which we were invited, but as the next morning was registration and I had to mind the folklore desk from 8 to 12, we thanked all and bade farewell."

I closed with my thoughts about the music business: "While the music end of the deal was not very rewarding, we had not expected it to be so, and we enjoyed the opportunity to thank Jimmy Nicholas. . . . And we were well-fed and paid. As far as trying to make money from Bluegrass, you can see that this sort of thing—earless audiences—even when they pay as well as this job did (which is not often) does not fill one with ambition to devote full-time energy to it."[4]

FALL 1962

Mocking Bird Hill

September 1962

TWO DAYS AFTER PLAYING for the truckers in French Lick, "White House Blues" research led me to Mocking Bird Hill for the first time. This was a country music park like the Brown County Jamboree and similar venues that Tom Adler describes at the start of *Bean Blossom: The Brown County Jamboree and Bill Monroe's Bluegrass Festivals*.

When I first heard of it in 1961, Mocking Bird Hill was presenting country music (including bluegrass) on Sundays from spring through fall. It followed a typical park schedule: two shows each Sunday afternoon and evening. Each show included a house band, other opening acts, and a featured popular recording artist, frequently an Opry star. I know nothing of its history beyond my own experience and running across it in published accounts by bluegrass pioneers like the Stanley Brothers who spoke of playing there regularly while on tour.

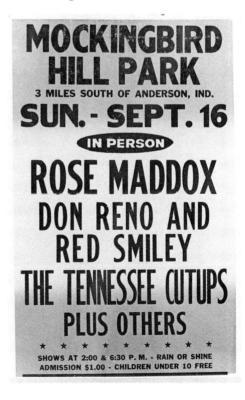

People who knew about Bean Blossom usually knew about Mocking Bird Hill. Located three miles south of Anderson, Indiana, 40 miles northeast of Indianapolis, it drew from the same demographic as the Jamboree. The park was not on a hill. Its name came from a song, "Mockin' Bird Hill," the 1951 Les Paul and Mary Ford number that Patti Page had a big hit with. Unlike the Jamboree, it advertised in Indianapolis on the radio and in the newspapers. So at Bean Blossom, people often spoke about who was playing Mocking Bird Hill this or next Sunday—often, it seemed, as an explanation for why attendance was down at the Jamboree: Johnny Cash, Reno & Smiley, or some other big draw was playing there today.

I first went there on September 9, 1962, to see Flatt & Scruggs. I don't recall how I heard they were coming. Possibly it was announced on the Opry, the only radio show to which I listened. Maybe Merce passed the news on when I dropped in to pick up beer and empty Cutty Sark boxes. Perhaps Marvin mentioned it at his jam.

I needed to talk with Lester Flatt and Earl Scruggs. Their new album, *Folk Songs of Our Land* (Columbia CL 1830) included "McKinley's Gone," their version of "White House Blues," the song I was studying. Their version was unique. I wanted to ask them the basic folksong researcher's questions about where they had learned it and what they knew about its history.

Naturally, I was excited to have an opportunity to see the most popular bluegrass band. I'd watched them on television and heard them on the radio, and I had their records and tapes of live performances. But I'd never seen them in person.

The park had an outdoor stage, in front of which were wooden benches. It was built onto the end of a long building with a low peaked roof, of newer materials but similar design to the Jamboree barn. The wall at the back of the stage was painted with floral designs. Around the edge of the stage was a low fence of fancy white wrought iron, the kind used to edge public flowerbeds. A door at the back of the stage had a big color painting of Marty Robbins on it.

On the front of the building to the right of the outdoor stage were food concessions. The stage door with its painting of Marty opened onto another stage inside the building that could be used for indoor shows. To the right, as you faced it from inside, was the dressing room.

Like the Jamboree barn, the inside of the Mocking Bird Hill building had a smooth cement floor suitable either for folding chairs or dancers. As at Bean Blossom, it could be entered from the side, as I discovered after the show when I went to see if I could talk with Lester and Earl about "White House Blues." The dressing room was crowded. Every member of the band was visiting with friends or fans.

I went back to the car, got my banjo, brought it in, and asked Earl if he'd autograph the head, which he did in a way that suggested to me that it wasn't the first time he'd had such a request. Thanking him, I told him I was enjoying their new album, and asked about "McKinley's Gone." He told me that they'd known that song, which he called "White House Blues," ever since they'd worked with Bill Monroe back in the forties. That was all he had to say.

I went over to Lester and asked the same question. Like Earl, he mentioned Monroe. I told him I'd heard Monroe's recording—Bill's words were not the same as his. Lester told me he got the words "from Louise." Louise, Earl's wife, was the band's manager. That was all I needed to know for now.

Earlier I had asked for and received permission to record the show. I had only enough tape—one blank second side of the tape I'd used to record the Stringbean show at Bean Blossom a month earlier—to record the first half of their show.

It was a typical F&S show. In the first half hour, they did eight songs and a lot of comedy. This was a hot band in which everyone had several jobs. All five band members sang, and each played lead or backup on different instruments. Guitarist/lead vocalist Flatt's smooth folksy emcee work, punctuated with smart-aleck remarks from bassist-comedian "Cousin Jake" Tullock, moved the show along briskly.

Scruggs spoke little but demonstrated the power and subtlety that had made him the undisputed fountainhead of bluegrass banjo playing. Buck "Uncle Josh" Graves played straight man to Cousin Jake while contributing his signature Dobro playing. Like Scruggs, he was the leading exponent of his instrument in bluegrass.

Many of their songs were familiar to me from recordings, but even the warhorses like Josh and Earl's "Foggy Mountain Rock" were filled with nuances reflecting the polish they'd given these pieces in frequent performance since the recordings had come out.

Lester spoke of playing recently in California, at the Ash Grove in Hollywood. In a couple of weeks they'd be recording their biggest hit, "The Ballad of Jed Clampett," theme of the CBS comedy show, *The Beverly*

Hillbillies, due to premiere on the 26th. No mention was made of this, even though CBS had discovered them at the Ash Grove.

At the end of the show, the park's emcee announced that next week's show would feature a double bill: country star Rose Maddox and bluegrass greats Reno & Smiley. Like Birch, he asked patrons to take along a few posters and put them in their favorite places of business. I took a poster and made plans to come next Sunday.

On the first of October, I wrote to Scott Hambly about the three Mocking Bird shows I'd seen in September. "Flatt and Scruggs were good but impressed me as being sort of cut & dried."[1] That's all I said.

On September 16, 1962, I drove up to Mocking Bird Hill for the afternoon. Before the show I wandered inside toward the dressing room. Before I got far I saw Don Reno, standing in the center of the floor in front of the stage. Reno was a close contemporary of Scruggs. He'd followed Earl in Monroe's band, thereby helping to enshrine that Carolina three-finger banjo style in bluegrass. He was highly regarded in this neck of the woods.

He was warming up on the banjo. Around him stood a crowd of men, circled a respectful ten feet away. Don was just noodling around when I joined at the fringe of the circle. Soon after someone said "That Earl Scruggs sure does a nice job on 'Farewell Blues,' don't he Don?"

Reno said nothing, just nodded his head and began playing "Farewell Blues." He did a couple of choruses in C (the key Scruggs had recorded it in back in 1949) then moved up to D, and finally ended in G. All of this was done in his unique style with single-note runs, fancy chords, muted percussive 5th string, and so forth, with wonderful mellow tone, and no retuning. It was very impressive, a statement about what Earl did and what Don Reno could do.

I wish I had recorded that day's show, for the music was great. They had a six-piece band, with guitarist/lead singer Red Smiley, Reno, his mandolinist son Ronnie, fiddler Mack Magaha, bassist John Palmer, and electric guitarist Steve Chapman.

On stage, Don Reno stood out. He was the only one wearing a hat—a Stetson like those worn by Monroe's bands in the forties—along with white cowboy boots and western twill pants. During the show, he strode dramatically around the stage, always managing to get up to the mike (sometimes from quite a ways backstage or sidestage) to contribute a banjo break or a tenor harmony.

As with Flatt & Scruggs, comedy played a prominent role in the show. But here the longest routine was contributed by Reno in drag as "Chicken Hotrod," playing Smiley's guitar and singing comic songs. Don Reno was instrumentalist, singer, comedian—cock of the walk on stage. After the show, I brought my banjo backstage and got him to autograph the head. As with Scruggs, it seemed a familiar routine.

I already knew from conversations with local fans that Reno & Smiley were very popular in Indiana. During these years, they generally played twice a year at Mocking Bird Hill. I don't think they drew any smaller crowd that day than Flatt & Scruggs had the previous week. At the end of the show, it was announced that next week's guest stars would be Jim & Jesse and the Virginia Boys.

When I wrote to Scott about Reno & Smiley's show, I called it "the best" and described it enthusiastically: "Man, don't ever miss a chance to hear those boys," I began. After a detailed description, I closed with an apology because my recorder "was screwed up, so I didn't get it on tape."[2]

But I did tape the third show, by Jim & Jesse, and sent a copy of that tape along with my letter. I knew this was the band Scott most wanted to see. This was the band I'd heard first on Pensacola television sound tracks that had come to me in a tape trade four years earlier. That was where I'd heard Vassar Clements and Bobby Thompson.

Jim McReynolds and his brother Jesse were Virginians who'd been in the country music business since their teens in the late forties. They recorded for Capitol in the early fifties and then lost their contract when rock and roll hit. In 1959, Starday began recording acts like theirs that didn't fit the new "Nashville Sound" mold.

They were a classic "brother duet," with Jim playing guitar and singing tenor and younger sibling Jesse singing lead and playing his very distinctive mandolin style, "cross-picking," a way of creating arpeggios that sounded like Earl Scruggs's fingerpicked banjo but were played with a flat pick. It was very different from Monroe's mandolin playing. Scott was a great fan of Jesse. Like many, he was trying to learn that style.

Jim & Jesse had been playing bluegrass in the deep south—Alabama, Georgia, and North Florida—and were little heard live outside that region until 1960 when they picked up the sponsorship of Martha White Flour, the same outfit that was sponsoring Flatt & Scruggs on the Opry. Soon after, they landed a recording contract with Columbia and, by Sunday

September 23, 1962, when they came to Mocking Bird Hill, they had a recent single, their second: "Sweet Little Miss Blue Eyes," on Columbia subsidiary label Epic. They were beginning to do guest spots on the Grand Ole Opry. That brought them to audiences in Indiana. Here, for bluegrass fans, they were a new thing, a regional band going national. They'd first come to Mocking Bird Hill at the beginning of July, and on this day there was a good turnout for them.

Vassar Clements and Bobby Thompson were no longer with the Virginia Boys. In their places were Jimmy Buchanan on fiddle and Allen Shelton on banjo. Bassist-comedian David Sutherland ("Joe Binglehead") and guitarist-singer Don McHan rounded out the band.

Before the show, I went backstage to get permission to record. I found Jim in the dressing room and got his OK to tape. Jesse was standing alone on the indoor stage, warming up on his mandolin break for "Air Mail Special," a barn-burner duet he and Jim had recorded ten years earlier.

The show opened with a couple of instrumental choruses of this song, played by Jesse and Allen Shelton. Like Monroe's "Watermelon Hanging on the Vine," a recording he'd made in the 1930s, this Jim & Jesse '50s oldie was now the band's theme. They ripped into it, showing the instrumental flash both would demonstrate throughout the show. Fully one-third of the numbers they did were instrumentals.

It was a tight musical package that focused on the singing: the brothers' Louvinesque country duets; Don McHan's country baritone voice, which, when added to the duet, created a perfect trio; and bassist Binglehead with his comic songs. Shining around the vocals were the instruments—Jesse's unique mandolin, Jimmy Buchanan's hot bluegrass fiddle, and Allen Shelton's bright, driving banjo, often described as "bouncy," with flawless rhythm, economical musical line, and great power. Shelton "sold" his performances with ease and flair. Tall—over six feet—lanky, freckled, red-headed—he was an imposing figure even without the banjo. What audiences saw first and loved was his big smile. If ever there was a banjoist who fit the "picking and grinning" stereotype, it was Allen Shelton.

Every time he stepped up to the mike to take a break, applause broke out. At this show, he featured three banjo pieces. His first was an instrumental version of Flatt & Scruggs's 1960 hit, "Polka on the Banjo," demonstrating his mastery of the Scruggs dialect. Next came a pop oldie he had put out on a single in 1958, "Lady of Spain," which incorporated chords in a manner reminiscent of Reno. Finally, he played "Grandfather's Clock" with a tightly arranged bridge: Jesse and Jimmy Buchanan plucked fiddle and mandolin in a fugue with the banjo to create a wonderful musical ticking clock. I'd heard Walt Hensley play "Grandfather's Clock" in the back room at Franklin last fall. Here, it was polished and promoted to a part in the show.

Although they played covers of Flatt & Scruggs, Mac Wiseman, and others, emcee Jesse mentioned only their own recordings. Like the other two bands I'd seen at this park in recent weeks, they never spoke of their music as bluegrass: it was country.

At this time, when many bluegrass acts had new albums, Jim & Jesse had only singles for sale to fans after the show (they also had pictures). But their new Epic album was due out soon. They played three songs from it, mentioning this each time.

There were a number of other banjo players at the park for this show. One of them, Mark Barnett, was a young man from north central Indiana who was invited on stage to play a few tunes with the house band. I have no memory of what he played, but I still remember thinking, this guy is fantastic and he's doing stuff I'd never seen or heard before on his banjo, one that had once belonged to Earl Scruggs.

In the dressing room after the show, Shelton seemed surrounded by banjo pickers. Jerry Waller, whom I'd met through Birch at Bean Blossom, was there along with his fiddler friend Lowell Denman. Lowell, not as shy as Waller, showed Allen Jerry's new Vega Earl Scruggs banjo, asking him to try it. Allen took it, played a tune; he praised it and handed it back. I asked him if he'd sign my banjo head and, like Earl and Don, he did. Then he looked at it, asked some questions, and began playing it.

While the bluegrass pioneers I'd seen the previous Sundays had all played prewar instruments, everyone in Jim & Jesse's band played fifties instruments. Shelton had a midfifties Gibson Mastertone archtop. It was OK, but he told me he really wanted a thirties flathead like Scruggs and Reno played. Like mine. He played it for about fifteen minutes and then handed it back to me saying "this is the best banjo in the room." I left Mockingbird Hill feeling good about the recording I'd made and about my backstage meeting with Shelton.

In three weeks I'd seen and heard a lot at that park. The shows by these top bluegrass acts gave me an education in bluegrass theater. After the shows they sold souvenirs: songbooks, records, photos. Much of what they did on stage was similar to what the audience expected from any good country act: tightly scripted (though not rote) presentations with costume, comedy, choreography, and musical specialties. But the audience was there to see and hear bluegrass. Many there were like me—performers coming to see the masters of this music.

A month later, Franklin Miller wrote us telling of his work in the film business and adventures with motorcycles and bluegrass. He reported briefly: "Saw Jim & Jesse in Cleveland a while ago—they are really tops. Perfectionists."[3]

Folk and Country
October 1962

BLUEGRASS WAS CONTINUING to grow in popularity with the folk scene. In September, Mike Seeger responded positively to my request for help on "White House Blues" with a letter in which he spoke of "the New NLCR." Tom Paley had been replaced by Tracy Schwarz: "We're doing some early Blue/grass now," he reported.[1]

On Saturday, October 6th, almost two weeks after my last trip to Mocking Bird Hill to see Jim & Jesse, the Pigeon Hill Boys were the featured act at the Phase III, a coffeehouse near the IU campus. We did four sets. That had us digging for repertoire. I brought my newly repaired mandolin along and played it on a few numbers. The college folk music audience—a full house—not only ate up our music, they even liked our comedy.

The next day, I went to Bean Blossom with my recorder to see Monroe. Harry Weger had promised Monroe would be there, but Bill didn't make it; the Barrier Brothers replaced him. That afternoon's show began with another bluegrass band, led by Roger Smith, that had dropped in and been invited by Weger to play on stage. The others in this band were new to me: Vernon McQueen, guitarist and singer from Connersville; Loren Rogers, a banjo picker from Tennessee; and Tom Ford, a bass player I'd met up at Mocking Bird Hill.

This was a pickup band. Rogers had played banjo with Jimmy Martin and was presently with a Knoxville group called the Pinnacle Mountain Boys. He was visiting Smith and McQueen, who often played together, sometimes as Blue Grass Boys. Tom Ford was a friend from northern Indiana. The music they made—half of it instrumentals—was brilliant. Roger responded to Loren's hot music with his own hot fiddle. Sadly, Loren, a great banjo player, died in a tractor accident soon after this performance.

Their ten-piece set was as exciting musically as anything I'd seen at Mocking Bird Hill the previous month. The only real difference was they didn't do any comedy. This was cut-to-the-chase bluegrass that made what we Pigeon Hill Boys had picked the night before—even though the audience liked our show—seem amateurish.

The Barrier Brothers invited Roger to stay on stage and play with them. Their show was similar to their July performance, filled with Flatt & Scruggs covers. Roger added a lot to their sound. He was a close follower of the style of Benny Martin, who'd fiddled on early Flatt & Scruggs records and on all of the Barriers's albums. As before, Uncle Herman Barrier provided plenty of comedy, at one point teaming up with Weger's comedian Country McCullough for a kazoo duet.

Two weeks later Mayne and I drove out to Bean Blossom to see Charlie Monroe. Again I brought my recorder. Bill's brother and former partner had rarely played the Jamboree. Eager to see this famous musician, we immediately headed backstage. Birch and Harry Weger were putting together a band for the afternoon's show. Along with Birch (fiddle) were Kyle Wells with his guitar, Jerry Waller on banjo, and electric guitarist Jim Ray Prior.

Weger remembered Mayne from our August appearance and asked if he had his Dobro along—he said he did and was invited then and there to be on the show. This impromptu combo opened the day's music on stage with an eleven-song set that highlighted Weger's vocals but also included a couple of banjo solos by Jerry Waller. One was "Grandfather's Clock," without the fancy bridge Jerry and I had both heard when Jim & Jesse did it the month before. Mayne sang harmony with Harry on "Precious Jewel," a favorite Roy Acuff piece.

After intermission, the same band came back to accompany Charlie Monroe. At the start, Charlie introduced another musician: singer-auto-harpist Wendell Allen, mayor of the Monroe family's Kentucky hometown, Rosine. Charlie, genial and jolly, presided over a show in which many of the musicians on stage were featured—Wendell with a song and an instrumental, Jerry Waller with a banjo instrumental, Kyle Wells with a gospel song of his own composition, and Birch with a fiddle tune. Charlie sang a lot of his old material and a few new things he was working on for an LP, his first, on REM, a Lexington label. He even had me turn off the tape recorder for one song he hadn't yet recorded.

October 1962. Charlie Monroe, supported by Jerry Waller, Birch Monroe, and Mayne Smith. (Courtesy of Jim Peva)

This was Charlie's first public appearance in some time; he wouldn't really do much performing again until over a decade later. It was fun to see him—so different than either of his brothers and a powerful singer and guitarist. He was playing his old prewar D-45 Martin, a rare and wonderful instrument, and was enthusiastic that college boys like Mayne could play his music. Out behind the barn after the show, Mayne and I played a number or two for him. He praised our music and spoke vaguely about having us help him out on his next record. That was the last we heard of that! We appreciated his encouragement.

The following Sunday (October 28) Bill Monroe and the Blue Grass Boys were back. Bill had a completely different band from the one I'd seen in August. Jimmy Maynard, who'd been there when I played in the band last year, was back as guitarist and lead singer. Bill introduced a new man, Lonnie Hoppers, as his first banjo picker from Missouri. Harry Weger filled in on bass. No one was playing fiddle.

Not only was this a hastily assembled band, the program was also hastily assembled. "We haven't picked out any numbers," Bill said at the start, "but we generally fill out a lot of requests while we're up here." After the eighth song Roger Smith walked on stage, fiddle in hand.

Bill welcomed him: "Well hello there! Boy, we've been looking for you for the last two hours here." Roger said he was late because he had business in Indianapolis. "Well while you're here now, get your fiddle, and let's fiddle a good one." He obliged with "Dance around Molly," then someone requested "Paddy on the Turnpike." Monroe liked good fiddling, and after Roger had finished that, Bill accused him of practicing.

"I bet you been easing down on the banjo, haven't you?" Bill asked.

"Yes I have," said Roger.

"Picking the fiddle there," Bill added.

"I've been easing down on both of 'em," Roger replied.

"No," Bill told him, "that fiddle's getting better."

The requests continued. When one came in for "Tennessee Waltz," Bill coaxed Roger into singing it, and later in the show again prevailed on him to sing lead on several requested hymns. The show ended with "Close By," a request: "Marvin Hedrick called for another one, wanted to know if we'd do it, back there, and since Roger is here, we'll try to do this for him. It's entitled 'Close By.'"

This was an unusual and spirited show, filled with the impromptu and the improvised. I was glad I had taped it; Marvin had also taped it, and Jim Peva had taken photos. Bill was hustling to put on a show that would appeal to the folks at the Jamboree; Bean Blossom was his musical home.

Backstage before the show I'd brought my newly refurbished mandolin in to show Bill. Sitting there in the inside room, under the little high window, he gave the old F—with its new blonde top, shiny finish and fancy inlays—a careful visual inspection. I mentioned that John Duffey had worked on it.

He took out a pick, played a few licks, and then pulled his right hand away from the strings. He directed my attention to the top of the adjustable bridge. The tops of the adjustment screws protruded above the top of the bridge. He admonished me curtly: Those screws shouldn't be so high, he said, you can hurt your hand or tear your clothes on them! Surprised, I promised to address the problem.

It had been created by my new adjustable bridge. How, I wondered, could I ever reduce the length of those screws? It would be easier to raise the action—which is what Bill was probably suggesting. For some reason—shyness I think or possibly because I might betray my foolish ignorance—I didn't ask him how to address the problem. I just said I would. That was all he ever said about my pretty old Gibson F.

After the show, browsing in Harry Weger's rack at the back of the barn I noticed a new Bill Monroe album: *My All-Time Country Favorites*. I could tell by looking at the titles that it was a compilation of unissued tracks and old singles. I was eagerly compiling a Monroe discography; finding this new album was like discovering 12 lost pieces fallen on the floor from a 500-piece jigsaw puzzle. I bought it and eagerly took it backstage for Bill to autograph.

When I handed it to him, it was at once obvious that he had never seen this particular album before. He put on his glasses, read the list of titles and the notes on the back of the jacket; turned it over and looked at the front picture, and then, shaking his head, carefully turned the cover back over and signed it so that the autograph was upside down in relation to the printing on the back. Here, I realized how distant Bill was from the companies who made his records, another challenge for the budding discographer.

Soon after this show, a package arrived from Jim Peva, the Indiana state policeman I'd met at the Jamboree last year. Every time I went to a show, he was there. Like Marvin and me he was taping shows. He was also shooting pictures with a high-quality State Police camera. This package contained big eight-by-ten-inch prints from last month's shows by Charlie and Bill Monroe. He wrote: "I think these guys are the greatest and if the history of hillbilly music is ever written they surely will be listed among the pioneers. My wife and I have enjoyed your group from the University too. I'm sorry that I didn't get some pictures of the Pigeon Hill Boys."[2]

He'd seen us at the Jamboree in August, and shared his thoughts about the venue: "I hope Bill keeps the old barn open next year. It's too bad they can't draw better crowds. The only country music radio station in Indianapolis (WGEE) devotes all its advertising of that type to the Franklin Jamboree."

At this time of year, in the late fall of 1962, the future of the Brown County Jamboree was a matter of speculation. But there was little doubt that the folk music fans from the University—IU—had become a part of the picture at Bean Blossom.

Two weeks later, my daughter Teya was born. Life at home grew complicated. An unexpected bonus was forced early risings for feeding; I set the clock radio on WSM and began listening regularly to Flatt & Scruggs's early-morning Martha White show. I began to like working in the early morning.

Not long after this, I set off to perform with the Pigeon Hill Boys at Antioch College over in Yellow Springs, Ohio.

College Folk, Bluegrass, Banjo Necks
November 1962

IN OCTOBER, a group of students led by Joe Hickerson founded the Indiana University Folksong Club (IUFC). Joe became president and Mayne, vice president. In November, the club began instrument "workshops"—lessons. I taught banjo. All fall, Mayne and I performed at campus venues advertised by the club. Up in Lafayette, Jim Work started a similar club at Purdue. Over in Columbus at Ohio State, folk was also popular.

That month, Franklin Miller wrote to say he was living in the elegant Columbus suburb of Worthington, rooming with an OSU faculty couple, Miles and Joan Gibbons. He was a graduate student in Fine Arts, studying sculpture and motion pictures. He'd spent part of the summer playing around Chicago with other recent Oberlin grads in Erik Jacobsen's new group, The Knob Lick Upper Ten Thousand: "They are making money now and they consist of Jake, Dwain Story and Pete Childs."[1]

Since then, he wrote that he was "tending more toward folk and away from B.G.—the local boys are too good." He was following the scene with interest, though: "FRANK WAKEFIELD who is really good is now living in Columbus so he can play with Sid Campbell."

Only a few weeks after Franklin wrote, Mayne and I joined him to perform bluegrass as the Pigeon Hill Boys at Antioch College in Yellow Springs, Ohio. We performed on the same stage the Plum Creek Boys had played in March 1960 to open for the Osborne Brothers. This time we opened for Sid Campbell and his Country Cut-Ups.

Beyond that, I recall little about others at this November 17th event. Joe Hickerson recently called it the "Antioch Folk Festival." The Antioch College *Record* listed it as "A Folk Jamboree."[2] Gus Meade, who had introduced me to old-time and hillbilly discography last year, helped organize the event. Gus had left IU for a job at Wright-Patterson Air Force Base and now lived in Yellow Springs. Hickerson described Gus as "a kind of guru for Antioch folkies."[3]

Gus asked Joe for assistance in finding other performers and hence we were invited, along with a popular new singer-songwriter on the IU campus folk scene, Greg Hildebrand. Joe may have also suggested Janet Smith, Mayne's sister, now in her final year at Oberlin and very popular on campus there. But the main attraction of the event was Sid Campbell's Columbus bluegrass band.

The Pigeon Hill Boys opened with a short set before Campbell and the Country Cut-Ups—Ross Branham, banjo; Danny Milhon, Dobro; and Frank Wakefield, mandolin—took the stage. It was a hot band! I was sorry to miss Campbell's usual banjo picker Johnny Hickman, spoken of highly in Columbus, but Branham was a solid picker, too. So was Dobro player Milhon, the best I'd seen since Josh at Mocking Bird Hill in September. Wakefield was already a legendary mandolin picker and didn't disappoint in this regard.

However, he was a bit over the top with comic antics. While Milhon was at the mike playing a Dobro break, Wakefield knelt down behind him and rolled up one of his pants legs. It got laughs from the audience but sympathy from me—I'd had a similar experience with Shorty and my pants in front of the microphone at Bean Blossom the year before. When I ran into Milhon at a jam session in Florida in 2007, he still remembered that evening. He told me that someone had brought a bottle of hard stuff in the car on the way from Columbus to Yellow Springs and the band had gotten pretty frisky. They sure played some great music.

That day, Franklin introduced me to some of his new friends from Columbus, among them the Gibbons, his landlords who owned the Sacred Mushroom, an off-campus coffeehouse near OSU.

Backstage before the show, he also introduced me to schoolteacher and Columbus bluegrass kingpin Sid Campbell, making a point of showing me the new inlays on Sid's Martin guitar fingerboard. Robby Robinson, a Columbus craftsman who'd apprenticed with Tom Morgan, had cut and inlaid them. Morgan was famous in the bluegrass underground for building instrument necks for bluegrass stars like Ralph Stanley and the Country Gentlemen. He'd even made a copy of Bill Monroe's old Lloyd Loar F5 Gibson mandolin, the first I'd ever heard of. He'd helped Duffey with the inlays on my old Gibson F. Robby was following in Tom Morgan's footsteps.

I asked Franklin if he thought Robinson could build a prewar style neck for my old flathead Gibson. I wanted something besides the too-familiar "bowtie" inlays of the '54 neck I had now, something more interesting visually and thinner to better fit my small hand. Franklin, ever the sculptor and instrument enthusiast, was studying Robby's work and assured me he could make a neck for me.

I returned to Bloomington with visions of a new old-style banjo neck with fancy inlays. In class that fall, I'd filled notebook margins with doodles of old banjo pegheads and inlays. I'd seen pictures of various old prewar Gibson Mastertones with ornate inlays and was wishing I didn't have that ordinary postwar neck on my banjo. These days, those old patterns are well known; many of them have standard names ("Flying Eagle," "Hearts and Flowers," "Wreath") and are associated with various model numbers. I knew nothing of that in November 1962; I was just focused on ornate.

When the IUFC began that fall, I'd volunteered to help out by giving banjo lessons. After Thanksgiving, one of my students, an IU frat boy from Chicago, showed up for a lesson with a banjo he'd gotten while home for the holiday. It was a 1920s Paramount with a neat resonator. It had been a tenor, but the neck had been broken at the nut so he got it for a good price and had a 5-string neck built. The new fingerboard was plain—no inlays, like a classical guitar or a violin.

I asked him: Why no inlays? Didn't he have the old neck? Oh yes, he said, I have it but it has all these ornate flowery inlays; too fancy for me. He gave me the broken neck and peghead.

I fell in love with the inlays at once—it was a Paramount Style B pattern—and envisioned them in my new banjo neck. Soon after I found an old Gibson tenor neck at Rone Music. Louis and I were talking instruments. He showed me a weird old instrument in the back room. A student had left it for repair or trade years ago and they didn't know what to do with it. He asked if I knew what it was.

It was a handmade mountain dulcimer. John Jacob Niles, the Appalachian balladeer who'd built his own versions of these instruments, would be giving a concert on campus on December 10th. I told him I might be able to find a buyer for this authentic instrument. Within days, a Folklore grad student had bought it. As a commission, Louis gave me the old Gibson tenor banjo neck I'd spotted in the back room. It had the hand-cut "Mastertone" inlay block on the fingerboard and twenties-style Gibson fiddle pattern peghead.

With these two, I had enough inlays for my new neck. Now, I wondered, how would I get this to Robby Robinson, whom I'd heard about but never met? I pondered this over the Christmas holidays—the first I'd ever spent with my own family.

SPRING 1963

On the Road
January–March 1963

ON SUNDAY MORNING, January 6, 1963, we drove to Columbus, Ohio. The Country Gentlemen were appearing that night at The Sacred Mushroom, the Gibbons's jazz-folk-beat coffeehouse located in the basement of an old theater near the university campus. We stayed the night in Worthington with Franklin. I brought along my banjo and the two tenor necks.

After a spectacular performance in a tight space, the Gentlemen came back to the Gibbons' for a postconcert party. Among the guests were musicians from the local bluegrass scene—Sid Campbell, Robby Robinson, and others—and members of the Knob Lick Upper Ten Thousand, the Oberlin/Chicago band Franklin had played with last summer. The Knob Licks were going big-time. They'd had just signed with and recorded for Mercury records. Al Grossman was their producer. It was a big party with multiple jam sessions, and much mixing and meeting.

Franklin introduced me to instrument craftsman Robby. A friendly and easygoing guy, he was an accomplished banjo and mandolin picker. We jammed some, and then began talking about a new neck for my banjo. I showed him the two old necks and said I wanted those inlays in a thin neck with the old style peghead. I wanted the new-style 5th string capos—little model railroad spikes (HO gauge) to slip the string under at the 7th, 9th, or 10th frets to facilitate key changes. He said he could do all that. He got my address and I left the necks with him. He would build the neck and let me know when to send the banjo.

I also spent time at the party conferring with John Duffey. I'd been lobbying the IUFC to sponsor a Gents concert in Bloomington. Up at Purdue University in Lafayette, old friend Jim Work was running a similar new folk club and was likewise hoping to bring them to campus.

Duffey had previously asked me for help in finding bookings at college venues. Now he told me that if I'd nail down these bookings he'd give me a 10 percent agent's fee. This was something new to me, but it sounded easy enough so I told him I'd see what I could do.

The following Saturday, the Pigeon Hill Boys appeared in the first of a series of folksong club exchange concerts between the IUFC and the University of Illinois Campus Folksong Club (CFC) in Champaign-Urbana. We shared the venue with Joe Hickerson and Greg Hildebrand. Mayne and I reinvented the band again. Tom Hensley played bass and Chuck Crawford came down from Ann Arbor to play mandolin and sing tenor. We opened our show with an instrumental version of "The Ballad of Jed Clampett," which was now at the top of *Billboard*'s country charts and climbing its "Hot 100," too.

Although this was the first time Mayne and Chuck had sung in concert together since 1959, we'd all had some practice in Bloomington when the Crawfords spent New Year's with us a few weeks earlier.

Illinois' CFC was the brainchild of folklorist Archie Green, librarian at the University's Institute of Labor and Industrial Relations since 1960. Archie knew that Mayne was not only playing bluegrass but also studying it. Last fall, Mayne had taken an introductory ethnomusicology course with a new IU prof, anthropologist Alan P. Merriam. Mayne's term paper was "Bluegrass as a Musical Style." Merriam agreed to act as his supervisor as he developed the paper into an MA thesis.

Archie set up a late afternoon seminar titled "Bluegrass Music in the Urban Revival" and advertised as "featuring IU Folksong Club members The Pigeon Hill Boys Mayne Smith, Neil Rosenberg and Chuck Crawford." In fact, only Mayne and I spoke, and neither of us spoke about the urban revival. Mayne read his paper, which was about defining *bluegrass*; I extemporized briefly about bluegrass history. My talk was unfocused and boring, Mayne's was sharp and engaging. The CFC published it in their magazine, *Autoharp*, just a few weeks later.[1] On February 16th, the club fulfilled their part of exchange at IU; the performers they sent also included a bluegrass band, The Champaign County Yankee Ridgerunners, led by mandolinist Mike Melford.

By then, my MA thesis work had come to an unexpected halt. I'd written my parents about this setback: "The White House Blues has been shelved for the time being." I explained that Richard Dorson, the head of the Folklore program, felt that: "[I]t concerned questions—mostly about the relationship of hillbilly music to folklore, a rather new and unproved line of research—which I should tackle after establishing myself in more basic areas."[2]

This was quite a blow—I'd been working away all fall under the impression that the topic had departmental approval. I had to move on quickly. I was taking a graduate course, "Seminar in Fieldwork," with Dorson this semester. My term project was a collection of jokes. Dorson had published papers on contemporary Jewish dialect joke traditions. He, like most of my fellow students, relished good jokes and told them often.

Academic studies of this narrative tradition were trendy at that moment. Dorson suggested a seminar paper: jokes involving talking parrots. I already knew several, and soon discovered such jokes in the repertoires of friends, relatives, and acquaintances. I was thus already working on a promising project that had the head's approval. It became my thesis topic.

Meanwhile, I'd written Robby to inquire about the neck. He answered in early February with questions about details needed to fit the neck to the body, and asked me to ship it to him no later than March 1st. I sent it by Railway Express on February 25th.

By this time, the folksong clubs at Purdue and IU had both decided to go ahead with concerts by the Country Gentlemen on April 19th and 20th. John Duffey sent me the contracts to be signed, and asked if I could find out if Mocking Bird Hill would be available on Sunday April 21st. "Personally," he wrote, "I'd rather work a college if possible. But anything will do." He urged me to "Keep working on it!!"[3]

At that point, I was focusing on my school work, spending long hours in the Folklore Seminar Room and Library on the 4th floor of the old University Library. But I was also writing about bluegrass. The IU Folksong Club was running a "Folksong Guide" in their new monthly newsletter. I wrote "Bluegrass: A Selective Guide" for their March issue. I prefaced the list of records with a brief history of the music and the word *bluegrass*.

Soon after that, returning home at lunchtime from the library, I stopped into the bookstore on Kirkwood Avenue to look at magazines. To my surprise I saw Monroe on the cover of the new issue of *Sing Out!*

Inside was an article by Ralph Rinzler, "Bill Monroe—'The Daddy of Blue Grass Music.'" This was, as Monroe biographer Tom Ewing later wrote, "the first full-length biographical article about Bill ever published *and* the first to discuss his primary role in the development of bluegrass."[4]

I read it eagerly. My interest in Monroe's recordings was growing as I collected information for the discography. I had a sense of him as a person, but I didn't find him easy to get to know. He was not one for small talk, and the Shehans's stories cautioned against asking him questions. I was impressed that Rinzler, whom I'd known of hitherto only as the mandolinist in the Greenbriar Boys, had been able to get Bill talking.

In my first season at Bean Blossom, I'd seen Monroe in action close-up. Like a sports player-coach, he inspired teamwork by his own performance, and as far as each show was concerned, it seemed to happen as he willed it. I had seen him at Bean Blossom at least six times in the past two years. Never did he have the same band. But they always sounded like Bill Monroe and the Blue Grass Boys.

Rinzler's article got me to comparing the Bill I knew, and tales of him, with Monroe's own newly articulated perspectives. I didn't know it at the time, but Rinzler had already moved from writing about Monroe to booking him at February folk events in Chicago and New York. By the end of that month, he was moving to Nashville to manage Bill.

On March 5th, Nashville was in the national news because of the small plane crash in Tennessee that took the lives of Grand Ole Opry stars Patsy Cline, Lloyd "Cowboy" Copas, Hawkshaw Hawkins, and the pilot Randy Hughes. Its impact on the country music world was, as I would gradually learn over the next few months, similar to that of the crash of four years earlier that killed Buddy Holly—a tragic reminder of daily danger in this traveling art industry.

The following Monday, Robby shipped my banjo back; it arrived on Thursday. The new neck was all I'd dreamed of; the only disappointment was opening the case to find that the head, with its autographs of Scruggs, Reno, and Shelton, was broken. I put on a new head the same day, and on Saturday the Pigeon Hill Boys played in Lafayette for the Purdue's Campus Folk Song Club. Chuck joined us again and played my shiny old F mandolin. The new banjo neck was a joy to play; it was a good night for our music even though the audience was small.

Before and after the show, I hung out with Jim Work, who was heading the club. The Pigeon Hill Boys were billed as "bluegrass" on the posters; no mention was made of "folk music." While we connected bluegrass to folk music, many of the students who liked folk music apparently did not.

Pigeon Hill Boys at Purdue, March 1963. Chuck Crawford, me, Fred Schmidt, Mayne. (Courtesy of Ann Milovsoroff)

Worried about attendance, Jim put "Bluegrass & Folk Music at Its Best" on his posters for next month's Country Gentlemen concert.

When I returned home from Lafayette, a long letter from John Duffey was waiting. He said they'd gotten a booking at the University of Michigan for April 21st, the day after IU. So that weekend was settled, he didn't need Mocking Bird Hill. But he was hoping for midweek college bookings at Antioch and Ohio State after that, asking me to help. He closed with the admonition: "work, work, work; hustle, hustle, hustle; REMEMBER YOUR 10%; go, go, go; pitch, pitch, pitch; REMEMBER YOUR 10%"[5] I referred him to others at those schools. I wasn't interested in becoming a booking agent—that now seemed like too much hard work.

The week after I returned from Lafayette, Marvin Hedrick called. He asked, "Have you heard Bill's new banjo player? He's from Boston." I hadn't. Marvin had recorded the Opry for Saturday March 23rd and told me I should listen. I borrowed the tape at his next jam.

Marvin had recorded the whole evening's broadcast, ads and all, at slow speed. As usual, a well-known country star emceed each half-hour segment. I listened a long time before coming across a segment starring Faron Young, whose biggest hit was 1961's "Hello Walls." Right after the Jordanaires, Young introduced: "the king of bluegrass music. Make welcome the one and only Bill Monroe! All right?"

Indeed! They played "Cindy," an old folksong Bill had recorded for the first time just a few months before that featured the fiddling of Kenny Baker. Eastern Kentuckian Baker had played briefly with Monroe in 1958, before returning home to work at mining, a more dependable source of income. Now he was back, playing as strongly and uniquely as always on this up-tempo folk frolic. Bill's new banjo player traded breaks with him, and I heard things coming from that banjo I'd never heard before—swooping melodic runs.

A little bit later in the segment just as Monroe was about to play "Goodbye Old Pal," Faron Young stopped him: "Hey, Bill, before you start into that I want to say something. This banjo player back here I haven't met but I've heard him and golly if he isn't about the finest I've ever—"

"He's the best," Monroe said.

Turning to the still unnamed banjo player, Young asked him: "Aren't you from up in Massachusetts or somewhere?"

"Yes I am," the banjoist answered.

"Where?" Faron asked.

"Boston," replied the stranger.

"Boston!" Young exclaimed. "Can you imagine, a guy from Boston, Massachusetts!"

"Bradford Keith," said Monroe, who was using Keith's middle name—his first name was Bill—so there wouldn't be two Bills in the Blue Grass Boys.

"Bradford Keith, and he plays that banjo like, the greatest I ever heard." Let's get 'em back up here with a big round of applause. Bill Monroe, come on boys."

"Goodbye Old Pal" was led off by Keith's banjo. A lifelong staple in Monroe's repertoire, it was a measure of banjo players, especially at the end of the second line where the melody passes through the 2 chord (let's say from G to A and on to D). In that section, he played a breathtaking run I'd never heard before. It was just one of many.

They finished to rousing applause. Young called Bill back to the mike: "Hey Bill, I, we're, we're running short but I want to get this boy up here, Bradford, to do that song—the other night he did a song called 'Fisher's Hornpipe.'" Monroe turned to Keith and asked, "can you get it, tuned like this?"

There was a hurried conference between Keith, Baker, and Monroe. Keith played the tune in the key of A, Baker played it in B flat, a fret higher. Keith would have to retune. While waiting, Faron plugged his own appearance on the Ernest Tubb Midnight Jamboree later that evening. In less than a minute, Keith tuned all five of his strings a half-step higher and stepped up to the mike.

"You ready, Bradford?"

"Yes"

"'Fisher's Hornpipe.' Get right up here,"

"'*Sailor's* Hornpipe," interjected Kenny Baker.

And they were off—three short runs through at supercharged speed with Keith leading off, Baker swinging into it the second time, and Keith ending it with another spectacular run in place of the usual shave and a haircut. It was amazing—an old fiddle tune played note-for-note on the banjo with all kinds of drive and invention. The impromptu performance was, to my ears, perfect: in tune, with no missed notes or dropped beats. Bradford Keith in the Blue Grass Boys was an unexpected revolution. I looked forward to seeing him in person with Bill whenever they got to the Brown County Jamboree.

Spring Pickin'
April 1963

I DIDN'T FIND TIME TO LISTEN to the Opry for further performances by Monroe and his new banjo player that spring, and had no news about when the Jamboree was opening. Busy with schoolwork, I was collecting parrot jokes for the fieldwork course.

GRAND RE-OPENING
BROWN COUNTY JAMBOREE
BEAN BLOSSOM, IND. - ON HIGHWAY 135
SUN 2 BIG SHOWS 3:00 & 8 P.M. APR 21
W S M GRAND OLE OPRY
★STARS★ IN ★PERSON
BILL
MONROE
BLUE GRASS BOYS
BLUE GRASS QUARTET
SHENANDOAH VALLEY TRIO

At the end of March, the IUFC voted in new officers for the coming academic year. Mayne was elected president; I became vice president. The Country Gentlemen concert was coming soon; I wrote a "Concert Preview" about them for the *IUFC Newsletter*.

Spring vacation began April 10th; I headed with the family for Cleveland, where I spent the week doing research in the Cleveland Public Library's special folklore collection. That Friday, we drove forty miles southwest to see the Country Gentlemen give their third annual Oberlin concert, the usual dynamic show. We spoke with

The Country Gentlemen at Oberlin College, April 1963. Eddie Adcock, John Duffey, Tom Gray, Charlie Waller. (Courtesy of Ann Milovsoroff)

Duffey afterward, arranging to record and photograph their forthcoming IU concert at the student union building in Whittenberger Auditorium.

That weekend, the *Indianapolis Sunday Times* featured a full-page story by their young music reporter, Walt Spencer, "Folk Music Is Everywhere." "Few folks know it when they hear it," the article began, but in fact Indianapolis is "surrounded by practitioners of the two basic forms of American folk music—white country or 'hillbilly' music and Negro blues and primitive jazz. Unfortunately, most of these performers are overlooked while we are bombarded with mid-cult pseudo-folk performers."

He told of locally audible radio from Wheeling, Cincinnati, and Waterloo, Iowa that played "commercial country" with "a lot of old-fashion authentic folk mixed in," and mentioned similar sources for African American music. Lamenting that local bluesman Scrapper Blackwell had recently died in obscurity while "fuzzy-cheeked young folk singers" pack local clubs, Spencer suggested an alternative:

"On a summer Sunday afternoon and evening, there is no better recreation than going to the bring-the-whole family all-star country music shows at Mockingbird Hill Park near Anderson, Plantation Park at Pendleton or the Brown County Jamboree at Beanblossom owned by Bill Monroe, the best mandolin player alive and the person who popularized 'blue grass music,' the only new true folk music form, an amalgam of hillbilly, western swing, popular country music and even jazz."

Even in Indianapolis, authentic tunes can be heard at "rough and tumble taverns . . . on the East Side," he said, mentioning as an example, "Shorty Sheehan, who is as excellent an old-time fiddle player as can be found anywhere." He also announced the coming Purdue and IU folk music club concerts by the Country Gentlemen, "one of the best blue grass groups . . . one of those phenomenons of the folk fad" who recorded "for the country music firm, Starday, yet played a concert at Carnegie Hall last year."[1]

A week later, just after we returned to Bloomington, another package arrived from Jim Peva. It contained a folded Hatch show print poster announcing the "Grand Re-Opening" of the Brown County Jamboree by Monroe on Sunday.

An accompanying letter contained Jim's request: "Birch Monroe gave me the enclosed card and I told him I would send it to you. Do you think the Union Building people would object if the card were displayed outside of Whittenberger Auditorium on Saturday evening? I'm sure that a lot of the people who will attend the Country Gentlemen concert would also be interested in Bill's show on Sunday. Birch says he has a banjo picker now who is better than Scruggs—some fellow from Boston, Mass."[2]

On Saturday afternoon the Country Gentlemen arrived at our home on East 2nd. They were in a big black Cadillac limousine—"passes everything but gas stations," Duffey told us at supper. As usual we got to talking mandolins, and John brought in one he was selling—an old 1920s Gibson Lloyd Loar F5 mandolin he'd found in Arizona; perfect except for a hole on the side near the end pin where someone had installed and later removed a pickup. Only $350! I didn't have that kind of money, of course.

Their concert that evening was the first professional bluegrass show on the IU campus. It drew a mixed crowd—students like Mayne's ethnomusicology grad student friend Charlie Keil and my new friends from the Jamboree, Marvin Hedrick (with his family) and Jim Peva. I set the poster for tomorrow's Jamboree on an easel outside the door.

The Gentlemen gave their usual great show, appreciated by an audience that applauded as enthusiastically after breaks and at the ends of songs as at a jazz or classical concert. After the show, the band came back to the house to unwind and load up to drive that night to Ann Arbor for their Sunday gig. We stayed up late talking, going to bed only after they left at 4 a.m. One of the topics was Monroe's new banjo player, who they knew because he had been performing in the Washington area prior to joining Monroe. They said I'd dig his unique banjo style.

The next afternoon, Mayne, Mike Melford of the Yankee Ridgerunners (who'd come over from Champaign for the Country Gentleman concert), and I were sitting in the front row at the Brown County Jamboree. My tape recorder was in front of me.

After the Monroe and the Blue Grass Boys came on stage and played the theme, Bill welcomed us—with excuses: "We're glad to see a good many folks out for the show. Wish we could have advertised it better but we didn't have a really good chance, and we got a lot bucking us today. They got a big show in Indianapolis with about ten acts from the Grand Ole Opry, they ought to have at least a couple hundred up there. And then Franklin, I believe, is operating today. I don't know whether anybody else got a still going."[3]

The excuses continued with the introduction of the band—his new guitarist and lead singer, Del (Bill called him "Dale") McCoury, was having eye trouble and wasn't feeling well; Roger Smith was filling in on banjo "'til my other banjo picker gets ready." But, Monroe said, "We're gonna fiddle for you today as we never fiddled before. I promise you that. We're gonna really get with it in a big way. Kenny Baker's feeling fine." The show began with Kenny's new number, "Big Sandy River."

After the enthusiastic applause died down, Bill spoke about how much he enjoyed coming to Brown County: "There's some wonderful people up here, and I like to visit with you, too, and talk with you." This summer, he told us, they were going to operate the Jamboree and put on some good shows, starting next Sunday with Don Reno and Red Smiley. He plugged their comedy show: "If you want to get some good laughs, now, to really enjoy yourself, you come on over and watch 'em work here." He added, almost as an afterthought, "They play some good bluegrass music."

For the next song, he asked if Del felt like singing, and Del did. After his solo, "Dark Hollow," Monroe continued speaking about local friends:

I'd like to put in a plug for Mr. Hedrick. He's a-furnishing our public address today, ain't that right, Birch?

(Birch): That's right.

Now there's another friend up here we couldn't hardly do without. He's helped us a lot over here, and a lot of time we might could not operate if we didn't have a good public address here. And he sells a lot of records over there, I believe, in his shop in Nashville, and I guess he's got some of the Blue Grass Boys' albums there and you might could buy one. I sure would appreciate for my sake. And, ah (laughing), let's see, he sells TVs over there, and works on radios. So visit him some time.

Several numbers later, Brad Keith snuck out of the cabin door onto the back of the stage, covering his face with his hat. As the audience laughed, Bill spoke to him:

I can't see good, but I can still see, he can't hide from me. Friends I want to welcome a boy here today and I want you to really give him a nice hand and listen to him pick. He's from Boston, Massachusetts and, ah, you know as well as I do there never been a lot of old-time string music come from the eastern parts of the country or the northern parts. I'm sorry that Indiana is up on this side of the river, wish it was down south. We gonna let him pick some here, he's been recording some with us, been on the Grand Ole Opry with us, I guess, a month or so; plays a different style of banjo from a lot of people. His name is Bradford Keith and let's give him a hand here today, what do you say? (applause) Now, the harder the numbers are to play, the easier he plays 'em, and the better he plays 'em and so he plays one called "Devil's Dream," let's listen to it.

It was a spectacular performance—not only did he nail the tune, which I'd never heard anyone play on the banjo, he had an ornate set of variations for his second break. It was a tour de force. "Mighty fine," Bill said dryly afterward as he launched into the main part of the show with his solo and a call for requests. After five of these (including my request for "White House Blues") he gave the Blue Grass Boys a break and introduced "two of the finest showmans in the country," Shorty and Juanita Shehan.

Today, they were laying the comedy on pretty thick, perhaps to remind Bill and Birch that they could be the perfect act for this year's house band. Following a string of one-liners and his opening "Orange Blossom Special," Shorty looked down at the front row and said: "I see we got some real young prospectives sitting in the audience out here—Mr. Mayne Smith and Mr. Neil Rosenberg, some real fine boys from over at Indiana University, president and vice president of the Folklore Club. . . . Boy they're taking up nice things in these colleges today, I wish I could erase a few years and go back. Woo, would I have a time!"

Juanita opened with Patsy Cline's "Sweet Dreams" in memory of the March tragedy in which Cline, Hawkins, and Copas had died. New tribute albums to these artists had already begun to show up at Rone Music.

After Shorty and Juanita's five-number set, Bill and the Blue Grass Boys came on stage again and Bill invited Roger Smith out along with his teen-age stepdaughter Cleata Carr to sing two solos—old pop songs like Connie Francis's "Lipstick on Your Collar" and Elvis's "Let's Have a Party."

Hymn time followed, with Roger helping with the baritone part and, as at the show in October, being drafted to sing lead on several of the four songs because Del, who'd been a singer-guitarist for only a month, hadn't learned all of Bill's songs yet.

This was a long show! More songs followed, and then Bill introduced "a banjo number here that a we, ah, that Brad put on record about a month ago and it'll be out before long now, called 'Salt Creek.' Well, it went by fast, but what a neat tune! I was glad I was taping the show, because I wanted to hear that one again.

Bill returned again then to the topic of next week's show by Reno & Smiley. He needed help to advertise the show:

> Ah, we have some cards of Don and Red, you know, and it's pretty hard for us to get 'em out up here, 'cause we live down in Nashville there. And some of us tries to farm, some fools with game chickens, and some just loafers around, you know, and—but we don't have much chance to get 'em out. My son, he come up here the other time and put some cards out for my show here, Jimmy Monroe and brother Birch here. And ah, they got the cards out for this show. So if you will take one or two of 'em, wherever you live at. And if you got a filling station where you buy gas, if you'll put one in it, I'll sure appreciate it a lot. And, ah, and we'll try to get out the rest of 'em. And that'll help Don and Red, that'll, ah, mean of course a little money for me, but it'll mean something for Don and Red and they have to come from, ah, Roanoke, Virginia, they work over in that part of the country.

Reno & Smiley were on his mind in another way because, as he explained, they were coming to Nashville next Friday:

> They plan on having, ah, the story of bluegrass music on the Friday before they come up here, if I can be there at all, why they gonna have the story

of the bluegrass music. They gonna have it from the time they first started, back in nineteen and thirty-eight right on up 'til today. And what I mean, the boys that's played with me. Like the first fellow that ever started like Cousin Wilbur, Clyde Moody, people like that. Fiddling Art Wooten was the first fiddler. Come on down through Chubby Wise, Big Howdy, Red Taylor; with the banjo pickers, Stringbeans was the first, Earl Scruggs was the second, Rudy Lyles was the third I believe, and Don Reno right on down the line. And they'll play records of how bluegrass music, it had advanced along from the first time it started up until today. And people like that I do have now, like Kenny Baker on fiddle and Brad Keith on the 5-string banjo. Some of the best. So if they do have that on the Friday before, and that'll be next Friday, why I want you to be tuned in on that.

It was unclear to me then—as it still is today—where in Nashville this event, presumably a broadcast, was to take place; perhaps at the Opry? In any case, this was the first I heard the phrase, "The Story of Bluegrass." It would become familiar a few years later when Carlton Haney, who had managed Bill in the midfifties and was, in 1963, managing Reno & Smiley, built the first bluegrass festivals around an event with that title. This was also the first time I'd heard Bill speak about the history of his band, naming some of the pioneer Blue Grass Boys and mentioning his records.

It was significant that Bill was now talking about bluegrass as a historical event. Was that the result of his newly published interview with Rinzler? Had he been talking about his "Story" with Carlton Haney? Perhaps it was just a reflection of how he felt that day, as he sensed a growing interest in his music: "This makes about a hundred and fifty times or two hundred times that I've played here and I don't really expect a big crowd when I come up here because you know when you've played that much you needn't to expect too many. But, ah, see this many out, I'm pleased to have you folks here."

The requests went on, and Bill did many of his best-known songs. When "Blue Moon of Kentucky" was shouted out, he again evoked his past:

That's, ah, that's a pretty number right there. Lester Flatt and myself on that number there. And, ah, I, we've sung it a many a time on the Opry, we hope you enjoy it here today. "Blue Moon of Kentucky," I'd like to do that. We want to do that in C sharp if you boys don't mind. Seem like I can do that a little better there than we've been a-doing it. [hits C# chord on mandolin] We've always sung "Blue Moon" in a C, so we've moved it up to

C sharp last night, it seems like it works a little bit better. For me. I don't know about the boys who play.

That was a bit of a tongue-in-cheek statement—of course C sharp is an unusual key, especially for Kenny Baker, who did all the solo work on that piece. But he and the rest of the Blue Grass Boys rose to the occasion.

After the show, I went backstage with my banjo, introduced myself to Keith and told him how much I'd enjoyed hearing him in person. We compared new banjo necks—he'd had Tom Morgan put a Hearts-and-Flowers neck on his late-thirties top-tension flathead. I had mine with its Paramount inlays and neck by Robby Robinson. We spoke of mutual friends; he told me Ralph Rinzler was now Bill's manager. That was news to me. Our meeting was brief; my friends were eager to hit the road.

As the show closed, Mike Melford urged us to come home with him to Champaign so we could meet and jam with a very fine mandolin player there, his mentor Nate Bray. Pat Burton had told me about Nate, who was in a band with brothers Harley and Francis and friend Red Cravens; they'd been the house band at Bean Blossom in 1960 and last year had made an LP under the name of The Bluegrass Gentlemen for the Liberty label.

It seemed like a good idea to us. After hearing a lot of top-notch bluegrass, we were all ready to do some picking. After stopping in Bloomington we headed west in Mayne's '51 Chev, a three-hour drive. It was about 11 p.m. by the time Mike got Nate over to his apartment. We jammed for a couple of hours—Nate was a very nice guy and a great musician—and then sacked out. Next morning, we hit the road home early. We had to make a seminar that afternoon: back to the reality of school after an amazing weekend of live bluegrass!

Later that week, I listened to the tape of Sunday's show, writing out a table of contents for it. I paused at "Salt Creek," listening to it several times. I really wanted to learn how to play that! I was looking forward to more good bluegrass at Bean Blossom.

Reno & Smiley

April 1963

SOME INTERESTING ACTS performed at the Jamboree in the first six weeks of the season. Was Bill doing the booking in consultation with Birch, or was his new manager, Ralph Rinzler, playing a role? At last week's show Bill spoke of Reno & Smiley in a way that now suggests he'd been talking about "The Story of Bluegrass" with Carlton Haney. Was Ralph involved in these talks?

We went to Reno & Smiley's afternoon show at the Jamboree on April 28. As at Mocking Bird Hill last fall, they drew a big enthusiastic crowd and put on their usual tight show. It began with the theme they used in their broadcast shows. Reno, glib and gregarious, quick with the humor, did most of the emcee work. As he introduced each band member, he'd call for "a welcome" or "applause." The band helped in the cheerleading—especially electric guitarist Steve Chapman, who had a

BROWN COUNTY JAMBOREE

BEAN BLOSSOM, INDIANA ON HIGHWAY 135

SUN. 2 BIG SHOWS 3:00 & 8 P. M. **APR. 28**

STARS FROM

NEW DOMINION BARN DANCE

WRVA · RICHMOND · VA.

DON RENO

—— AND ——

RED SMILEY

two-bar fanfare for every one of Reno's introductions and jokes: a cue for laughter and applause.

Don and Red opened with a recent duet, and then each band member was introduced and did a "solo," covering a wide variety of material, from very old fiddle tunes done up-tempo like "Paddy on the Turnpike" by Don's teenage son Ronnie on the mandolin to bassist John Palmer's performance of Buck Owens's 1961 hit "'Til These Dreams Come True."

Each solo was executed in a style befitting its origins. Don Reno and fiddler Mack Magaha added hot bluegrass breaks to "Paddy." The band laid down the perfect contemporary country walking beat for Palmer's Owens cover while electric guitarist Steve Chapman expertly re-created both its steel guitar and lead guitar breaks.

Of the four top bluegrass bands at this time (Monroe, Flatt & Scruggs, and the Stanley Brothers were the others) only Reno & Smiley had an electric guitarist. Except for his fanfares, a fingerpicked version of "John Henry," and breaks on a few country hits, he stayed mainly in the background, playing percussive rhythm. Added to the bass, mandolin, and Smiley's booming guitar, he helped create an extremely solid rhythm section capable of playing anything from old-time country to rockabilly.

Chapman's "solo" was a cover of "Wolverton Mountain," a recent country hit for Claude King. Ronnie and Mack joined in with a responsorial chorus that parodied the original:

"The bears and the birds," sang Chapman.

"The buzzards and the bats," replied Ronnie and Mack, adding: "The doggies and the kitty cats."

"I thought I heard some odd words in that song," said Don afterward.

At midshow, Birch Monroe came on stage to speak with Don about the Jamboree. Before they spoke, Don invited Roger Smith to come up and perform. Then Birch asked Don to "help me advertise our show for next week."

That was his cue for Don to identify the act: Charlie Monroe with his band the Kentucky Pardners. "Charlie's kind of a legend in our time and you don't want to miss him. That's next Sunday, right?

"Next Sunday. Three and eight," said Birch.

"Three and eight. So you folks be sure and turn out and see Charlie Monroe. Some time this summer I'd like to see Charlie and Bill together up here, you know," Don added. The Monroe Brothers had been hillbilly stars in the late 1930s but had performed together only a few times in the mid-1950s. "They gonna be up here Don," Birch chimed, "they're gonna have a Monroe Day here 'fore long." At this time, I had no idea I'd be involved with Monroe Day when it finally took place.

Birch moved then to a new topic: "The dance we have on Saturday night . . . we want to work it up to a big dance." It runs from eight until midnight and, he said, "we've got some old-time musicians and we're gonna have a rock and roll band." That was the first I'd heard of a rock and roll band at Birch's dance!

"And a one thing sure," he added, "we gonna have good order because the sheriff's brother, he's gonna deputize his brother. And when you got the sheriff behind you, you can do a lot of things." Hedrick, who knew the sheriff, had told me of fights and drinking at the dances; Birch was addressing rumors about this, which he worried were cutting into attendance on Saturday nights.

Reno agreed with Birch and pushed the subject toward the comic: "Oh you ain't kidding! You, you, you really don't know what you can do, 'til you get the sheriff behind you!" Laughter broke out as Birch moved on to yet another topic.

He first complimented Don and Red—"You can't beat 'em"—and urged them to sell their pictures and songbooks. And then he turned to their connection with Bill Monroe. Don had already mentioned that Bill was tutoring Ronnie whenever he could. Now Birch told him, "you come up under the right kind of a man to play this kind of music, didn't you?" Don spoke of how Bill "learned me how to do everything from play ball to the 5-string banjo—almost," he added, reminiscing about his times together with Birch in the Blue Grass Boys.

Birch left the stage, Roger came up with his fiddle, and he and Magaha, along with the rest of the band, played virtuosic versions of two Monroe instrumentals: "Panhandle Country" and "Roanoke." After that, the show carried on with hymns from their latest album, both sides of their new single, audience requests, and, to close the show, an appearance by Don in drag as Chicken Hot Rod, doing comedy and then taking Red's guitar and singing "Mule Skinner Blues"—another piece associated with Monroe—with added comedy verses.

As the audience filed out to a fiddle tune, Smiley spoke over the applause urging people to pick up "some of the advertising cards for next Sunday's show. If you have someplace to put 'em, a service station or some place you might know where they'll let you put the advertising card up we'd appreciate it."

So when, a week later on May 5th, Charlie Monroe played the Jamboree, I knew about the show, but for reasons now forgotten I didn't go. Having missed that show, I was out of the loop and never did learn who played on the 12th. The Jamboree was advertised only by word of mouth and posters.

Stonemans, Banjo Contest

May 1963

I DID HEAR ABOUT THE following week's (19th) show, when I saw a poster at Marvin's for the Stoneman Family. From the Washington, D.C., area, they'd made their first album last year for Starday and had begun touring. The Stonemans had been in the music business for a long time.

Father Ernest V. ("Pop") Stoneman and his wife Hattie, from Galax, Virginia, were pioneer hillbilly recording artists of the 1920s. By 1952, when Harry Smith included two of their recordings on Folkways' *Anthology of American Folk Music*, they were living in the D.C. region, where Pop worked as a carpenter. They raised a large family, and many of the children joined them in playing music at events in the region.

In 1957, Folkways released an album produced by Mike Seeger and Ralph Rinzler: *The Stoneman Family/Old-Time Tunes of the South* (Sutphin, Foreacre

BROWN COUNTY

JAMBOREE

BEAN BLOSSOM, INDIANA ON HIGHWAY 135

SUN. 2 BIG SHOWS 3:00 & 8 P.M. **MAY 19**

IN PERSON

POP STONEMAN

and the **STONEMAN FAMILY**

STARDAY RECORDS

FEATURING

SCOTT STONEMAN

WORLD'S CHAMPION FIDDLER

DIRECT FROM WASHINGTON, D. C.

and Dickens). One side was devoted to Ernest and Hattie and included a track featuring them playing at a dance with Pop's family band, the Little Pebbles.

On Seeger and Rinzler's other 1957 Folkways production, *American Banjo Scruggs Style*, the first bluegrass LP, daughter Roni (billed as Veronica Cox) was the only woman included.

Along with her sister Donna and various brothers, she'd become part of the Bluegrass Champs, a Stoneman family band that had played the bars of Baltimore and other country music venues starting in 1956 and won a national television talent show. The band's membership varied.

In 1962, the Bluegrass Champs moved briefly to Nashville. In a guest appearance on the Grand Ole Opry, they stopped the show with their performance of "White Lightning No. 2," a comedy cover of George Jones's hit of a few years earlier. Shortly after that, Starday Records contacted them, and their first album for that label, released in November 1962, was titled *Ernest V. Stoneman and the Stoneman Family (The Bluegrass Champs)*.

By the beginning of the year, they were appearing at both country venues and folk music events. They arrived in Bean Blossom that Sunday after having played for the University of Illinois Campus Folksong Club the night before. Archie Green, who'd interviewed Pop Stoneman a few months previously, had arranged the concert. He knew Rinzler and helped them land a booking the next day at the Jamboree.

Their show featured the five youngest of thirteen surviving Stoneman children, aged between twenty-two and thirty-one, with their sixty-nine-going-on-seventy-year-old father. Each had their role in the family band.

Van, the youngest, played guitar, sang lead, and acted as the emcee.

Next in age came sister Roni, who played banjo and did comedy. She was sassy—mouthing off and acting out on stage. Decades later, she would become "Ida Lee Nagger," a regular character on the long-running television country music comedy show "Hee Haw."

Jim (later known as "Jimmy") played bass—he had a percussive double-time slap rhythm that really took charge of the sound. He also sang solos—sophisticated arrangements of old folksongs like "Poor Ellen Smith" and "John Henry."

Older sister Donna played an F5 mandolin with a pickup. That was off-putting to me—the sound was tinny. She used the pickup because she did a lot of dancing on stage. Now, when I get beyond the electrified tone and listen to what she was playing, I realize she was deeply into Monroe's mandolin style, doing creative stuff with it. In contrast to Roni, Donna was pretty, sweet, and demure—hardly speaking at all.

The oldest of the five was fiddler Scott. He was a championship fiddler who did a trick routine with his version of "Orange Blossom Special." He was also a superb accompanist—a D.C. bluegrass recording session veteran—who had, by this time, been in and out of the band several times because of a solo career and a serious drinking problem.

I hadn't heard their new Starday album, but I had run across Pop while researching "White House Blues." In 1927 and '28, he'd recorded his version of this song, first as "The Road to Washington" and then as "The Unlucky Road to Washington." Even though it was no longer my thesis topic, I was eager to ask Pop about this.

I met him backstage before the show. He was friendly, quite willing to answer my questions. I told him I had heard his '20s recordings of "White House Blues" and wondered where he'd learned the song.

"From Charlie Poole," he said. I asked how come his words weren't always the same as Poole's. He laughed and said: "You could be in the same room with Charlie Poole and not understand what he was saying!" He promised to sing the song on the show.

They opened with a lively rendition of "Old Joe Clark" featuring Scott's amazing fiddle work and a mandolin break by Donna.

Van ran a fast-paced show peppered with jokes and comedy bits. After singing "Old Slew Foot," an up-tempo song that Donna had recorded with Rose Maddox while they were in Nashville, Van gave a comic thank-you for the enthusiastic applause: "Thanks. I'm telling you, sure appreciate that. Just as nice as snuff, and not half as dusty."

Then he introduced Pop and the rest of the family: "We're gonna call on Pop, the father of all the band, Pop Stoneman, to do one for you. As the poster says out there, the Stoneman Family, well we really, each and every one of us up here, are all brothers and sisters with the exception of Pop, and he's our son."

After the laughter subsided, he continued: "I'm sorry, I should have introduced the band earlier, before we got started so fast. I'd like to take time out right now to introduce the band." What followed was a classic comedy routine from the swing era, with Van introducing band members to one another and everyone shaking hands. Afterward, he seriously introduced the band and then turned to Pop.

"Here's one we're gonna call on Pop to do for you, one that he recorded in nineteen and twenty-six. He recorded it as 'The Unlucky Road to Washington' but it's been recently recorded not too long ago as 'The White House Blues.' So here he is." Pop sang eight verses, including ones that I'd never been able to decipher from Poole's 1925 recording. Pop had been an early hillbilly cover artist; his cover was easier to follow than the original.

The rest of their performance showcased the family's singing and picking talents, with one banjo piece for Roni, and two each featuring mandolin and fiddle for Donna and Scott. One of Scott's performances was his "Orange Blossom Special," which reviewer Fritz Plous had seen the night before in Urbana and called "a classic exhibition of trick fiddling—holding the bow between his knees and moving the fiddle over it, lying on the floor and arching his back while he played the fiddle under his 'bridge,' playing the instrument while holding it behind his back."[1]

Their repertoire, both instrumental and vocal, was largely traditional, salted with a few recent Monroe and Scruggs pieces. Comedy was built around the players' family personas: sassy Roni, demure Donna, and Scott the drinker.

At the end of the show, just before introducing Scott's rendition of "Listen to the Mockingbird," Van announced: "Friends, I would like to say that next Sunday here, they gonna have a banjo-picking contest. There'll be fifty dollars first prize and also a second and a third prize. So don't forget to come around and be with them here, a banjo-picking contest. And every Saturday night they have a dance here, so always come around."

After the show I bought a copy of their Starday LP and took it to Roni for an autograph. I told her I played the banjo and really enjoyed her picking today. We talked about banjo pickers—Don Stover was one of her favorites; he was one of mine too.

This was the only time I saw the Stoneman Family, who were at the start of a successful concert and recording career that led to a popular syndicated television show in the seventies. Pop died in 1968; Roni is still going strong as this is written.

I was looking forward to next Sunday, and began practicing for the banjo contest. Bill announced it on the Opry the night before, and one contestant drove all the way up from Tennessee to enter.

As usual, the event was judged by applause. It was as much an audience duel as a musical one. I took first in the afternoon, narrowly beating a local

With Mayne at the Jamboree's May 1963 banjo contest; several people taped the event. (Courtesy of Ann Milovsoroff)

fellow who'd brought a substantial claque with him. Once I'd gotten my first place, the audience that had rooted for me switched their applause to contestant Jim Looney, who'd driven up all the way from Lawrence-burg, Tennessee. He was not playing as much fancy stuff as I was, but I made mistakes and he didn't. Winners were supposed to stay to defend their place at the evening show but Looney had to hit the road after the first show to drive back to Tennessee, so Birch gave him the second place money before he left.

The other fellow and his claque left at the end of the afternoon show with a provisional third place. At the evening show, there was only one other contestant, Leonard Burton, Bryant Wilson's former partner, a solid picker and a very personable character. I picked well, maintaining my first place and securing the $50 first prize; Birch awarded Leonard third.

I don't recall what I played, but at contests I usually chose one fancy old pop piece with lots of chords like "Lady of Spain" and a more straight-forward old-timer like "Little Maggie" or "Darling Pal of Mine." Mayne accompanied me.

The next day I finished my coursework for the spring semester; summer school would be starting the middle of next month. At the contest, we'd learned that Bill Monroe and the Blue Grass Boys would be coming back to the Jamboree next week, on the 2nd of June. It was another chance to see Bill's amazing new banjo picker, and the start of a very musical summer.

SUMMER 1963

Meeting Ralph Rinzler
June 1963

ON SUNDAY, JUNE 2ND, the day I met Ralph Rinzler, Monroe was at the Jamboree as advertised. A big crowd came from IU; word had gotten around about his new banjo picker from Boston. Mayne and I were there, as was Joe Hickerson, eminence gris in the Bloomington folk scene, folklore PhD candidate, soon to depart for work at the Archive of Folk Song in the Library of Congress.

Before the show, I went backstage to get better acquainted with Brad Keith. He congratulated me on my victory in the banjo contest and showed me the new tuners he and Dan Bump had invented that put the function of Scruggs tuners right inside regular tuning peg gears. We examined each other's banjos, talking about setup. I asked him to teach me one of his unique runs, and he did so patiently. Our conversation ranged beyond musical matters; we had much in common—the same age, graduates of small coed liberal arts colleges, nonsoutherners who'd gotten into bluegrass from folk. The Boston and Berkeley scenes he and I were part of had many connections. We quickly found mutual friends. We worked up some twin banjo pieces and Bill invited us to play them after the intermission.

There was no fiddler with the Blue Grass Boys today. Roger Smith, who usually filled in when this happened, wasn't there. Keith was called on for lots of instrumental breaks. I taped both shows that day. The afternoon show started with just Bill, Brad, and Del. They played the first part of the set—sixteen songs—alone. In some ways, this was a typical show—Bill soon called for requests. He was working hard to make up for the missing fiddle.

They had just returned from California where they had been since early May, playing festivals and concerts. This was the first time many of the young California folk musicians—like Ry Cooder, Jerry Garcia, Chris Hillman, David Lindley, Herb Pedersen, and Sandy Rothman—had a chance to see and hear Monroe with his new band.

They'd headed back East on Monday the 20th, and were in Nashville by the end of the week. On Saturday the 25th, Bill was on the Opry. He'd announced that there would be a banjo contest in Bean Blossom the next day.

A week later, the California trip was still fresh in Monroe's memory. He had done workshops—his first—at both festivals. He was speaking on stage more frequently about his past and the meanings in his music. He'd begun re-creating the old Monroe Brothers duets with Doc Watson. He was aware more than ever of the young documentarians like me, seated in the front row with a tape recorder attached to an onstage mike. As soon as the show opened and he introduced the band, he spoke to us tapers from the stage: "You boys, you folks that's doing some taping here today, we don't have a full band and it won't really sound as good as we probably could do it if we had a fiddler. Kenny Baker's not with us today and we'll have to make out with Brad Keith doing a lot of banjo picking. 'Course he can really turn loose on it and, ah, I hope you gonna en-, like it, the way he does it."

Throughout the show, Bill praised Keith's picking, telling of how the old-timers at the Opry appreciated his old-time notes. He spoke of an album in the works: "He's a-making a banjo album, that everybody's interested in—some NEW type of bluegrass banjo picking."

After five pieces, Bill spoke to me from the stage: "This microphone on the right's the one you're taping with? It needs to be put here because you'll hear so much tenor singing you won't hear any of the lead or the baritone there. [I moved it.] That'll make it about right I believe, there."

After the tenth piece, "Paddy on the Turnpike," Bill spoke to me again:

Now that's the kind of number you want to take down on your tape because there'll be days when there won't be people around to play them for you, and a it'd be good to know.

And the older the notes are, that you put in numbers like that, it's better, it's gonna make the number and I've done all I can for 'em. And if you boys that's gonna learn 'em, if you'll play as close to the way that I play 'em and then put a lot more in 'em, why it'll help the numbers along and it won't die out on you.

Following this succinct statement of his musical philosophy, he quickly moved on with the show: "Anybody else got a request?"

I called out "White House Blues."

"That's, that's a mighty fine banjo number right there," Bill said dryly, "and it's got a little singing in it." [laughter]

Relishing Keith's banjo work, with interesting twists and turns in every break—I was glad to be getting this on tape. They did sixteen numbers before taking an intermission.

After the intermission, Jim Bessire (on bass) and I joined Del and Brad on stage. Keith and I did our banjo duets, swapping lead breaks, with Brad playing the harmony on the twin breaks. It went over well.

Monroe returned to the stage with Brother Birch, who joined the Blue Grass Boys to sing bass on a couple of hymns. Jim Bessire stayed on, playing bass. Monroe then called for requests, performed one side of his latest single, a duet with Del called "There Was Nothing We Could Do," and closed the show with a speech that focused on his present band:

> I'll be back on the Grand Ole Opry this coming Saturday night; Del and Brad's going on a little vacation, they'll be back in two weeks down there.
>
> And I want you to kindly keep them close tabs 'cause they're gonna make two wonderful Blue Grass Boys. Del's coming right along with his guitar playing and gonna make a wonderful singer.
>
> And there's not a banjo picker in the country—and you better mark my word down for it—if Brad'll stay with me a year they won't be a banjo picker in the country that'll beat him and there's a lot 'em won't beat him right today, and along on a lot of numbers today the best ones won't beat him.

After the standard mention of his records and the Opry History Books, he plugged the show for next week and promised to return soon: "I'll be back in about a couple of weeks, something like that, two or three weeks and they'll have some good shows coming in for you. Speaking for all the gang now it's time we're saying 'Y'All Come' [plays and sings it]. So long!"

I stayed at the Jamboree between shows, picking up a hamburger and a Dr. Pepper for supper from Mrs. Logston's concession stand at the back of the barn. Joe Hickerson came over and said, with surprise in his voice, that Ralph Rinzler was here. He'd known Ralph from the midfifties when he and other Oberlin College folksong enthusiasts went to the big Folk Festival at Swarthmore College, where Ralph was then a student.

He took me up to the front of the barn by the cabin and introduced me to Ralph. I knew who Ralph was: the mandolin player for the Greenbriar Boys, Vanguard Records artists from New York, who had recorded some songs with Joan Baez. Ralph's recent interview with Bill Monroe in *Sing Out!* was fresh in my mind. I knew him also as the producer of field recording albums for Folkways. One of these was *Old Time Music at Clarence Ashley's*, the album that introduced the blind singer and guitarist Doc Watson to the world outside Western North Carolina.

Ralph was busy backstage putting together the evening show so we only spoke briefly. He had prepared a set list, which Del was to keep on the guitar and read off to Bill, who didn't wear his glasses while performing; he depended on the Blue Grass Boys to do the reading when something written came to him on stage. Ralph was anxious for Del to learn the words to Bill's older songs.

He was working on a Bill Monroe discography and beginning to edit albums reissuing classic Blue Grass Boys performances of the fifties. He hoped a set list would direct Bill and his audience to this repertoire and help Del get up to speed on Bill's early classics.

Bill opened the evening show with the typical introductions and then turned to McCoury and asked "What is the first one?" Throughout this first half of the show, his introductions were like that—brief, perfunctory. After each song he turned to Del for the title of the next piece. Gone was his usual shift of focus into requests after the first few numbers. Eventually, he referred directly to the list: "And we've got down on the list an old-timer called "Little Joe," he said, punctuating the title with a mandolin chord—a signal to the band of the key the song was in, but also, in its insistence, a sign of impatience with the list.

Almost all of the pieces in the set were ones Bill had recorded, but they were pieces like "Blue Yodel #4" and "Memories of Mother and Dad," not often heard or requested at Bean Blossom. Two others Bill had not yet recorded, although both were already familiar to bluegrass audiences: "Love Please Come Home" and "Soldier's Joy"—the former popularized by Reno & Smiley, the latter by Flatt & Scruggs. They were pieces Ralph, Del, and Brad knew.

He chose two hymns. Again, they were not ones Bill usually did or were requested at Bean Blossom. First came "Life's Railway to Heaven." He invited Rinzler to join the band for it:

"Ralph, you want to join in with us on this? You know this one. Ralph Rinzler is the fellow that does the booking for the Blue Grass Boys—and he sings some bass, and you used to work in a group called the—" [Rinzler:] "The Greenbriar Boys." [Monroe:] "The Greenbriar Boys and they've played all over the country, lot of our universities."

Ralph knew the bass part because the Greenbriar Boys had recorded the song. Next came "Were You There When They Crucified My Lord." Bill had recorded it in March as "a solo number with some fiddling on it. We'll try to do it for you tonight." He was not happy to be doing it without Kenny Baker there with the fiddle to help him.

By the time they came to the end of the list, Del was prompting Bill: "Little Georgia Rose."

"Little Georgia Rose," Bill replied, "Yes suh!"

Though it was addressed to Del, the "Yes suh" seemed aimed at Ralph, too, reflecting Bill's impatience with the list. The intermission was announced. I went backstage to tune up for another set of banjo duets with Keith.

When our duets were finished, Bill came on stage with Birch, and they did two hymns with Birch singing bass. Afterward Bill invited him to fiddle with the band: "I don't know what number he's got picked out. Birch will you bring your fiddle on up here and tell us what you'd like to play?"

"Ah, Bill something you fellows can help me with the most," Birch replied."

"All right," said Bill, "you just name it, we'll do our best to help you on it."

"What about 'Down Yonder'?" Birch suggested.

Bill answered: "'Down Yonder's a good 'n. It lets me and the banjo picker have a little of it, too, will you?"

Birch promised: "You'll sure get your part of it."

Birch left after a couple of fiddle tunes, and Bill called for requests, taking on almost all, even those that were usually led by the fiddle.

"'Mule Skinner,' Bill answered to one request. "It's hard to do that number without a fiddle but we'll, we'll, we'll tackle it. I'm gonna try a little break in it, and a Brad'll get a good one, and we'll try to make out." Then someone wanted to hear his latest single, "Big Sandy River," and Bill confessed, "I hate to record one and can't play it, so we'll try it. That is really a fiddle number right there, and it's pretty hard to handle with a mandolin, I know myself here, and I guess it's pretty rough on Brad."

Bill closed the show with the promise of "good shows coming in," again apologizing about the lack of advertising, mentioning that Clyde Moody, who'd sung with the Blue Grass Boys in the forties, would be at the Jamboree for a show.

Whatever the future held, this was a good show musically. Bill and the Boys played boldly and adventurously and kept their young audience enthusiastically involved for the whole evening. There was lots of applause for banjo and mandolin breaks, which were often novel.

At the end of the day, I invited Ralph to come back to our apartment in Bloomington. We stayed up late talking. He told me about what he was doing. I was fascinated to hear about it, and he was happy, I think, to have a kindred soul to tell about his adventures and problems. There were few people around who shared our intense involvement in the music of Monroe and saw it as we did—related to all kinds of folk music. He spent the night with us and left the next morning.

I learned that Ralph had moved to Nashville and was managing Bill; that he'd been responsible for booking Reno & Smiley and the Stonemans into the Jamboree last month; and that he'd helped resolve the dilemma earlier in the year in Nashville when Brad arrived in Nashville to find Monroe had also invited another banjo picker—Del McCoury—to join him by suggesting Bill try Del as a guitarist and lead singer.

He was dealing with Monroe's career in other ways: Kenny Baker, who'd been with Bill since the previous fall and played a key role in bringing Keith into the band, had left at the end of May when they finished touring California because he wasn't making enough to support his family. Ralph was helping Bill search for a new fiddler.

He told of his frustrating visit to Decca producer Harry Silverstein to renegotiate Bill's contract only to find that Bill had re-signed last year for five years. He was encouraged, on the other hand, to be able to go into the Decca offices and study the company files documenting dates and personnel for each of Bill's recording sessions. I told him of my work on a Monroe discography, saying that the information he was unearthing would help me move forward on it. I was disappointed that he declined to share it with me, saying that it would soon be published in a new songbook he was working on with Bill.

He was booking Bill on the folk circuit: coffeehouses, folk festivals, college concerts, and the like. He told me about their trip to California. Doc Watson, whom Ralph was also managing and booking, played the

June 1963. A few days before I went to Mocking Bird Hill, Art Rosenbaum, Pete Siegel, and Pat Dunford, on the road collecting Indiana folk music, dropped in for a little jam. (Courtesy of Ann Milovsoroff)

Ash Grove with Clarence Ashley and his band the week before Bill appeared there. Ashley had gotten laryngitis and Watson had, of necessity, stepped up to fill in with vocals. He was a big hit—it really marked the start of his ascent as a solo star in the folk world—and, Ralph said, Ashley was jealous and angry.

They were staying in Malibu with Ash Grove owner, Ed Pearl. Ralph got Bill singing the old Monroe Brothers duets with Doc, first at Pearl's, then backstage, next onstage at the Ash Grove, and finally at the Monterey Folk Festival. Ralph had fond memories of seeing Bill and Charlie Monroe perform together in 1955 at New River Ranch, a park like the Jamboree in Maryland. He mentioned that he and Bill were planning a Monroe Brothers day at the Jamboree. This would be a one-time thing, but he was working to get Bill and Doc together to play similar duets regularly for recordings and concerts.

He wondered if the IU Folksong Club might be interested in having Bill and Doc give a concert. I said that sounded great, but I'd have to run it by the other members of the Club's executive. He mentioned that he'd be with Bill at Mocking Bird Hill the Sunday after next—the 16th.

The following week, I wrote to Ralph about points that had come up in our conversation. I began by relaying the information that I'd "told the executive board" of the Folk Song Club "about the Doc Watson–Bill Monroe tour in the fall, and everyone was enthusiastic."

But bringing Bill in was a challenge. Judging by the turnout for the Country Gentlemen—both IU and Purdue clubs had lost money on them—Indiana University students weren't into bluegrass as much as those at Oberlin, Antioch, and the Ivy League schools. Monroe appeared several times a year just over in Brown County, so seeing him at IU would be no big deal locally. Doc Watson was virtually unknown.

I told Ralph that to cover the cost of a Bill and Doc concert, we needed to have a big-drawing star first. Knowing Ralph had worked with Joan Baez, I asked his help in getting in touch with her to do a concert at IU and suggested that Purdue might also be interested. I said I would get the president of Purdue's Campus Folksong Club, Jim Work, an old friend, to "drop over to Anderson next Sunday so we can discuss this."

The rest of the letter was about Bean Blossom:

> I have been trying to think of various other suggestions that might help you in your new job and here are some that came to mind. Both Reno & Smiley and Flatt and Scruggs carry copys of most of their LPs and the latest single, and members of the band sell them during intermissions. You'd be surprised how many albums are bought at a show, since most record stores don't stock "grass" consistently and since most people don't mail-order for records. The other thing that came to mind is that at most parks the MCs announce bookings for the following two or three weeks in advance. At Bean Blossom Birch sometimes doesn't know for sure who is coming the following week on many occasions, and this cuts down attendance. On a well-publicised show by a popular group, people from all over Indiana, and from Ohio, Kentucky and Illinois will show up. Last year when it was thought Bill was going to be there for a show, people from Chicago came down to dig and tape; it turned out that Bill wasn't coming (the fellow who ran the jamboree last year had hoped to get him on a weeks notice and failed) and the show was given by a comparatively colorless group, the Barrier Brothers. The point here is that the people from Chicago would probably not venture so far again because of that experience. And little screw-ups like this have been happening often enough at Bean Blossom

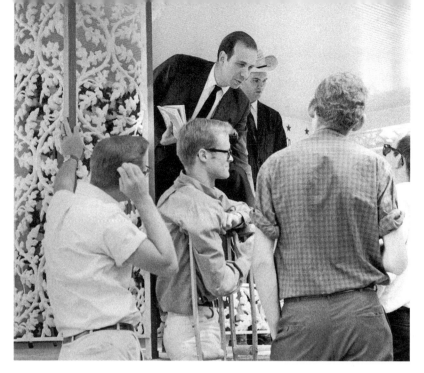

June 1963. Folksong Club business with Rinzler at Mocking Bird Hill. Keith is onstage behind Ralph. At the front of the stage are Joe [?], Jim Work (with crutches), Mayne, and me. (Photographer Unknown. Courtesy of the Jim Work Collection.)

in the past few years so that many potential customers don't feel it's worth the trouble to drive over. I think that publicizing bookings in advance and making sure the dates are certain will help build up the attendance there.

Jim Work, Mayne, and I went to Mocking Bird Hill that next Sunday, June 16th. Bessie was playing bass, and Bill included Melissa on the show, too. Also with the Blue Grass Boys was Billy Sage, a fiddler that Del knew, who was auditioning for Monroe. After the show, I introduced Ralph to Jim Work.

Jim wrote soon after, beginning with a report from friends who'd seen Monroe and Watson at Gerde's Folk City and thought they were "a little rough." He recounted his conversation with Ralph: "I told Rinzler that anything was OK with me as long as we made [a] profit in excess of $750 (The minimum price on Watson, Monroe and the Blue Grass Boys) off of the Baez concert. I was blunt; I told him that I thought that we would lose money on Doc, Bill, etc. This caused an elevation of his eyebrows."[1]

We'd meet with Ralph again soon. Bill and the Blue Grass Boys would be at the Jamboree the following Sunday.

Ralph Fires Birch
June 1963

UNTIL I BEGAN WORKING ON THIS BOOK, memories of my hiring as manager of the Brown County Jamboree at the end of June 1963 had withered down to a few "facts," trotted out for those who asked: Rinzler was managing Monroe; he couldn't get along with Birch handling the chores at Bean Blossom because Birch treated him with a kind of bumbling hostility. Bill's companion, Bessie, was there, too, and in fact it was Ralph and Bessie who hired me; Bill was at first angry about that.

When I identified the date, I dug out a tape I'd made that Sunday. Of the many tapes I've made of Monroe shows, I'd listened to this one least of all. It was flawed—my recorder was on the fritz and the music sounded awful. I made a table of contents, shelved it, and did not copy it for anyone. When I finally re-listened, I discovered that while the music was messed up, the recording of the show was filled with talk that freshened memories. One thing that immediately struck me was Monroe's mention of a visitor traveling with the band: Brad Keith's former roommate and musical partner Jim Rooney.

In 1979, Rooney wrote about his experience that Sunday at Bean Blossom in *Baby Let Me Follow You Down*, the history of the sixties folk revival he coauthored with Eric von Schmidt. The following account draws, then, from the aural history of the tape, Rooney's memoir, and my own memories of that day and of what Ralph said about it the next day when he told me: "I can't work with Birch, I need a manager at Bean Blossom I can work with." It was a story meant to talk me into taking the job.

The Piano

Ralph booked Bill at the Jamboree on Sunday June 23rd, only a few weeks after his last appearance. Worried that he might not draw a very good crowd coming back so soon, they booked another act: Grand Ole Opry piano star Del Wood. Bill said there was a piano on the stage at Bean Blossom. Ralph called Birch, who assured him that there was indeed a piano on stage.

It was on stage right against the wall. Birch failed to mention that it was, at best, badly out of tune. I think that it was worse than that—some keys didn't work, that sort of thing.

Did Birch know the piano was so bad? In the two years I'd been coming to shows at the Jamboree, I'd never seen anyone play it. Birch must have known. But he didn't say. And that was part of Birch's modus vivendi. He gave the impression of stupidity or slowness when in fact he knew very well that, by his silence, he was allowing you to walk into some kind of minefield. This happened often, and in many ways, whenever someone came between him and Bill. That's why Bessie didn't like to come to Bean Blossom. Ralph could see that Birch was running this kind of trip on him.

They arrived early in the morning from Nashville—there was a one-hour time difference, as Nashville was on Central while Indiana was on Eastern, so they would have left after midnight and gotten in around 7 or 8 a.m. And when Del tried the piano, it was unplayable.

So Ralph had to find a piano. I recall a pickup truck with a piano arriving before the start of the afternoon show, and a piano getting manhandled on the stage. But my memory can take me only so far.

The Show

Luckily, Rooney's account fills in the picture. It includes a few erroneous details, mentioning for example a sign on the roof that wasn't there at the time of his visit, and including Kenny Baker, the fiddler who'd left the band weeks earlier, in the roster of musicians and camp followers who'd come with Monroe. Minor lacunae aside, he captures well the spirit of the day.

Quite an entourage had come from Nashville. In addition to Ralph, Bill, Brad, Del, and Bessie, there was Bill's daughter Melissa and two visiting friends: Brad's Boston pal Rooney, and Ralph's English folk music friend Barry Murphy. Barry was sharing an apartment in West Nashville—they called it "The Blue Grass Rest Home"—with Brad, Del, and Ralph. He had built a 12-string guitar that Bill was enthusiastic about. Also traveling with them was Del Wood. She and Bessie were old friends. Nashville-based singer and instrumentalist Benny Williams was also present.

Exactly how each of these people got there from Nashville is uncertain. Rooney's account doesn't account for everyone, but he mentions that Ralph, Bill, Del Wood, and Bessie were in Bill's Olds station wagon while he rode with McCoury in Keith's car. I don't know about the others from Nashville—Melissa, Barry, and Benny. Later, in introducing Bill at the afternoon show, Ralph mentions that he was "picking people up who'd arrived late" before the show, so perhaps that's who he was referring to.

There was no regular house band that Sunday. The show opened with what was sometimes advertised as "The Shenandoah Valley Trio"—the Blue Grass Boys without Bill. Bill still had no regular fiddler, so Roger Smith was filling in on fiddle, joining Del, Brad, and Bessie in an opening set. Bessie sang tenor on one number, a trio version of "Columbus Stockade Blues," and Melissa came to the stage and sang two songs. Ralph acted as emcee.

For the next set, a visiting bluegrass band from the small town of Servia in North Central Indiana, the Moore Brothers and the Pike County Hikers, performed. Next on my tape is a performance by Benny Williams singing one song accompanying himself on guitar with Roger Smith playing fiddle. Williams worked off and on as a Blue Grass Boy—I'd seen him with Bill here the previous August—playing the fiddle and doing comedy.

Ralph's introduction to Bill's portion of the show on the tape begins:

> He'd be out there driving spikes just like everyone else was, get that tent up in time for the show, and a few people from the town would usually join in with him and they'd look around, they'd say, "say, you know when Bill Monroe's gonna get here?" And Bill would look at them and he'd say "Don't you worry, he'll be here for tonight's show." [laughter] That's about like this afternoon. Here was Bill, moving pianos and picking people up who'd arrived late. But he's finally here and he's about to burn up this microphone. The king of blue grass music, Bill Monroe! [applause].

I was not at both shows; my recording is only of the afternoon show, after which I left. I didn't record Del Wood's performance, which must have come after Bill's show; I think my tape recorder had packed it in by then. However, Rooney was there for the evening show and tells what happened:

"That night Bill did another show. This time there were only about fifty people, but he still did a full show, and it was getting on towards eleven when it was finally over."

Bill had asked Del McCoury to stay over and help Ralph do some painting at the Jamboree. Del Wood was scheduled to go back to Nashville that night with Rooney in Brad's car. Keith was waiting for Monroe to pay him before he left. Rooney recalled:

> Monroe and Ralph were over in the shed talking. As we sat there we could hear snatches of the conversation. Ralph had a tendency to huff and puff when he got excited, and he was huffing and puffing a lot. He was talking to Bill about Brother Birch and how slow he was and how the park needed a live wire to run it and build it into something. Ralph was treading on dangerous ground. Before we knew it, Monroe materialized at the car. "Miss Del, you're going to stay up here tonight and go back with Bessie tomorrow. I'm going now." That was that. He didn't ask. He just told her. She was great. She just got out, and he got in. He closed the door and said, "I'm aggravated. Let's go." He didn't say another word until we got to Nashville.[1]

I Become Manager

The next morning Ralph called. He, Del, Bessie, and Del Wood were staying at the Orchard Hill Motel, just down the road from the Jamboree toward Nashville. We discussed his dilemma—Birch had to go. Who could be manager? He asked if I would be interested. I immediately suggested Marvin Hedrick, a local musician who knew the Jamboree, understood Bill's music, and was an experienced businessman. I'd already introduced him to Ralph.

Ralph spoke with Marvin, who said he was too busy to take on the job. But he told Ralph that if I did it, he'd help me as much as he could. Ralph told me this when he called back to say that Hedrick had said no. I then spoke with Marvin, who confirmed directly that he'd assist me. By midday we had agreed: I would become manager. Marvin would help as best he could and would sub for me a month during August and September when I would be on a family vacation. Birch would continue to run the dances on Saturday nights.

Around noon, I drove out to the Jamboree and met Ralph. He and Del were painting the johns. As he was getting ready to go with me, I told him about the IUFC's recent concert by the Country Gentlemen. He said he hated that band—he didn't like their shows or what they were doing to the music—too "commercial" for him. We began our rounds setting up my manager's business. While we shared a deep interest in Monroe, clearly our musical tastes diverged on some points. That wasn't a surprise after what I'd heard from Duffey about his New York experience in 1961. I didn't let it bother me since I wasn't doing the booking for the Jamboree.

I left my car in Bean Blossom; we spent the afternoon riding around in Monroe's Olds with Ralph, Bessie, and Del Wood. We went to the Nashville State Bank and opened a bank account in the name of "Bill Monroe's Brown County Jamboree," with the address of Bill's box at WSM in Nashville, Tennessee. Ralph and I had signing powers. We did other business in Martinsville and Morgantown, stopping at least once for strawberry pie a la mode. Bessie and Del Wood, just along for the ride, were enjoying themselves. Bessie and I hit it off.

Ralph filled me in on the details of running the Jamboree. He had contracts and publicity kits for coming shows. We needed a house band. He wanted to experiment with radio ads. Hedrick told him about the need for regular newspaper ads so that patrons would know for certain who was appearing each week. My letter of the previous week to Ralph reflected our shared concerns and seemed to fit his business model.

A Business Model
June–July 1963

I NEVER LEARNED EXACTLY what Ralph and Bill were arguing about the day before, nor did Ralph linger on why he couldn't work with Birch. But certainly the documents he gave me that afternoon of Monday June 24th played a part. He had two fat envelopes that had been sent to him last Wednesday by the Jim Denny Artist Bureau, the Nashville agency that booked Bill. As he handed them to me, he explained how they fit into his business plan for the Jamboree—particularly those parts I'd be expected to look after.

One, with a covering letter from Denny Bureau head Lucky Moeller, contained seventeen AFofM union contracts for performers to appear at the Jamboree from next Sunday (30th) until early September (8th)—eleven Sundays, with just one open date, on Labor Day weekend.

He and Bill (who'd signed the contracts) had booked two Grand Ole Opry performers for each weekend at an average cost of just under $400 a Sunday. Each week's two performers—usually called "stars"—contrasted in some way: a male singer paired with a female, or a serious star with a comedian. Ralph believed the Jamboree would attract bigger crowds with these pairs. None were bluegrass.

All of the booked acts except one (Bobby Helms, who was coming next week) had a clause in their contract calling for the Jamboree to furnish "musical assistance by union band at no cost." The Jamboree needed a house band.

Ralph had lined up a country band from Indianapolis for that task: the Russell Brothers and the Wabash Valley Boys. They had a new record out on Nabor, a local label. If they were union members, I never knew about it. Ralph paid them separately, so they may have been. No one ever spoke to me about the union during my season as manager.

Ralph had also arranged for Indianapolis country music DJ, Bob Todd, to act as emcee. He was taking out ads on WGEE, the station Todd broadcast from, so that in addition to the regular ads, Todd would let his listeners know he'd be at the Jamboree each Sunday—valuable publicity.

Ralph's other big envelope contained publicity kits (glossies, bios, and photo mats) for each of the contracted acts. Most of this stuff (the sort of thing artists put on their websites today) was neat, interesting to read, and pretty much useless to me over the season. For us, advertising meant getting out the names of the performers to "regulars," fans and enthusiasts who frequented the Jamboree. They knew the names from radio and records; we figured if they knew someone they liked was coming to the Jamboree, they'd come, too.

Drawing and keeping an audience was also the idea behind Ralph's innovation of a third show, a special open-mike show for local talent (later in the season, we began calling it the "hootenanny"), to be held at 6 p.m. He thought it would attract a crowd including fledgling or amateur performers and their friends who would stay for the often sparsely attended evening show.

Each Sunday's featured acts would expect to be paid at the end of the show. That was my job. I would also be paying other workers as needed. I would be arranging and paying for radio and newspaper ads and overseeing the upkeep of the property. Each week, I was to deposit in the Nashville State Bank the money collected from the gate and from our percentage, a third, of the Logstons's food and soft drink concession profits.

In creating a business plan for the Jamboree, Ralph drew from what he'd seen at other country music parks, especially New River Ranch in Rising Sun, Maryland, where he'd often visited and which I believe was where he got the idea for the six o'clock show. He'd also been to Mocking Bird Hill and other parks during his brief tenure on the road with Bill.

There were many operating details to be decided. My salary was $15 dollars a week—$60 a month.

The next day, a letter to my folks carried the news that I had just been made manager of the Jamboree, and aside from that my only responsibilities this summer consisted of two six-week courses, eight hours a week as a graduate assistant in the folklore library, and running the mail-order folk album sales business, which I'd taken over when Hickerson left town.

None of this contributed much money, but we were chalking it all up to experience and I was enjoying the challenge. My main duties at Bean Blossom were to keep the barn clean, run shows on time, and manage the cash; Monroe's manager would handle the contracting. I explained in detail:

> While the Jamboree thing may sound "crazy" to you both it is for me something with quite a bit of meaning, etc., for many reasons. This is the first time Monroe has attempted to run the place on a feasible financial basis. Heretofore there have not been records, receipts and so on, to make it possible for Monroe to declare a tax loss. Monroe's brother has mismanaged the place badly, etc. A group of friends in Nashville are interested in seeing the jamboree become a respectable institution, etc., so I have much support and help. The situation, I am confident, is not too much for me, and I accepted it because I felt it would not interfere with schoolwork. I *have* resigned my vice-presidency in the folksong club and backed out of the radio shows, making this my only extra-curricular activity. I hope I can describe the whole situation to you in length in August. I will by then have a better idea of what's happening, etc.

The next day, I began getting down to business. I'd worked various jobs over the past ten years—grocery bagging, Fuller Brush delivery, gas station attendant, and musical performer—but had never been in such a position of responsibility.

The first thing I did was create written records, a set of lists. I didn't have any Jamboree stationary, so I typed "BILL MONROE'S BROWN COUNTY JAMBOREE/ BEAN BLOSSOM, INDIANA" at the top of each. Adding Monroe's name was part of Ralph's plan—what we'd today call a re-branding. He wanted Bill to be better known. Bill himself, Ralph told me, was not as enthusiastic about the idea as we were, but we would use that name in our advertising for the rest of this season.

I made four lists: (1) car use records—I was paying myself five cents a mile and keeping track of the mileage; (2) phone calls on the credit card that we'd taken out using my phone number so Ralph could do Jamboree phone business; (3) contact information for the house band and other local musicians needed to fulfill our contracts; and (4) a list of the contracted star acts, giving the cost of each, for the first eleven weeks. This was based on a schedule Ralph had given me along with the contracts.

I kept that list with the contracts. It represented my most important responsibility: handling the advertising, running the stage, and paying the stars. The list began with the coming Sunday, June 30: the Carlisles ($175) and Bobby Helms ($200). After typing it up, I went looking for contracts and found nothing for the Carlisles, an act that had been on the Opry since 1953.

I had to write Ralph quickly in any case, for he'd left me with the task of calling Birch to fill him in on details of our new arrangement. In my card to Ralph, I reported that Birch wasn't happy, but we'd "arrived at an 'understanding,' altho he sounds a bit irked. I will see him on Saturday and hopefully we can remain on terms, even if I have to sound like the unwitting tool of villains in Nashville."[1]

Then I added a question: "I notice no contract for the Carlisles is included amongst the sheaf you gave me. Is this O.K.?" Ralph called back the next day with the news that the Carlisles were off the list and would be replaced by Gordon Terry.

I knew of Terry as a fiddler who'd recorded with Monroe in the fifties. Shorty had told me about helping Terry with his break when they recorded "Christmas Time's A-Comin'." Ralph told me more: Gordon had been a prominent Nashville sideman and studio musician before moving to LA in 1958, where he was on several weekly TV shows, and had gotten into western and adventure films. He'd had some modest hits as a rockabilly singer and had recently moved back to Nashville. His solo act combined rockabilly singing and old-time fiddling. He would bring along the money I needed to have to pay the stars.

Bobby Hits the Barn
June 1963

IN THE FEW DAYS LEADING UP to my first Sunday, I began organizing ads and preparing for operations. I bustled about setting up business. Ralph wanted me to keep track of "comps"—complimentary tickets given to promote the show. I bought tickets from a theater supply place in Indianapolis and had a rubber stamp made up; at the top was the geometry term "Complementary," a misspelling friends who received the comps teased me about for the rest of the season.

Help was needed to take tickets at the gate, keep the barn and grounds clean, and so on. I asked two young men I knew from Bloomington, budding bluegrass pickers Peter Vitaliano and Virgil "Virgie" Neawedde Jr., if they would help me at this. They worked as I had when playing with Shorty and Juanita in 1961—in exchange for free admission. Both lived in Bloomington.

Peter was an IU student whose parents were professors. He had been taking banjo lessons with me. These lessons were my contribution to the IUFC; Peter was my most enthusiastic student. He'd really gotten into bluegrass. He was a quick learner and soon was showing me stuff.

Virgie was the youngest brother of Jim, the guitarist and lead singer in the Pigeon Hill Boys. He had been following big brother's music from early childhood, and now, at thirteen and in high school, he was just blossoming into a hot flatpick guitarist. He, too, was a bluegrass enthusiast.

Neither had a car. I would pick them up at their family homes late Sunday morning and we'd drive out to Bean Blossom to begin setting up for the day. I dropped them home Sunday night after the show was over and we'd cleaned up.

A typical Jamboree Sunday began when I arrived at the entrance, stopped the car, got out, and unlocked the beat-up old cable across the driveway. Then I'd drive to the north end of the barn, unlock the door, go in, and turn on the power. We then set up some 300 metal chairs in the dance floor area. Last night they had been folded and stowed against the wall for Birch's dance. We aimed at having that finished by 1:00.

The next arrivals were Dessie and Jerry Logston, who operated the food and soft drink concessions at the north end of the barn. Jerry, 70, sold Coke products, and Dessie sold hamburgers, popcorn, pie, and a few other things.

The afternoon show started at 3:00. Musicians began arriving around 1:30 or 2:00. There was lots of socializing in and around the backstage rooms at the south end of the building.

Since 1961, I had spent many hours in these rooms as a musician, focused on my performing job but also interested in meeting and listening to other musicians. Now this was my business workspace. We had a show to organize.

This was my first Sunday and the house band wouldn't be coming today, so I was particularly anxious for the stars to arrive. Gordon Terry rolled in first, in a new pink Cadillac convertible with California plates. He introduced himself and handed me an envelope from Ralph.

In it was an 8–1/2-by-11-inch flyer from the Ash Grove for the month of May, On its back was a hastily typed message:

"Neil. . . . . This is the money for Bobby Helms. . . . Gordon will do the emcee work if Bobby Todd is unavailable. We'll call you Monday morn. first thing. Sorry for all the confusion . . . will try to avoid getting this on your back from now on . . . [signed] Ralph" Below this was handwritten in ink: "P.S. Bill will pay Gordon in Nashville—Don't worry about that."

By "Bobby Todd," Ralph meant the WGEE DJ Bob Todd. I don't recall ever hearing him called "Bobby" but I didn't listen to WGEE! As I explain later, Todd was unavailable, so emceeing was the first thing Gordon and I discussed.

Terry was friendly and polite, a handsome, poised, hunk of a man in his early thirties with an infectious smile. He was easy to talk with. We waited there in the back room for the other "star," Bobby Helms, to arrive.

Helms was well-known in southern Indiana. Born in Bloomington to a musical family, he was a teenager when he joined the house band of "Hayloft Frolic," Uncle Bob Hardy's long-running country show on Bloomington television station WTTV. Hardy's contacts opened doors for Bobby in Nashville; a background vocals session with Ernest Tubb led to a Decca contract and, in 1957, when he was 24, he had three giant hits: "Fraulein," "My Special Angel," and "Jingle Bell Rock."

Now, in 1963, he was locally known as a three-hit wonder: still familiar enough to be a star but no longer heard much on radio except for "Jingle Bell Rock" at Christmas. "Fraulein," a song about an American serviceman in love overseas, was becoming a bluegrass standard. Later that season, I noticed it written neatly on a list of songs taped to the side of one singer's D-18 Martin guitar: "Fraw Line."

It was the last day of June, very hot and humid. I was standing outside at the backstage door to catch some air when I spied Helms's car, a black Cadillac limousine, enter the drive and speed around the barn in a cloud of dust. Bobby was at the wheel. He headed to park, nose in, at Bill and Birch's old horse barn. He slowed down but didn't fully stop before hitting the barn with a thump.

The car sat there for a few minutes. As the dust settled, the passenger side door opened slowly and Joe Edwards stepped out. Joe was a fiddler and lead guitarist who'd grown up playing with Helms on the "Frolic." I'd heard about him from Shorty—he'd played fiddle in Shorty's western swing band—and from Tom Hensley, who'd heard about his fancy guitar playing at Don Sheets's studio.

My narrative is uncertain here: had I already met him? I *did* get to know him better later. He walked over to me as I stood outside the back room. We went inside, to the inner room.

Quiet, smiling, black hair carefully combed back, wearing glasses of a style I associated with my engineer uncles— black plastic top and sides, with wire frames below—smoking a pipe, Joe (who'd studied physics at IU) filled me in on Bobby. "He has these allergy pills he's got to take, and today, because it's so hot, he had a beer and it caused a bad reaction with his medication." He assured me that Bobby, with his backing and that of their bass player, would do the show as advertised.

Eventually, they got Bobby out of the car and into the back room. He was comatose—could hardly walk or talk. Luckily, Gordon Terry was ready to go on and open with a good solo show. He sang his rockabilly hits and some contemporary country stuff and then switched to the fiddle, doing, among other pieces, his fancy version of "Johnson's Old Gray Mule," a song he'd recorded. It was well-received; some people in the audience remembered seeing Terry perform at the Jamboree with Monroe seven years before.

After the intermission, he introduced Helms, who still seemed pretty stoned. Edwards helped Bobby onto the stage and pointed him toward the mike, and he did his hits and more recent recordings. The show was livened by Edwards's guitar playing. Even then he was one of the few guitarists mentioned in the same sentence with Chet Atkins.

Today, Edwards is still active in his '80s, recognized for his skill by induction into the Thumb-Picker's Hall of Fame. He was often on television as the leader of the staff band on the Grand Ole Opry from 1968 to 2000.

After the show ended, Gordon Terry invited me to go for dinner with him at the inn down in the center of Nashville. It was a kind gesture that I appreciated, what with the day's stressful beginning. We rode down in his car, he bought me a nice meal, and told me about his life. I knew that he'd fiddled with Bill in 1951 but nothing beyond that.

He had just moved back to Nashville after five years in southern California. He'd had considerable success, both in music and in the movies. But he had grown disillusioned with the way of life in California and decided to return to the South.

A native of northern Alabama, he'd bought some property south-southwest of Nashville in Loretto, just above the Alabama line, not far from his hometown. He was planning a western-style theme park. It would reflect his considerable experience in Hollywood westerns, and there would also be fiddle music. The park, "Terrytown," would be opening next year.

I don't recall telling him much about what I, a folklore graduate student, was doing. He knew I was working for Bill and that bluegrass was popular with the folk music crowd in southern California, but we didn't discuss those things. What impressed me then was his friendly way and the intensity of his feelings about returning home. Now, looking back with the benefit of knowledge about his career, I'm impressed with his modesty. He could have told me about how he played the Opry at the age of nine with his family's band, of the extent to which he was a key player in Monroe's triple fiddle recordings in the early fifties, or how he went from being in Faron Young's band to working in the Hollywood western where Faron starred as "The Young Sheriff." He could have mentioned his subsequent movie and TV career and his years of touring with Johnny Cash. But he wasn't into dropping names, he was following his dream.

This respite with Terry made the rest of my first Sunday pass more easily. I had five more Sundays of country shows ahead before Monroe was due to return.

Two Country Sundays
July 1963

AS MY SECOND WEEK BEGAN, I realized that advertising would be a big part of my job. I took time off from classes to arrange for newspaper ads in Bloomington and Columbus. I also wrote to the only newspaper contact I had, Walt Spencer at the *Indianapolis Times*:

> I have recently taken over as manager of Bill Monroe's Brown County Jamboree in Bean Blossom. Being a bit new at this sort of thing, I am hunting for the best ways to advertise, etc. Could you be so kind as to send be [*sic*] a list of the column-inch rate for the Times? Also, if I were to send you a list of some of our upcoming acts, would it be possible for you to mention them in your column. Some of the shows, especially the Monroe Brothers reunion planned for this fall, are of interest which transcends that of the usual country music fan.[1]

It would be a while before I heard back from Walt. Meanwhile, I learned Bob Todd's nonappearance on Sunday was connected to a problem we'd experienced with their advertising on his station, WGEE: they'd mislaid the check Ralph had sent to pay for last week's ads. On Tuesday, station operations manager Stan Barton wrote me that they were giving us double coverage to atone for the oversight and acknowledging that they'd be working with me on a weekly basis.

On Wednesday the 3rd, I wrote Ralph to tell him the costs of the radio and newspaper ads, and that, on Friday, I would be helping Marvin Hedrick install a new sound system.

Marvin and I had pressed Ralph to do this—the old system consisted of an amp at the front of the stage connected to wall-mounted speakers on either side of the stage and a single microphone at the front. Pretty much the classic P.A. setup of the era, it had been through quite a few seasons, survived a fire, and was weak.

Marvin's business was the logical place to go for a new system—local, with previous experience at installing systems. Plus, Marvin knew the inside of the barn well and understood what was needed to get the music across. He'd worked on the old system over the years. He was eager to do the work. But there was a cost—several hundred dollars.

Ralph worked out a deal between Bill and Marvin to cover the cost of the new system. Bill had an old Gibson F4 mandolin. Marvin's son Gary, who was taking mandolin lessons from Roger Smith, needed a better mandolin. If Ralph could get Bill's F4 for Gary, Marvin would install a sound system. Bill agreed to the swap. Now—how to get the mandolin to the Hedricks? This was being worked out as the new sound system was installed.

Marvin moved the amp from the front of the stage to the control room at its side and installed a speaker on the roof of the barn right over the room facing toward the park's entrance. He also installed a 45-rpm turntable. From now on, passing traffic and entering customers were treated to the sound of bluegrass 45s before shows *and* the shows themselves as they were happening.

Sunday's extreme heat got me to thinking about ways to improve the flow of air into the barn. Having the side doors open and a few fans in the stage area helped some, but more was needed. Marvin directed my attention to the north end of the barn. At the top of its outside wall were two large sets of movable louvers that covered large exhaust fans inside, up in front of the rafters.

Marvin recalled times in the forties when those exhaust fans ran on hot days, helping considerably to cool the barn. We discovered the 3/4-horse electric motor that ran them was still in place but its wiring was disconnected. On Friday, while we were at the barn working on the sound system, an electrician came by and gave us an estimate to hook up the cables and repair the motor. I called Ralph with the cost, he OKed it, and we were ready with new sound and airflow for Sunday's show.

Week Two

Things ran more smoothly this Sunday. Bob Todd showed up to act as emcee, and the Russell Brothers were on hand to open the show and help back the two stars, Billy Walker and Grandpa Jones, both of whom were sober and gave good performances.

I knew little about Billy Walker beyond the fact that he was on the Opry and that last year he'd had the biggest hit of his career, "Charlie's Shoes." We got to talking backstage between shows. I told him about my other job—graduate student in folklore. He was interested in folk music and spoke fondly of the traditional songs he'd learned growing up in Texas. We talked particularly about one he was performing regularly, "Wild Colonial Boy." It was a revelation for me to learn that this modern pop country singer was interested in and knowledgeable about musical traditions.

Like Gordon Terry, he said little about his career. He'd started in honky-tonk, been at Hank Williams's last show and Elvis's first, rubbed elbows with Buddy Holly at a recording studio in Clovis, and narrowly missed being on the plane in which Cline, Copas, and Hawkins died earlier this year. But I recall only a bit of the last fact: he, like everyone else, sang a song in memory of the recently departed Opry stars.

Grandpa Jones was much more familiar to me. When I first got interested in bluegrass, I'd quickly discovered his popular King recordings from the forties with fine old-time banjo playing and traditional songs. He'd been around since the thirties. Shorty and Juanita had Grandpa Jones stories; he was famous for his temper, which was easily lost.

These days he was with a new label, Monument, pursuing a new direction in his music. He'd had a hit last year with Jimmie Rodgers's "T for Texas," complete with yodeling and his own expert twist on Rodgers's blues guitar stylings. I plugged his music at an IUFC event during that week, and a few students who were into old-time music came to see his show at the Jamboree.

I learned firsthand about Grandpa's temper at the end of the day when I got around to figuring out the take at the gate. Usual practice was to pay the stars with a check, which we would then cash for them. Tonight, Walker cost $150, Jones was $250.

I had only a little over $200 on hand. I figured I could only cash one of the checks—Walker's. That's what I did, and then I told Grandpa that Monroe would cover the cost of his check in Nashville tomorrow. He was not happy. Looking at me coldly, he said: "Young man, I've got two trunks at home filled with uncashed checks." I repeated my assurances about Bill—that was all I could do. It was an uncomfortable moment.

Week Three

I sorted out the Grandpa Jones mix-up over the phone with Ralph early in the new week. My third Sunday lay ahead, with Loretta Lynn and Jimmy C. Newman scheduled. At some point during the week, we learned that Lynn had a conflict and would have to be rebooked for later in the season. Her agency, Wil-Helm, substituted another "girl singer" from the Opry, Margie Bowes.

On Saturday, I had news of another change in the lineup—the Russell Brothers would be unable to make it. I hired Shorty and Juanita, along with Dewey Harris, a lead guitar player from Bloomington, to take their place. Shorty gave me some interesting news about our advertising on WGEE—he said that this summer the station was playing Monroe's records for the first time in three years.

I recall vividly from this Sunday my conversation between shows with Jimmy C. Newman. Newman was a Louisianan who'd joined the Opry in 1956 and had a string of country hits. Monroe had recorded covers of two of his biggest ones, "A Fallen Star" and "Cry Cry Darling." I had heard Jimmy on the radio but he had not attracted my attention.

Raised in a bilingual Cajun family, Newman was proud of his heritage but until recently had mainly performed in honky-tonk style. But this year, he'd released a new Decca album, *Folk Songs of the Bayou Country* (Decca DL 4398), which had several songs in French and featured top Cajun instrumentalists Rufus Thibodeaux and Shorty LeBlanc. He was now including Cajun songs in every performance. By the time of his death in June 2014, Newman had become, in the words of Marty Stuart, "the Cajun fellow at the Opry."[2]

As had happened in previous weeks, I got acquainted with one of the stars in the quiet of the late afternoon after the first show. Folk music was very popular at this moment, and Terry, Walker, and Newman were all curious as to why a folklore graduate student had become manager at a country music park.

Hip guys in country music were trying to find ways to cash in on the new folk trend. It was selling well to middle-class college students whose musical tastes had not previously included country music. It was clear that bluegrass was ahead of the game in this aspect of the music business. They knew I was working for Monroe and his new manager and were curious to talk about folk music with someone who was studying it.

In my conversation with Newman, the name of the most successful folk act of the day, the Kingston Trio, came up. I don't recall exactly what I said to Jimmy about the Kingston Trio, but it was not complimentary. I felt about them sort of the way Ralph Rinzler felt about the Country Gentlemen. I thought they were promoting watered-down stuff as authentic folk music, and I didn't like it. Newman disagreed: "I'm like the Kingston Trio," he told me. He explained that he was using the Nashville sound to introduce the folk music of his home to new audiences. He saw nothing wrong with this as a way of educating people, opening doors to a new market.

What he told me didn't make me like the Kingston Trio any better, but it was a revelation in my thinking about the ways of folk music in the world of popular music.

Getting to know the stars between shows like this was a learning experience. Up to that point, I'd had little close contact with mainstream country music except as a distant listener. What the insiders thought about the music I was interested in—that was new to me.

In terms of this job, this was a bonus and it was something that didn't happen very much. Increasingly, my mind was occupied with matters pertaining to the management of the Jamboree. Things that needed fixing somehow, things I would have to resolve with Ralph and Bill.

Conversations with Ralph
July 1963

BY MID-JULY I was halfway through a couple of summer school courses, laying plans for travel to Berkeley as soon as summer school finished, and hustling to keep up with Jamboree business. On the Monday after the Jimmy C. Newman–Margie Bowes show, I typed a long letter to Ralph—three pages, single-spaced, with two pages of operating statistics, all about the Jamboree's working needs. To begin with, we would need $300 by the end of the week to cover the costs of this week's stars, George Morgan and Dottie West.

Next, I conveyed a message from Birch—please call him. Then I listed some pressing needs to discuss: a lockable gate, trash cans, plumbing work in the men's john, and repair (or replacement) of the popcorn machine. Mrs. Logston sold a lot of popcorn every Sunday—now she was using a borrowed machine.

I also raised some long-term needs that reflected Bill and Birch's infrastructure neglect: paint on the inside of the barn, covering the gravel portions of the interior floors with concrete, replacing the broken-down old theater seats at the back of the audience section, a general rewiring inside, and installing lockable doors on the johns. This was not the last time such needs would be mentioned.

I turned then to advertising, suggesting newspaper ads in Indianapolis and recommending that we join the Brown County Chamber of Commerce in order to better exploit the county's substantial tourist traffic, a point Marvin Hedrick had been pressing for from the very beginning.

Finally came two urgent requests: posters for the next four weeks, and the mandolin for Gary Hedrick, which I'd already mentioned to Ralph in a phone conversation:

> You expressed surprise that Hedrick (whose first name is Marvin, by the way) was annoyed at the non-arrival of the instrument. The explanation lies in the fact that he has often put up equipment and time for the Jamboree but has only been paid cash once. Several times, he has removed speakers, etc., and in general has not had good luck in business relations with the Jamboree. Thus, while he has confidence in both you and Bill, he nevertheless feels a little edgy, this situation being too similar to others he has faced. But don't let it bother you; I explained to him the difficulties you all have had in getting the instrument and everything is smoothed over.[1]

My hope seemed justified when, on Sunday morning just before I left for the Jamboree, a special delivery letter came from Ralph, saying he had just put the mandolin, along with the posters, in George Morgan's car.

At Bean Blossom, we waited expectantly for Morgan to arrive but were disappointed when he came. He'd forgotten to bring the mandolin! All we had were the posters—jumbo size cards from Hatch Show Print, with names of the stars for next Sunday and the three Sundays after that. Their monthlong shelf life greatly simplified the business of poster distribution.

I still recall when I first heard George Morgan sing, way back in 1948 when I was nine. At home in Olympia, Washington, my brother and I were in our room after dinner just before bed listening to NBC's Grand Ole Opry on our Philco Bing Crosby radio. Emcee Red Foley introduced the Opry's newest member, singing his big hit "Candy Kisses," George Morgan. I was impressed with the intensity of the audience's response—an ovation with an encore.

Morgan was still on the Opry, and would be there for the rest of his career. A country crooner in the style of Eddy Arnold, he had a string of hits in 1949 and then the occasional charted record. His most enduring hit was "Room Full of Roses."

By contrast, I knew nothing of Dottie West, although she'd been working as a songwriter in Nashville for several years, part of a coterie whose other famous members included Willie Nelson, Roger Miller, and Harlan Howard. Mentored by her close friend Patsy Cline, her performing career had just begun.

Like Billy Walker, she had a story to tell about the crash in which Cline died. She and her husband, steel guitarist Bill West, had invited Cline to travel home to Nashville with them in their car but Patsy chose to fly.

One vivid memory from that Sunday is of my surprise that West had one of the men in her band tune the guitar for her. I assumed that happened because she couldn't tune it, but I really don't know if she couldn't or just wouldn't, for there was something of the diva in her demeanor.

The following Tuesday, I had a collect call from Ralph. He was in New York City, at the Gotham Recording Studio on 2 West 46th Street. Bill and the Blue Grass Boys, in New York to record a segment on Oscar Brand's syndicated radio show "The World of Folk Music," were headed for the Newport Folk Festival. Ralph was elated to have finally found a good fiddler for Monroe, Kenny Baker's cousin Billy. The band was getting hot!

I told Ralph about last Sunday: we had taken in $125 less than the cost of the two acts, and the mandolin was, once again, a no-show. We discussed plans for the coming Sunday.

The stars would be old-time vaudeville comedian, the Duke of Paducah, and Little Jimmy Dickens. Dickens had a string of novelty songs in the late forties, the best known of which was "Out behind the Barn," which Juanita Shehan had often sung at the Jamboree. In the forties, he'd become familiar to Indiana audiences when he worked at an Indianapolis radio station. He was one of the first to perform at the Jamboree when the barn was opened in 1943. Last year he'd had his first hit in over a decade with "The Violet and the Rose."

My vivid memory from that day is that it was very hot, a fact Dickens noted in a ribald comment as he and the Duke entered backstage: "Boys, I'm hotter than a fresh-fucked fox." As usual, the performances went over well, and once again we took in less than half of the cost of the stars at the gate.

Ralph, still on the road, called Monday from Dublin, Virginia. I reported on our bank balance, the gate, and how much extra cash I'd need to cover next Sunday's show by Lefty Frizzell and Martha Carson, one of the most expensive of the season.

In response to my laments about the mandolin, he suggested we meet on Wednesday night at Corydon, down in southern Indiana near the Ohio River, where Bill was giving a show at the Harrison County Fairgrounds. He would bring some cash and the mandolin. After his call, I sat down and wrote Ralph a long letter. Then I made plans for Wednesday evening.

That last day of July was hot and muggy. I drove to Corydon, eager to see and hear Bill and the Blue Grass Boys for the first time in over a month. I had not spoken with Bill since Ralph hired me.

Bill and the Blue Grass Boys were in fine shape. Del and Brad were playing and singing well, getting into Monroe's grooves. Brad's banjo picking was changing. He didn't use the fancy stuff on every song as he had at earlier shows. I no longer recall the rest of the band from that night—Bill and Del, of course, but was Bessie there? Probably. I don't think they had a fiddler that night, but if they did he was only a stand-in. After the show, Ralph told me Billy Baker was great but he didn't want to move to Nashville—the pay wasn't attractive enough. They were still looking for a fiddler.

Backstage, Bill took me aside and said quietly but sternly: "Never pay Grandpa Jones with a check." Billy Walker, he explained, would have been OK with that—I should have given Grandpa as much cash as I could. Ruefully, I agreed. The rest of my backstage conversation was with Ralph. This was a major disappointment—he didn't have the mandolin! Ralph had been on the road with Bill until the day before and when they got back to Nashville, George Morgan was out of town. I told Ralph he'd be getting a letter soon with my latest report.

One bit of news I had for Ralph came from a recent Jamboree Sunday when a small group of young black people arrived (the first and only I ever saw there), bought tickets, and took seats in the audience. This was a "sit-in," a civil rights activist test for patterns of discrimination against African Americans in public places. Not long after they arrived, two older women, regular patrons whom I recognized, approached me, the manager, with worried looks on their faces. One said, "I'm sure Bill" (he was not there that day) "wouldn't want colored here at the Jamboree." I told them Bill hadn't said anything like that to me, and while they weren't happy with my answer, they did nothing further. It was a busy day for me—I didn't know when the sit-in ended.

Now I told Ralph about it. He'd had his own experience with the impact of the civil rights struggle. Traveling alone in a small Mississippi town doing promotional work for Monroe, he—a young man with longish hair driving a car with New Jersey plates—was pulled over by a menacing county sheriff who demanded to know what he was doing here. Ralph said that he was Bill Monroe's manager, in town working on a booking. Skeptical, the officer asked for proof. Ralph showed him posters and promotional literature and his demeanor transformed from menacing to good ole boy. It was a scary tale, and not the only one he had about working out of Nashville that summer.

Week 6 and the Letter
July–August 1963

LAST MONDAY, after we talked, I wrote to Ralph. I drew upon five weeks of management to suggest changes at the Jamboree.

I gave good news about the new show he had initiated: "The 6:00 local talent show is starting to draw a crowd, and Mrs. Logston does her best business at that hour, which is reason enough for continuing to have it. The Russell Brothers and I put together four or five bluegrass numbers for that show, and this induces grass fans to stay around. So, although I must admit I was dubious about that idea, it seems to be working out very well."[1]

Then came the bad news—the average weekly crowd was 225, at a buck a head not enough to pay for the stars we had already contracted. I had discussed this with Marvin Hedrick, who was preparing to manage the Jamboree while I was on vacation next month. He knew the Jamboree's history well. I told Ralph: "We both feel that at least in some cases, one artist would have drawn as much as two. I think this is particularly true for Grandpa Jones and Jimmy Dickens. Perhaps one $250 artist a week, combined with a second house band or something of that sort, would draw as well as the two-artist setup."

Finally I weighed in on the type of music we were offering: "Of course we want to draw the same sort of crowd that Mockingbird draws by having the various 'popular' artists, I think the present group of bookings does not have the proper amount of bluegrass/type acts."

I'd broached this subject with Ralph before. So, aware that he didn't agree with me, I anticipated his argument:

Hootenanny at the Jamboree, July 1963. I'm backing up our house band, the Russell Brothers, in a bluegrass set. (Neil Rosenberg Collection)

Mockingbird Hill averages two bluegrass bands a month, and while I know that bluegrass bands have much repertoire in common, as you mentioned, all the pops performers we have had at Bean Blossom in the weeks I have been managing it have been performing the same hit numbers—"Sweet Dreams," "Six Days on the Road" and the Hank Williams standards. In short, every band does the same ol' stuff to some extent, and the crowd—many of whom are regulars—eats it up. And the same ol' jokes, week after week, get laughs. People come at least to some extent because they will hear what they know. Now, granted, the "stock" numbers of a grass band are not the same as those of a regular country act, still they are accepted in the same way, as the "stock" numbers of the country act. And, although you and I tend to do so, the average person attending the jamboree does not think of bluegrass as being something far-removed from country music; it is just different as Grandpa Jones' act is different from Margie Bowes'.

This was our first push toward Ralph and Bill about reshaping the programming to include bluegrass. We'd already made a step in that direction by featuring it at the new 6:00 show.

I wrote next about what I called "the problem of advertising," again mentioning Marvin Hedrick, who felt that "the real gold mine is in the thousands of tourists who come into Brown County (most of them driving past the Jamboree) every Sunday." I suggested three ways of exploiting this traffic. Take an ad in the Brown County Democrat, the local weekly that was given free to tourists at motels; join the Chamber of Commerce so we're listed on their tourist maps and mailings:

> Start selling Bill Monroe's Brown County jamboree the way the rest of the Brown County businessmen do—as the real McCoy, 100% authentic head-quarters for the good old-fashioned stuff that the pioneers reveled in. Like Don Pierce writes up his record jackets. And perhaps booking bluegrass will help emphasize this, since it draws both the folk and the country crowds. But not even this is necessary—it's the package, not the contents that will get people in; and they come to Brown County to dig the old-time, and country music can easily be sold that way.

I also suggested advertising in the Indianapolis newspapers—costly but they "might help." I turned then from the issue of the Jamboree's public image to its business image:

> Amongst Brown-County people in general and any . . . who have had to do business with it [there is] no "good-will" left. Birch has gotten the reputa-tion over the years of being the hardest person in three counties to collect money from. And too often, shows have started late or no one has showed up, or so on—so that no one will give the Brown County Jamboree the benefit of a doubt in any direction. This makes it hard business-wise and I'm pretty sure it cuts into our attendance. Too many years of not handling things right cannot be corrected in six weeks.

I told Ralph: "In order to get the place running right it will be necessary to invest in more than acts," and I passed on suggestions Marvin had made to me about financing "necessary improvements on the property." It would be some time before these suggestions bore fruit.

Once again, on Sunday, August 4th, we had two big stars: Lefty Frizzell and Martha Carson.

Texas honky-tonk singer Lefty Frizzell was thirty-five when he took the stage at Bean Blossom that Sunday. His last big hit, "Long Black Veil," had come in the summer of 1959 when I was just starting to listen to country radio and records, so it was familiar to me. He'd had a string of hits in the early fifties, and a much-admired and widely emulated singing style. I'd heard backstage jokes about his drinking that made me worry about a repetition of the Bobby Helms incident. But his show went well and he did "Long Black Veil" along with his older hits.

Kentucky gospel star Martha Carson was forty-two. Like Frizzell, she'd had her biggest hits in the early fifties—songs like "Satisfied" and "I'm Gonna Walk and Talk with My Lord"—before leaving the Opry to move to New York in 1955 and embrace a pop-influenced style for her recordings. By 1963, she'd returned to her roots with a program of gospel songs and country standards. I have a memory of her performance as being powerful— a great singer who belted out the music with both voice and guitar. She went over very well.

Once again, we had to pay more for the stars than we took in. The next day, Ralph called collect from Kalamazoo. He was very excited; at last night's show a man had come backstage with a mandolin for sale—Gibson F5 like Monroe's built in the twenties and signed by Lloyd Loar. Ralph already had one, but this one, he told me, was better. He bought it.

I filled him in on our costs and mentioned, for the first time, the name of fiddler Roger Smith. I'd hired him to play backup with the Russell Brothers and paid him ten bucks. Roger would soon become an important part of our show. I thought I would be seeing Ralph the next Sunday at Bean Blossom, but he wasn't there with Bill and the rest of the band that day.

Mandolin Sunday
August 1963

ON SUNDAY AUGUST 11, 1963, the day before leaving on a month's vacation, I arrived to find Bill, Bessie, and the Blue Grass Boys already in Bean Blossom. They had played last night in Columbus, Ohio, and driven over afterward. Everyone was in high spirits. At last they had a full-time fiddler: Joe Stuart. Joe had played with Bill in the fifties; I'd heard Hedrick's tapes of him at the Jamboree back then. He was a jovial, outgoing guy; the archetypal bluegrass sideman who'd worked with everyone in the business—played bass with Flatt & Scruggs, every instrument (even mandolin) with Monroe, and much more.

Before the show started, Brad Keith and Del McCoury told me that last night in Columbus, my friend Franklin Miller had showed Monroe a mandolin he'd made himself and had Bill autograph its back with a beer can opener! That sort of thing didn't happen at every show. Most fancy instrument backs like that were only autographed inadvertently by belt buckles. They enjoyed telling this story of voluntary desecration.

Attendance was the best of the season: 470. It was drawn, it seemed, by today's two stars—Monroe and Jean Shepard. Shepard was the third star we'd contracted with close ties to March's fatal plane crash. Joining the Opry at twenty-two in 1955, she'd married fellow cast member Hawkshaw Hawkins in 1960. When he died in the crash, she was pregnant with their son, born in April.

According to *The Encyclopedia of Country Music*, following the crash, Shepard, "devastated, . . . gave up singing for several months."[1] Back in June when Ralph and Bill signed the contract for her to play today, that must have been one of her first bookings. I wonder if she even knew about it, for she was the only star we advertised that failed to appear.

Of course we didn't know that right away. Ralph wasn't present and there was other business to address. Hedrick was taking over the management at the end of the day for the next month; we were conferring with Bill and Bessie. What Bill said from the stage that day reflected our backstage conversations.

The Russell Brothers weren't here; Bill had decided the Blue Grass Boys could provide backup for Shepard. Three o'clock came; she hadn't arrived. Someone had to open the show. Marvin suggested Roger Smith. Bill turned to Roger, who was there in the back room with Vernon McQueen and Tom Ford, the guys I'd seen with him at the Jamboree last year with Loren Rogers. Bill said "Can you boys play a few songs?" Smith said yes and asked me to join them on banjo.

Roger and Vernon told me the songs they were doing. I knew them all. Talk turned to arrangements. Roger told me, "You sing baritone on 'All the Good Times.'" I said I knew the song, but didn't know how to sing baritone. That surprised him. Didn't all bluegrass banjo pickers know how to sing baritone?

Roger took me into a corner: "Here, sing along with me." He sang the part several times and I sang along in unison. That was my first lesson in bluegrass baritone harmony singing. Our little set went over well, and I came away with a sense of empowerment with my new vocal skill. Roger, Vernon, and I would play and sing together a lot in the next five years.

Monroe's shows that day were taped in the control room on my Wollensak, plugged into the new P.A. amp Marvin had installed. This was the first time I'd done that. The recording was supposed to convey the sound as heard over the P.A. by the audience. I wasn't around to monitor the taping, and the recorder's input volume was set too high, distorting the music but catching clearly every word spoken off-mike on-stage.

Throughout the show, Bill, full of energy and enthusiasm, mentioned friends who were in the audience; this began right after the first number, when he lectured the band:

"You boys better do your work good here today, because Mr. Hedrick's over here, the fellow that has the radio and television shop, in Nashville, ah, Indiana, and he's probably setting down all this stuff and I like to do it pretty good if a man's gonna put it on tape. So you boys sing good, hear?"

He dedicated the next song, "On and On," to "a mighty good friend of mine, Herbert McQueen." McQueen, from McKee, Kentucky, was Vernon's older brother. He often taped shows.

Bill was now promoting Brad Keith's soon-to-be released recordings with him: "I say there's not a man in the country can play these old-time fiddle pieces like Brad will play 'em for you. He recorded a number with me, it'll be out before long . . . Devil's Dream."

As this tune finished, fiddler Stuart began to play his other role in the band—noisy smart-aleck comedian. He took his fiddle break, solo, after everyone else had stopped. "Now just a minute here!" Monroe shouted at him in mock anger. "He started before I did, I wanted to catch up with him," Stuart explained to the laughing audience.

For the rest of the show, Stuart lobbed off-mike wisecracks between songs. He wasn't a fancy fiddler like Kenny Baker, but he knew Bill's repertoire, sang bass in the quartet, and played strong soulful breaks on the songs. He sang well on a rockabilly solo in each show to his own stout rhythm guitar.

Brown County was on Bill's mind that afternoon. He mentioned Hedrick twice from the stage, and dedicated songs to local friends the Hammonds family and fiddler Thurman Percifield. After a spate of requests and dedications, Bill rested the music, did a comedy routine with Joe, and then turned to promotion, asking people to follow our ads on WGEE. Next he spoke as usual about Birch's dances, followed by an unusual soliloquy on his love of dancing:

> Used to be, when I was young, I really liked to go out and square dance, especially on Saturday night, I looked forwards to that, and back in my younger days we used to dance for WLS in Chicago. And we worked for them a long time back in the early thirties. But I really like old-time square dancing, and that's where I first learned how to play behind the finest old man from the hills of Kentucky, a uncle of mine called Uncle Pen Vandiver. And, ah, I'll never forget him, one of the finest fiddler players in the country, and he played the *best* time. He had a shuffle up on that bow that, ah, that just no fiddlers today that can do it right, play the, do that shuffle like he played it. And it wasn't a Georgia shuffle, it was just a shuffle that he had of his own there, and played the best time in the world, and I learned to play from him. And I think, today, [speaking very quietly] I-play-better-time-than-anybody-of-course.

Bill often spoke onstage of Uncle Pen and his fine time, but I never had heard him connect it so directly to his own time. In fact I only really heard it when listening recently to this tape, for he seemed to be saying it for himself—half in earnest, half in jest. His six months with Ralph was beginning to show in his onstage demeanor, a new public pride and warmth.

After Joe sang his rockabilly piece, an old Ernest Tubb honky-tonk boogie, Bill spoke about a local dance that competed with Birch's:

"Friends, our good buddy Mister Hedrick from over at Nashville and his band plays over at the Brown County State Park, they have a dance there every Saturday. And I'd like to see how many of you folks that was over there. . . . Anybody was over there, would you hold your hand up if you come on over today. Yeah, I see some hands back through there. We're glad you folks come over and we hope you enjoy the show here today." Hedrick had told Bill before the show that they advertised the Jamboree to the tourists who came to their square dances at the Park. This was Bill's response.

More comedy followed, then hymn time, and a few final requests, including a version of "Roanoke" that was quite different from the recording, where the fiddle predominated with the banjo and mandolin just taking short breaks. Now Brad was playing the whole tune note-for-note like the fiddle, and Bill, not about to be outshone by his sideman, was also playing the full tune. They were getting hot. Not only was Del's singing improving, his guitar rhythms and runs were precise and sharp.

Bill closed the afternoon show with an invitation to stay: "We're gonna see you tonight around eight o'clock. So stick around here and make yourself at home. And if you want a hot dog or a hamburger, or a coke cola, whatever you'd like, ham sandwich, why they've got it back there in the back and they really taste all right 'cause I done been back there and sampled some of 'em." Bessie joined in: "Home-made pie!" Bill added: "Home-made pie and cake, Bessie says. Yes. Yeah. That'll really put the weight on you, though, you better watch that." Finally, at Bessie's prompting, he gave me some much-appreciated praise from the stage: "Neil Rosenberg's doing a fine job here taking care of things."

I was trying, but it was a difficult day. Now Bill's show was over, but there was still no sign of Jean Shepard. People in the audience were asking where she was. Buying time, we asked Shorty and Juanita, who were visiting that day but not playing on the show, to help out. Shorty borrowed

Joe Stuart's fiddle and they did a set. Finally, Bill came out on stage and announced that he was very sorry but it appeared there had been a mix-up, Jean Shepard was not here, and he would gladly refund the admission price to anyone who wanted that. He had one taker.

By the time the evening show got under way, things were much more relaxed; the crisis had passed. A fair crowd had stayed from the afternoon, vindicating our feelings that most people, like Jim Work who was there taking photos, came today to hear not Jean Shepard but Bill Monroe. His show opened with his usual pattern—fiddle tune, a vocal solo by the guitarist, and a trio.

At the end of the third song, a trio of teenage girls sitting in the front row—Roger Smith's stepdaughter Cleata and her friends—decided to pretend they were at a rock concert by screaming their approval after every song. Monroe was amused but not perturbed by this, but it was hard on the other patrons in the front of the audience and I was glad when they tired of it after five songs.

Meanwhile, Bill asked Brad to do "Sailor's Hornpipe." Keith was reluctant, wanting to do "Blue Grass Breakdown." Monroe persisted, saying he'd give him time to tune because he'd promised they'd do it: "A lot of people down on the Grand Ole Opry thinks this is the best number Brad plays. Roy Acuff and a bunch of them people—Big Howdy [Forrester]—they think Brad is really tops on this number."

Keith no longer had to tune to B flat now that Kenny Baker wasn't with the band, so he did "Sailor's Hornpipe" as he had been doing it with Jim Rooney before coming to Nashville, in the key of A as part of a medley with "Devil's Dream." It was well-received by the audience, and Stuart, introducing his solo, another rockabilly standard ("That's All Right") began by adding his praise to Bill's:

> That's some mighty fine banjo picking and I'll tell you what, I'm one that knows, 'cause I loves to hear it. You really get your money's worth when that boy steps up in front of a microphone, that's one of the, one of the new styles that he's developed it all himself and you never hear nobody else playing it throughout the country. I don't care where you go and he really knows what to do with it when he steps up in front of a microphone. Let's give him another big hand on that. You got two for one on that time.

For the rest of the show Bill fielded requests until he recalled: "They want me to play one of the numbers I have wrote about Brown County."

Both Marvin and I had asked for these compositions he'd recorded some time ago that Decca hadn't released. Ralph had discovered them that spring while working on Bill's discography; they would later appear on an album he produced.

First came "Stoney Lonesome," named after a little town on the road between Nashville and Columbus, Indiana. Bill had never played it with this band before, so did it as a mandolin solo. "Brown County Breakdown," a tune that Stuart knew, came next.

Bill was really feeling his oats on the mandolin. When a request for another tune was handed to Stuart, Joe told Monroe, "They want 'Chicken Reel,' I said that I can't cut that." Bill said, "'Chicken Reel'—I, I'll play 'Chicken Reel' if you'll dance it." And Stuart, who'd been doing comedy all through the show, thanked him and danced to Bill's brilliant mandolin.

As the end of the show approached, Bill announced that there was a lady in the audience who played the 5-string banjo. He invited her to come up and "play a number." This was Ginger Callahan, a radio DJ from WTMT in Louisville. Bill asked her what she wanted to play. She said: "We'd like to do a little foot-patting tune. I think you did it a while ago as sort of going off the stage—I don't know, I'm ashamed to play, you know [laughs]—this boy back here, he's terrific, he's really the greatest I've ever, ever heard, really he is."

Bill responded simply: "What key?"

"G" she replied and launched into a version of "Y'all Come," singing all the verses and playing clawhammer old-time banjo breaks. The audience loved it and called for more.

Bill spoke to her at once: "Ginger, that's fine. That's really mighty fine picking and singing there. Ah, if I could pick and sing like that I wouldn't be ashamed to play in front of anybody. What would you like to do for the next one, now?"

She wasn't sure, so Bill asked for "John Henry." She demurred at first—it was in the wrong key, A. Bill asked band members to help her retune the banjo—he wanted to hear that song: "Now you're gonna hear some good singing, 'cause when you put that up A, that's moving on up in the country there." Again, the audience responded enthusiastically to her performance.

As she started to exit the stage, Bill called her back. He thought he'd seen her perform once at the Opry, and asked her if that was so. When she said it was, he replied: "You really sang fine here, you done better right here than you did on the Opry." Ginger thanked him and then invited people to listen to her radio shows. Bill, preparing to end the evening, asked where she was from, and she said she was originally from West Virginia. "Come back and be with us again," he told her, "Don't let this be the last time."

The show was the first in my tenure as manager to turn a profit. As the band was leaving I gave my old F mandolin in its new case to Brad Keith for him to drop it off with master instrument repairman Tom Morgan, Robby Robinson's mentor. The neck Duffey had repaired was starting to come up. Keith had boarded with Morgan before joining Monroe; the Blue Grass Boys were on the road to D.C. where Morgan lived. Brad had agreed to drop off the mandolin for a further repair job.

Several months later, I received a letter from Franklin Miller giving me the story of the mandolin that Bill had autographed:

> By the way I made an "F" style mandolin this summer. Not bad for sound—little soft tho! Trouble is that I screwed up and made the fingerboard too narrow and the bridge too high. I figured that I would go Duffy one better and make *my* mandolin *totally* unplayable. Robbie says I set all-time world record for *HIGH BRIDGE*. Any way, I can't string it up cause I broke the neck off (stepped on the goddam thing)—so I gave it a shot of Elmer's, and off to Monroe to get God to bless it. Carved his name in the back with a beer-can opener—let me play his fine axe. He (Monroe) is without doubt the *one* person who stands for all that is good in *grass* today. He doesn't *lead* his band, he *presides* over it.[2]

Berkeley Bluegrass

August–September 1963

THE ECHOES OF Sunday evening's raucous show with the screaming teens, Bill and Brad's hot picking, and Ginger Callahan's high lonesome "John Henry" were still ringing in my head as we headed West the next day for a long-planned family vacation. I was looking forward to a musical reunion with my old Berkeley pals, Mayne Smith and Scott Hambly. Mayne had gone home to Berkeley for a summer job. He wrote enthusiastically several times over the summer about his musical life. He was playing regularly at Berkeley's newest coffeehouse, The Cabale. He arranged gigs for us the Friday after I arrived and the two following Sundays—August 16, 18, and 25.

Although we were three of the four original members of the Bay Area's first bluegrass band, the Redwood Canyon Ramblers, the Cabale did not use that name in advertising us. Instead, the flyer simply listed: "Mayne Scott and Niel [*sic*]." I hadn't been part of that band since 1960. Scott and Mayne had carried on with Pete Berg, the fourth original member, on banjo until Mayne moved to Bloomington in 1962. After that, Scott and Pete had run the band with a new singer-guitarist, Al Ross. This latter aggregation had been playing until recently at the Cabale and elsewhere in Berkeley—this was the Redwood Canyon Ramblers as the band's fans knew them now.

In May, Scott had joined the Air Force. He spent the summer at officer training school in San Antonio, Texas. After being commissioned August 6th, second lieutenant Hambly came home on leave. Mayne, now concentrating on the Dobro, asked Sandy Rothman, the seventeen-year-old guitarist with a new Berkeley band, the Pine Ridge Ramblers, to join us on guitar. We'd all met Sandy several years earlier.

Our first night, a Friday (16th), the Cabale was jammed with an audience that included friends, acquaintances, people who'd heard about us, and the usual patrons. Sandy was already well known. He had played there with Rick Shubb in the Pine Ridge Ramblers for a month at the beginning of the summer. Mayne, too, was a Cabale regular that summer. Scott, who'd gigged around Berkeley more than any of us, was well remembered. I hadn't performed in public here since 1960, so for me tonight was mainly an evening of meeting new people.

Our music went over well. Sandy played solid guitar and featured vocal and guitar solos in each set. Like many of his friends, he was listening closely to the two most prominent California bands—Vern and Ray, and the Kentucky Colonels—and had met Bill Monroe and Brad Keith when they played California in May.

Scott's solid rhythm was central to our sound; his unique cross-picking mandolin style (inspired by Jesse McReynolds) amazed us, and his high tenor voice was in good shape. He emceed part of the time, in brief, always to the point—wry, acerbic introductions in the style he'd developed playing this country music for young urban westerners.

Mayne had developed a unique repertoire of old country and folksongs that fit the music he was studying for his MA on bluegrass. Singing well and now beginning to write songs, he knew the house better than any of us. He did much of the emcee work, talking about bluegrass history—

The Redwood Canyon Ramblers at the Cabale Coffee House in Berkeley, August 1963: Tom Glass, Mayne Smith, Scott Hambly, me, Sandy Rothman. (Neil Rosenberg Collection)

especially pertaining to Monroe, whose repertoire we drew from extensively. Mayne did most of the lead singing and, as the evening unfolded, did several comedy routines with me—stuff we'd learned from the Barrier Brothers, Shorty and Juanita, and others at the Jamboree.

I had been playing banjo every Sunday all summer at the Jamboree and had spent considerable time hanging out with Keith. I'd been learning his fancy licks and used them a lot that night, to good audience response. Vocally, I debuted my new skill, singing baritone harmony parts. I did some emcee work, too; some of my introductions included facts that Rinzler had gleaned from his interviews with Monroe and told me about.

I'm able to write in such detail because Scott sent me copies of a fan's tapes of all three sets this evening, and one set on each of the two following Sundays.

We were joined on the first Sunday by bassist Tom Glass, who'd played with us in 1960. The following Sunday, Pete Berg joined us for a set—playing guitar and singing a solo, a duet with Scott, and a trio adding Mayne—and then reminisced with me about our band history.

Scott, Mayne, and I played as much music together that month as we could. We hung out in the Hamblys' basement family room where we'd been jamming since high school. Scott's parents hosted us at a patio party.

Scott invited the young bluegrass musicians he knew, like Herb Pedersen and Butch Waller, and we all came with our families.

I also visited the now-flourishing Lundberg's Fretted Instruments, where I found and bought an old Epiphone banjo with a Gibson RB-100 neck, at a price acceptable to Pete Vitaliano, who'd commissioned me to find him a better axe. I also had Jon Lundberg install one of the new geared 5th-string pegs on my banjo—that made tuning a lot easier!

During that vacation, I taught myself how to play "Soldier's Joy," a fiddle tune I had on a 45 by Gid Tanner and the Skillet Lickers. I'd heard Keith play it with Bill in June. "Soldier's Joy" is always played in D. Brad had been telling me backstage about how Allan Shelton played a lot of D stuff with the banjo uncapoed except for the fifth string up two to A (DBGDA instead of the usual DBGDG). I assumed Keith was playing "Soldier's Joy" in that tuning, so I worked out my own version. I learned later that Keith played "Soldier's Joy" like Scruggs did, in C tuning with dropped 4th string and capoed at the second fret. So I'd stumbled into inventing my own style of playing open in D. Having Keith as an example led me to try new things, pushed me to stretch and develop my music. He, like Roger, was a teacher in that way.

Recently Scott found some home movie footage taken that afternoon at the Hamblys'. It includes shots of the three of us playing, surrounded by family and friends young and old. Singing and picking for "company" on the family patio was, like our jamming, one of those things we'd been doing together since high school days.

Our time together was brief—by the end of the month Scott's leave was over. His first posting was to Tyndall Air Force Base in Panama City, Florida. We returned to Bloomington on September 7th, a Saturday. That Sunday, Carl and Pearl Butler were playing at the Jamboree. I didn't go. IU courses would begin in a week; I was preparing for a busy fall.

Around the same time, Mayne left Berkeley in his '51 Chev, heading to Bloomington. His passenger was Sandy Rothman, eager to explore the bluegrass scene back east. In the trunk was Pete Vitaliano's new banjo.

Musical friendships had kept Mayne, Scott, and me in touch for nearly a decade. Now we three old friends were on different paths. The Cabale gigs were the Redwood Canyon Ramblers' last public performances until 1991.

Marvin Takes Over

August–September 1963

AS SOON AS HEDRICK TOOK OVER for me at the Jamboree he began making changes. Some were urgent tasks I had not been able to address, like properly cleaning the grounds. While Birch's mower sat idle, Marvin rented equipment and cleared tall grass and brush around the fences so the park would look more attractive to passing tourists. In the same spirit—a chamber of commerce awareness of the County's main source of income—he added new outdoor lighting.

The first Sunday's show (August 18) featured two Opry stars, comedian Archie Campbell and "girl singer" Loretta Lynn. Then thirty-one, Lynn was a protégé of the Wilburn Brothers, on the Opry just a year and with her biggest musical successes still ahead of her. She, too, had a connection with March's fatal crash—Patsy Cline had been her best friend.

Marvin told me nothing about the Lynn and Campbell show. But the advertising copy he drafted for this show reflected a big change we'd been pushing for: in caps, at the bottom of the newspaper ads, was a new slogan: "BLUEGRASS

BILL MONROE'S
BROWN COUNTY JAMBOREE
BEAN BLOSSOM, INDIANA ON HIGHWAY 135
2 SHOWS 3 & 8 P.M. EVERY SUNDAY
- *Featuring* - The RUSSELL BROTHERS and the WABASH VALLEY BOYS
—— PLUS SPECIAL GUESTS FROM ——
WSM GRAND OLE OPRY
SUNDAY AUG 25
STONEWALL JACKSON
SUNDAY SEP 1
THE CARLISLES
SUNDAY SEP 8
CARL & PEARL BUTLER
SUNDAY SEP 15
COUSIN JODY & DEL WOOD

HEADQUARTERS FOR INDIANA." In addition to the stars, the ads listed "Roger Smith and Verne McQueen along with Bob Drise and his Rock-A-Teens."

Drise and his band was a one-time shot, but with Smith and McQueen, Hedrick was assembling a new house band that played all bluegrass. The Russell Brothers were still being advertised, but this was their last appearance.

The next week, Marvin revised the advertising copy for the coming Sunday (25th), listing "Roger Smith and Vernon McQueen" and revising the slogan to "Bluegrass and Folk Music Headquarters in Indiana." "Local Talent Hootenanny at 6 p.m." was added.

That Thursday (the 22nd), Marvin sent Ralph Rinzler a one-page "update since Neal's last report."[1] He said Roger Smith was now the emcee and was organizing a bluegrass band on the show. Also, following Bill's example of several weeks earlier, Roger was now polling the audience regularly from the stage so we could evaluate the effectiveness of our advertising. He was being paid $25 a week for all of this—more than I was getting!

In addition to cleaning the property and installing new lights, Marvin told Ralph, he had developed a poster distribution system utilizing two Brown County musicians, both regulars at his weekly jams, Jim Bessire and Charlie Percifield (Charlie was Marvin's employee at this time).

Another one of Marvin's promotional ideas, again aimed at finding out more about our audiences, was the creation of a "guest book" which was kept on a picnic table in the barn between the audience area and the food concessions. He'd pitched this idea to Ralph; now it was up and running, the start of what was hoped would be a mailing list.

Much of Marvin's letter consisted of complaints about Birch and his dance. Now that we were members of the Chamber of Commerce with local ads mentioning the dance, Marvin said, we had to consider how hoped-for tourist patrons would respond. He pointed out that the dance contributed no revenue to the Jamboree, but it did create trash and disorder. His cleanup of the grounds revealed many empty bottles, and his friends in the sheriff's office reported being called to deal with a drunken brawl last week.

He closed his letter to Ralph by saying: "Most of the things yet to be done fit two classifications, those that cost lots of money and those that take hard work and detail."

Sunday the 25th, the show was headlined by yet another Opry star, honky-tonker Stonewall Jackson. The same age as Lynn, he'd been on the Opry since 1956; his biggest hit to date had come with "Waterloo" in 1959.

The following Saturday (31st) Marvin wrote me a letter with management recommendations. The biggest problem, he told me, was the restrooms, which needed more attention from employees who are "not holding their end of the cleanup."[2] He also advised me to hide restroom supplies from Birch and let him do cleanup, too. Dust was another issue he mentioned—I needed to keep it down. A very leaky roof also needed fixing.

In addition to his advice about maintenance, Marvin had suggestions relating to the content, timing, and advertising of the shows. We needed to utilize more local talent, but not for lengthy performances; and we needed more bluegrass. And Roger's polling had shown that the radio ads on WGEE weren't worth it, especially when the last two weeks' shows had each drawn less than 300 customers.

The day after he wrote me, another Opry act, The Carlisles, was featured. The show made a profit for the Jamboree, only the second time that had happened since I'd taken over as manager. A week later, on Sunday the 8th of September, Carl and Pearl Butler, also from the Opry, were the star act. Both acts were old friends of Monroe, who'd gotten songs from Bill Carlisle and used Carl Butler as his guitarist on his 1960 LP, *Mr. Bluegrass*. I heard nothing about these shows beyond the attendance figures. Both drew somewhat larger crowds, in the mid-300s.

We got back in Bloomington late on the day before Carl and Pearl Butler played the Jamboree. I didn't go. IU courses would begin in a week; I was preparing for a busy fall. I saw Marvin during the week. On Tuesday, he gave me a copy of a two-page single-spaced letter filled with recommendations that he'd sent to Ralph the day before.

In it he again raised the issues of cleaning, maintenance, and Birch's negative input. Turning to advertising, he asked for posters to come earlier and suggested handbills would be useful locally. He also repeated recommendations he'd made to me: changing show times, getting more local acts, promoting the Hootenanny, dropping the radio ads, etc.

Marvin was working to bring the local grassroots more firmly into the running of the Jamboree. So far, as manager, I was the only local worker receiving a salary; everyone else was given a free pass in exchange for working, as I'd done in 1961. The first change to this came with Roger's recent hiring; Hedrick suggested expanding this policy: "Serious thought should be given to taking a little money each week to pay the help Neil uses [as] well as the local musicians that have their following who pay faithfully each week."[3]

He knew local audience tastes were important. The hootenanny was developing in a promising direction, drawing new patrons: "I have to admit I thought your idea of a HOOTENANNY was for the birds but you were right far more than I imagine even you thought. The last two weeks Jim Bessire has worked this into a thing with at least a hundred people sitting thru the entire thing. Strictly as a guess I would say that it is bringing in at least an extra 25 that come to see their kids, friends, and relatives perform and many of them leaving as soon as this alleged HOOTENANNY is over."

Hedrick accomplished a lot in his four weeks. "It has been one hell of an experience but I wouldn't go thru this again for $150.00 per week and Mr. Rosenburg deserves cooperation you and all the other people connected with the business can give him." He closed his letter with a tirade: "P.S. I just found out this last Sunday that the place has no insurance of any kind and especially no liability insurance. This is the Damndest most stupid thing I have ever [heard] of an adult doing. Birch says Bill can't afford it. So I told him if they were ever sued he would damn well find out he couldn't afford not to have it. Had I [known] this was the case I would never have consented to take Neil's place for I value my neck too highly." Marvin wrote very much as he spoke; he loved the Jamboree as a local institution but he was dismayed by the shoddy business practices behind it, and he spoke in anger, hoping the message would be heard.

FALL 1963

Back to the Barn

September 1963

ON SEPTEMBER 15TH, I returned to the Jamboree. This week's Opry stars were steel guitarist and toothless comedian Cousin Jody and pianist Del Wood. Troupers who'd been around since early postwar years, people Bill and Bessie knew well, neither had current or even recent hits. It was one of the best business days of the season. Summer vacations were past and people were getting back to school and work, ready for musical entertainment. Over four hundred came. The Jamboree turned a profit.

What was new that day for me was playing banjo in the house band Roger had assembled at Marvin's behest. Advertised as "Roger Smith and Vernon McQueen," it was the guarantee for our new motto, "Indiana's Folk and Bluegrass Headquarters." The other band members were Jim Bessire on bass, Gary Hedrick on mandolin, and David Hedrick on banjo. Marvin's sons Gary (twelve) and David (eleven) were both studying with Roger. On each show, Roger's stepdaughter Cleata K. Carr and sister-in-law Carol Logston joined us separately to sing one or two songs each.

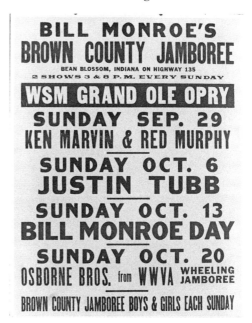

BILL MONROE'S
BROWN COUNTY JAMBOREE
BEAN BLOSSOM, INDIANA ON HIGHWAY 135
2 SHOWS 3 & 8 P.M. EVERY SUNDAY
WSM GRAND OLE OPRY
SUNDAY SEP. 29
KEN MARVIN & RED MURPHY
SUNDAY OCT. 6
JUSTIN TUBB
SUNDAY OCT. 13
BILL MONROE DAY
SUNDAY OCT. 20
OSBORNE BROS. from WWVA WHEELING JAMBOREE
BROWN COUNTY JAMBOREE BOYS & GIRLS EACH SUNDAY

In the next two months, I had the pleasure of working twice every Sunday with this band. It was a pleasure because of Roger. He was comfortable as an emcee, and he knew what he wanted in the music. Roger taught me how to play banjo in a bluegrass band. He didn't show me licks—I knew enough of them—he coached me on what and what not to play, when and where. He knew too what was needed vocally and helped me with parts.

A band with two banjos was unusual, but I'd been playing harmony banjo since I started, and had jammed with David at Marvin's so we already knew some tunes to play together. They became part of our show.

Along with the weekly pleasure of playing came new managing challenges. I don't know exactly when or why Ralph moved back to New York. I'm pretty sure part of the "why" was a lack of income; however, there were other reasons. Years later, speaking about his time in Nashville, he told an interviewer: "It was a world that I could not adjust to. But I was there just long enough to get him [Monroe] rolling."[1] Ralph continued to advertise himself as Bill's manager, but was also working with Nashville agent, Ken Marvin, another one of Bill's old pals from the Opry.

Meanwhile, I embarked on initiatives to improve the Jamboree. Hedrick told me he'd learned from his business that the Coke people were always ready to help with signage as long as you let them include their logo. The Jamboree barn already had a big white coke sign that faced the road. "BROWN COUNTY JAMBOREE" was written on it in faded red letters. Here was a chance to assert our rebranding. I called the Coke man and asked if they could repaint the sign so it read "BILL MONROE'S BROWN COUNTY JAMBOREE." Sure thing, he said, I'll send a man out to do that right away.

Later that week, I drove out to Bean Blossom and there was the newly painted sign—but with a mistake: instead of "JAMBOREE" the painter had put "JAMROREE." I called Coke about this error, asking to have that "R" changed to a "B." They promised it would be fixed. The next Sunday, the 22nd, I arrived to find the sign read: "BILL MONBOE'S BROWN COUNTY JAMROREE." Bill and the Blue Grass Boys were already there, enjoying the sign's spelling mistakes. On Monday, I drove out to Bean Blossom to photograph the sign at Brad Keith's request, and called Coke to make the sign right. Later I sent Keith a print of my photo. Jim Rooney saw it and incorporated it into his 1979 narrative about his June 1963 visit to Bean Blossom.

September 1963. I photographed the "corrected" sign before asking the Coke people to make it right. A print went to Bill Keith. (Neil Rosenberg Collection)

We didn't have as many people this week as last, but it was an unusually diverse crowd. Mayne and I had been telling our campus folk music friends about the Jamboree and Monroe's hot band. The growing popularity of bluegrass among the folk crowd and Bill's appearances at folk festivals and coffeehouses earlier in the year drew new fans.

Barbara Wallace, an undergrad in the IUFC, took a journalism class that summer. Her class project was a two-page photo essay on the Jamboree. It had pictures of The Russell Brothers, Little Jimmie Dickens, women and children in the audience, and the overgrown woods out back that, decades later, became the Festival site. She offered to print up copies. We kept them in the barn by the guest book for patrons all fall.

Another one of the IU students at the show was Peter Aceves Narváez from New Jersey. He was just starting as a folklore grad student. As a teen, he'd played rock and roll (Alan Freed produced his band) and then heard Dylan in New York and got interested in folk music. He'd heard the folk buzz about Monroe—who'd (amazingly, to him) played in New York at Carnegie Hall. Peter had never seen Monroe, so Mayne gave him a ride to Bean Blossom that Sunday. He brought his guitar and harmonica. I gave him free admission in exchange for help in setting up chairs before the show and cleaning up afterward.

After setting up, with time to kill out in the parking lot before the first show started, he took his guitar and harmonica and began playing and singing. He was playing a song he'd learned from Dylan's first album, "Gospel Plow," when "this old farmer with overalls comes up to me and says, 'Now,' he says, 'I know that song but it's got a different tune.' He says, 'But I don't have the lyrics, I don't have the words.' He says, 'Could you give them to me?' So he pulled out a scrap of an envelope or something and anyway, wrote it down, the words, and then he sang me his tune, with those words. And you know, I was just getting into folklore studies, I was very excited, this is fantastic, a farmer comes up to me."[2]

As the "farmer," who was wearing thick glasses, turned to go, Peter spoke to him: "I say 'Excuse me, my name's Peter. What's yours?' And he turns to me with a quizzical look on his face and says 'Monroe. The name's Bill Monroe.'" And he shook Peter's hand.

Monroe enjoyed checking out the grounds this way before the shows, noting license plates and meeting newcomers. During the show, he reported his findings: "We have folks here that's caught our show all over the country. Now, there's a gentleman and his wife, I guess, here that caught our show out at San Marcos, Texas, at the University out there, and they're here in the Brown County Jamboree, today.[3] Then there's a gentleman, a boy here from California where we played out there,[4] and we, we're glad to have you folks and always come back and see us."

Bessie Lee was absent, so house band bass player Jim Bessire sat in again with the Blue Grass Boys. Bill plugged the hootenanny, urging anyone who wanted to participate in it to see the bass player after the show.

Bill's 45 with "Devil's Dream" had just been released so Brad got a lavish introduction. Monroe was enjoying working with him. Bill opened the show with their new version of "Roanoke" and did "Raw Hide"—in which Brad had a spectacular break—twice, saying after the first time: "Tell you the truth, I didn't play that right, we'll do it again for you." And he did it again, faster.

Bill also spoke from the stage about his special show at the Jamboree next month. It was one that Ralph and Birch had both mentioned in public that spring, a reunion between Bill and his brother Charlie. He spoke of it as if it was a contest:

Now the day that we have, will be the Monroe day here, I'll have a lot to work against that day so I want all you folks out here pulling for me. Now don't let me down on that day, because brother Charlie will be here, and Charlie's a wonderful singer. And Melissa, my daughter will be here, and I, I figure she's a fine singer, too. So I'll have a lot to work against. Of course brother Birch will be here with his fiddle, and I pick a little on mandolin. We won't have so much competition with each other there. But I figure where the competition'll lay be between me and Charlie and Melissa so I want you folks out here really pulling for me, cause they're, ah, kindly foreigners here, you know, they don't come up here much and I'm up here a lot. I figure I'm like one of you and so I want you out here.

I was surprised by the way Bill viewed the event, since I thought of it as a historical commemoration rather than a competition. That night, I asked Bill about this and other Jamboree business. Ralph's departure had left me in the dark about bookings for the coming weeks—I had no signed contracts. We exchanged phone numbers and agreed to confer tomorrow.

Monroe Day

September–October 1963

IN THE DOCUMENTS saved from my season as manager of the Jamboree, I find rough notes scribbled on the back of a 5-by-8-inch calendar page, made during a call to Bill Monroe on a weekday following the September 22nd show. This was our first telephone conversation. I wrote down four dates.

We began by discussing next Sunday, the 29th. Bill said it would feature comedian Red Murphy, who was to be paid $35 after the show, and someone I noted as "Ken—?"

This was Ken Marvin. New to me but an old friend of Bill's, his real name was Lloyd George. The original "Lonzo" of Lonzo and Oscar, a popular country comedy team on the postwar Opry (their hit: "I'm My Own Grandpa"), George took the name Ken Marvin when he began a modest career as a country

SAT., OCT. 5—TIMES
FIRST PROOF—TIMES

BILL MONROE'S

BROWN COUNTY JAMBOREE

BEANBLOSSOM, INDIANA

Sunday, October 6

Grand Ole Opry Star

JUSTIN TUBB

Bluegrass Music

Roger Smith & Vern McQueen

Local Talent Hootenanny
at 6:00

Bluegrass and Folk Music
Headquarters in Indiana

Dancing Every Saturday 8-12 p. m.

singer that was pretty much over by 1963. Marvin was now acting as Ralph's Nashville agent for Monroe.

The next date, October 6th, our Nashville star would be Justin Tubb. The son of Ernest Tubb, he'd been on the Opry since the age of twenty. On the day of my phone conversation with Bill, Ken Marvin had signed Monroe's name, initialing "KM," on the AFofM contract for Tubb's Jamboree appearance on the 6th.

Then we turned to the week after that, the 13th, when the Monroe Brothers reunion was scheduled. Here my notes read: "Monroe's—|Birch/Melissa |Mike Seeger." Bill said that Charlie wouldn't be participating. I expressed regret, and he somewhat defensively and quite brusquely told me it would still be a Monroe family day—brother Birch and daughter Melissa would be on the show. He didn't explain why Charlie was out of the contest, as it were, and I thought it best not to ask.

Later, Brad Keith told me of being at Bill's place and overhearing an angry phone conversation between Bill and Charlie about this event. He couldn't, of course, hear what Charlie was saying, but he did hear Bill's unsuccessful attempt to get Charlie to appear for free, as a sentimental family gesture. Charlie, it seemed, would not agree to that.

The project of reuniting the Monroe Brothers was more important to Ralph than to Bill. In the spring Ralph had booked Charlie into the Jamboree, and he'd arranged for Bill and Doc Watson to re-create the Monroe Brothers sound. In July, RCA Victor released a budget-line reissue album, *Early Blue Grass Music*, with long-out-of-print Monroe Brothers recordings from the '30s. Although fan interest was growing, Bill and Charlie wouldn't reunite on stage until 1969 when Ralph brought them (and Birch) to the Festival of American Folklife in Washington, D.C.

I'm at a loss now to explain why Mike Seeger's name is in my notes— I guess that Bill and I agreed that he and his band, the New Lost City Ramblers, might add to the appeal of that Sunday's show. My note shows that I called Mike, he was out of town, and nothing more came of it.

The last of the shows we spoke about, October 20th, would feature The Osborne Brothers. Before this call, Bill and Ken Marvin had contacted Sonny, who handled their bookings, and Sonny had already sent me a contract. Hedrick and I had been lobbying to book big-name bluegrass bands like them. They would be the Jamboree's first bluegrass stars (other than Monroe) since last spring. Now that we were calling ourselves "Bluegrass and Folk Music Headquarters in Indiana" we wanted to live up to our motto.

Our conversation ended with local budget items. Bill authorized me to hire contractor James P. Schrougham to pour a cement slab over some gravel portions of the barn's interior and to pay Jim Bessire for his work running the hootenanny. That was done the following week. Jim would be on the payroll for the rest of the year, as would Virgie and Pete, who'd been working as volunteers since I started managing.

When I hung up after this long conference with Monroe, Ann teased me: "You're beginning to talk like him!"

A package of four-week posters arrived at the end of the week from Hatch Show Print. They listed the four shows we'd discussed. Sunday October 13th was described as "Bill Monroe Day."

The show on the 29th by Ken Marvin and Red Murphy drew just a little over a hundred patrons. The following Sunday we did better, with 224 souls, for Justin Tubb.

Justin was a successful country songwriter who'd recently had one of his few charted hits, "Take a Letter, Miss Gray." We had an interesting backstage chat about bluegrass and songwriting. Tubb sang in the traditional country honky-tonk style of his father, but had recently composed novelty songs about bluegrass' newfound uptown cachet, which he recognized was now newsworthy to Nashville's music marketers. They included "Bluegrass Fiesta," which Mac Wiseman had put on an album last year, and "Bluegrass Music's Really Gone to Town," due out soon on a new Osborne Brothers' album.

Although Bill told me that Melissa would be at the Jamboree on October 13th, I find no evidence that she was there. Birch was the only other Monroe on stage for "Bill Monroe Day." The show drew one of the biggest crowds of the year, a little under 400. In the audience, the folk and bluegrass scenes in Ohio, Indiana, and beyond were represented.

The Day was, not surprisingly, filled with bluegrass. Our house band, advertised in the papers and on the radio as "Roger Smith and Vernon McQueen," opened.

Next came a short set by a guest band from Hamilton, Ohio, Dave Woolum and the Laurel County Boys. Southern Ohio bluegrass scene veteran Woolum made his first recordings in Cincinnati in 1951. This was his first visit to the Jamboree.

The Jamboree house band on Monroe Day. Teacher Roger Smith (fiddle) proudly watches Dave Hedrick (banjo) as Jim Bessire, Gary Hedrick, Vernon McQueen, and I provide support. (Courtesy of Ann Milovsoroff)

Bill's hot band was drawing fans. Brad was featured in a variety of fiddle tunes. He introduced a new one this day, Fiddling Arthur Smith's "Blackberry Blossom." Hanging out backstage at the Opry with fiddlers one night that fall, Keith had a chance to play it for Smith. Brad told me his rendition brought tears to Smith's eyes.

Quite a few people in the audience were from IU, Purdue, and other schools where interest in bluegrass was growing. Bill mentioned the significance of the event only once, calling it a day that "makes two hundred times that I've played here." To recognize it, he said he was "trying to pick out some new numbers, and, ah, I don't know whether to start on 'em or not."

At Bessie's urging, he picked new songs from his own folk traditions, which Rinzler had pushed him to explore. First came "Pretty Fair Maid," which he'd done at Newport in July and since then at "college[s] throughout the county." He followed with his version of last month's encounter with Peter Aceves Narváez: "Ah, the last Sunday I was up here they was a boy here I heard, he was playing a banjo out here singing this song, and when I was a little kid in Kentucky I learned this song and, ah, I hadn't sung it in so long, why, I forgot some of the words. But he had some good verses. So I got some of his verses and he taken my tune. (chords mandolin; laughter) So we made a swap there. And it's entitled 'Gospel Plow.'"

Bill spoke to the young folk and bluegrass fans at the show with such songs. But both he and Birch also made a point that afternoon of welcoming the longtime regulars in the audience like fiddler Thurman Percifield, shop owner Marvin Hedrick, and faithful patrons the Jim Peva family.

Soon after the beginning of the evening show, Bill brought on stage a local man I'd heard about but never met, Denzel W. Ragsdale. Locally known as Silver Spur, Tom Adler has described him as one of the Brown County Jamboree's key original figures. I'd been hanging out at the Jamboree for two years. So far, I'd only heard about Spur from Marvin Hedrick and Roger Smith.

As Adler notes, he was a "colorful local character,"[1] who'd worked as a promoter and emcee for Monroe during the fifties. Silver Spur hadn't been at the Jamboree in a long time; Marvin and Roger played a role in getting him to come in today. He showed up backstage before the show, and Bill invited him on for a public reunion. There he reminisced with Bill and Bessie about their tours all over the United States from the Far West to Key West and up to the Northland.

Bill thanked Spur for bringing his aged parents to the show, and called for "a little banjo number." Brad had been cornered backstage by a man from Indianapolis who'd just gotten a new Gibson Mastertone banjo and wanted him to play it on a tune in the show. Keith politely agreed even though it wasn't easy for him to play like that on an instrument he'd never tried. He rose to the occasion with a very hot "Lonesome Road Blues."

My attention at the time was drawn to Keith's often spectacular banjo playing, but listening to this show now reminds me of how well Monroe was playing the mandolin. He was energized. When he stepped up to the mike for a break on this tune, he picked a hot chorus that closed with a final four beats rapped with his knuckles on the front of his instrument. It was a move he would use often in later years when playing "Blue Grass Breakdown"; I'd never heard him do it before.

An evening of insistent requests began with a small boy marching up to the front of the stage and speaking to Monroe: "I want you to play happy birthday for me." Bill obliged, and the clamor of titles after that and every song for the rest of the show suggests the diehards had stayed from the afternoon for the evening show.

The audience was enthusiastic and knowledgeable, old Monroe fans and new bluegrass fans. Among the many requests were ones (always politely declined) for other performers' hits like the Stanley Brothers' "White

Dove," and "Bringing in the Georgia Mail," a song of Charlie's that Victor had mistakenly included on the new Monroe Brothers album.

Both Bill and Roger encouraged the audience to come out next week to see and hear the Osborne Brothers. Bill spoke at length about them in the afternoon, placing them within his own bluegrass story:

> The Osborne Brothers gonna be here next Sunday and that's their first trip to ever make here. Sonny Osborne used to work with me on the Grand Ole Opry when he was a real young boy about sixteen years old, and his folks fixed it so he could come down and work with me a while. And his brother Bob will be along and they have another boy that works with them, a trio, and they will be here next Sunday. They do some wonderful singing and they play bluegrass music, that's what they learned to play and that's what they'll be playing when they come down here. And they're from down in the mountains of Kentucky and they will, they will try to, I know they will fill your requests just like I have here all the ways along. And I know they'll have a fine show for you here next Sunday.

This was a long day for me. At the end of the evening, I sat alone at a picnic table inside, near the new guest book, counting the day's receipts. When I'd finished I looked up to see Monroe standing nearby. He walked over and said quietly, "You should never count your money in public."

Point taken! I packed everything up and we started walking toward the stage, headed to the back of the barn. We spied a poster on an interior pole near the guest book table. It was for a Flatt & Scruggs concert next week at a local college. Bill wondered if the students had asked anyone before they put it up. No, I told him, this is the first I've seen it. He shook his head as I pulled it down. "They just don't play it right," he said.

Bluegrass HQ
October–November 1963

FLATT & SCRUGGS introduced bluegrass to folk music fans. Last year, after four years of listening to their recordings and broadcasts, I saw them live for the first time and described the show to Scott as "cut & dried."

Monroe's shows were full of musical electricity that gave them an element of mystery. With Monroe, it seemed bluegrass could go many directions. He was now speaking more of his beliefs about the music, beginning to accept the vision of young revivalists that he was the teacher, headmaster, choir leader, conductor and first chair, and above all, an artist. We were now Indiana's (self-proclaimed) "Bluegrass Headquarters." We wanted fans to experience bluegrass as interpreted by others.

In early October, I placed a brief notice about the Jamboree in IU Folksong Club's first newsletter of the fall. Giving location and show times, it listed only one group: The Osborne Brothers.

I'd been a fan of their music since I heard their first albums, classic bluegrass of the early and midfifties. We met in 1960, when the Plum Creek Boys helped open for them at Antioch College in Yellow Springs, Ohio. Their signature sound was a vocal trio in which the melody was carried at the top by Bobby Osborne's high tenor.

By 1963, The Osborne Brothers show featured just three singer-instrumentalists: Bobby sang lead and played mandolin, his younger brother Sonny played banjo and sang baritone in the middle of the trio, and rhythm guitarist Benny Birchfield sang a low tenor below him. What made their sound memorable was the way in which they sang their parts in chords that moved one or two notes at a time, in the style of then-new pedal steel guitar chords. Their songs often had ornate vocal trio endings.

They'd had two hits on MGM. "Ruby" (1956), a fast banjo-sparked solo, featured Bobby's dazzlingly high clear voice. "Once More" (1957) introduced their high lead trio. What first attracted Scott and me—typical California jazz-oriented bluegrassers—to the Osbornes was their instrumental prowess. Sonny's banjo and Bobby's mandolin were models of great bluegrass picking.

I'd lobbied Ralph and Bill to book them, so I was really happy to be backstage at Bean Blossom on Sunday, October 20th, 1963—the first of many times they would play the Jamboree. Coming into the back room, I didn't expect they would remember me from Antioch, three years ago. When I reminded Bobby, who acted as emcee, that we'd met in Yellow Springs, he did a double take. He called Benny and Sonny over and we reminisced about the event before turning to talk about the present.

The Osborne Brothers had been on the radio jamboree at Wheeling since 1956. They'd become unhappy with MGM, who didn't seem to know how to promote their career. With the help of Opry stars The Wilburn Brothers, they'd changed labels and booking agencies in Nashville. They were promoting their first Decca single at this show, and touting their forthcoming final album on MGM at the same time. Their career was on an upward trajectory; they'd join the Opry in less than a year and have a series of hit records, the biggest being "Rocky Top" in 1968.

Playing at Bean Blossom was a big deal for them. The whole Osborne family, along with old friends, had driven over from Dayton. They were, as Bill had said last Sunday, "from down in the mountains of Kentucky"—Hyden, in Leslie County—but they'd been living in Dayton since the war. Monroe's "mountains of Kentucky" evoked an image of Dogpatch to me and indeed, during the show Bobby quipped at the start of the evening show "we're just plain old hillbillies."

But they came from a hardworking family—schoolteachers, storekeepers, farmers, skilled factory workers—and brought the sophistication, skill, and ambition they'd grown up with to their music. Before the show, I told Sonny about my friend Scott Hambly, who was in the Air Force in Florida and had asked me to tape the show for him. Sonny actually announced this on stage.

I am glad I taped the show, for it still sounds good to me today. They did many of their trademark trios. I was just beginning to learn to sing in trios; their vocal work was awesome. Most inspiring to me that day was the way Sonny played the banjo. It was not just *what* he was playing—although that was amazingly creative—it was how he played, putting the English on the banjo.

The metaphor *putting on the English*, from baseball, means to throw the ball with a spin, imparting a curve, an act that requires careful handwork. Sonny put the English on the banjo neck and strings, pushing and pulling and moving to create unique music. It was inspiring, and I learned a lot watching him find notes I hadn't imagined.

They played a lot of requests—some coming from me, obscure stuff they hadn't done in a long time like "Poor Old Cora," "Auld Lang Syne," and "Little Maggie." Others came from an enthusiastic audience, many returning after last week's Monroe show and quite a few staying for both shows. A gate of 229 was, in terms of how things had been going, not too bad.

In addition to my taping, Ann, who'd also met the trio at Antioch in 1960, was there with her camera and took a bunch of photos of the show. We sent some prints to Sonny, and he ended up using one in 1964 when he published his banjo instruction book.

The following week's show was by another group of bluegrass-playing brothers, the McCormicks. Originally a guitar and mandolin duet featuring Lloyd and Kelly, they'd added banjoist Haskell along the way and, by 1963, a fourth brother, William Harold, was on bass.

From central Tennessee near Nashville, they'd had some success in the midfifties with records on Roy Acuff's Hickory label. But they weren't well known in Indiana. Not regularly on the radio, they had no current record releases. Our gate was down nearly 100 from last week. I recall most clearly from that Sunday a backstage seminar with Haskell, who was featured prominently on their records, about playing old-time fiddle tunes on banjo.

I didn't tape the show that weekend, for I was preoccupied about writing an academic paper—my first, on parrot jokes—which I read at the Hoosier Folklore Society's annual meeting in Indianapolis the following Saturday. The next day, Jim & Jesse and the Virginia Boys were coming to the Jamboree.

I'd seen them last year at Mocking Bird Hill and was impressed and excited to have them at the Jamboree. Like the Osbornes, they were Opry-bound. They were still working for Martha White Flour, the company that sponsored Flatt & Scruggs. When Lester and Earl went on tour, Jim & Jesse took their place on the Opry.

The Osborne Brothers debut at the Jamboree. Bobby and Sonny with Benny Birchfield, October 1963. (Courtesy of Ann Milovsoroff)

They were working a circuit of television stations on the Georgia-Alabama-Florida border, and found Bean Blossom quite cold on that November Sunday. They had been in Nashville the day before at the big annual DJ convention and brought guests from Twangtown with them on their bus: Ralph Rinzler and Brad Keith.

The only change in the Virginia Boys since Mocking Bird Hill was one less member; second guitarist Don McHan was gone. Fiddler Jimmy Buchanan was singing the baritone part in the trios, which were less common than duets this day.

Last year they were talking about the imminent release of their first album; now, they had two LPs out. The title of the latest was *Bluegrass Classics*. In 1962, they had not mentioned bluegrass, but this year they did. The evening show was filled with requests from Ralph, me, and the other bluegrass fans who stayed for both shows and the hootenanny.

A highlight of the evening show was the introduction of "Billy Keith, from Bill Monroe's band." He did a very nice banjo duet with Allen on one of Jesse's compositions, "Dixie Hoedown," after which Jesse asked him to do his new record with Monroe, "Devil's Dream." As he stepped up to the mike this cold night, Jesse asked "You thawed out a little bit?" and Keith answered "I don't know."

This was the best crowd of our three bluegrass brother Sundays, at 250. Next week would be the last of the season; posters advertising Monroe along with special attraction his daughter "Milissa" were already out there.

In listening to the recordings of these two shows I notice something I hadn't given much thought to before—the extent to which both the Osbornes and Jim & Jesse focused their shows on their harmony vocals, the meat and potatoes of their repertoires. Most songs had just one or two verses and a fancy harmony chorus. Both bands often opened the song with the chorus, and then moved to the first verse and another chorus. The lead instruments shared ("split") a single instrumental break. A second verse followed (if there was one), closing with the chorus. Short and sweet, over in two minutes and few seconds: radio-ready.

Keith's "Devil's Dream" had a few clams that night—it *was* cold for picking. Jesse McReynolds and Bobby Osborne both mentioned Monroe during their shows, reminding the audience that Bill would be back next week for the last show of the season.

Bean Blossom Hop

November 1963

ON THE FINAL DAY of the season, I got good recordings of the parts of the show involving Monroe, including the hootenanny. Photos taken that day show a poster for the IUFC's concert by the NLCR a week from the next Friday hanging onstage at the front of the cabin between the coonskins on the wall.

Monroe gave the usual two shows that day but also appeared on the 6:00 hootenanny. The substantial crowd—close to 350—included quite a few young college bluegrass fans. Toward the end of the afternoon show, Bill sent Joe Stuart out into the audience to sell Grand Ole Opry History Books. Afterward he reported on stage to Bill that he'd met people from four different universities: Purdue, Michigan, Illinois, and Florida.

The afternoon show had begun with an impromptu band. Bill explained: "We went out to Mr. Herb Hammonds to have a dinner out there, and Brad Keith

BROWN COUNTY
JAMBOREE
BEAN BLOSSOM, INDIANA ON HIGHWAY 135
SUN. NOV. 10
W S M GRAND OLE OPRY
PRESENTS - IN PERSON
BILL
MONROE
AND THE BLUE GRASS BOYS
—— EXTRA ADDED ATTRACTION ——
MILLISSA MONROE

and myself, we come on back, after we got through, we thought we'd done him all the damage we could. And all the carload—Bessie and Melissa and Del McCoury—they haven't got over here."

He expected them soon. Meanwhile the show got under way with Joe Stuart playing guitar, Roger Smith playing fiddle, and Vernon McQueen playing bass for the first six numbers. The band was hot; Bill and Brad were in good form, striking sparks off each other all day. They opened with "Roanoke," now a transformed showpiece. Hot picking on it and the two that followed, both sides of their new single, were enlivened with some very good fiddling by Roger on "Devil's Dream." Even Bill's "Footprints," which he did virtually every time he performed, had a unique feature this time—a banjo break.

Bill called for requests. The first one was for a tune he'd recorded, the still unissued, "Brown County Breakdown." When Roger told him he knew it, Bill said: "This is a number that, ah, I wrote, and titled it 'The Brown County Breakdown,' so we could say that we had wrote a number about Bean Blossom here. Next one'll have to be the 'Bean Blossom Hop' or something like that." [laughter]

When Del, Bessie, and Melissa joined the show, Bill playfully teased Del for his lateness. Later in the show, he mused about the event. It was the first time I can recall him speaking from stage about his musical invention:

> Friends, with starting bluegrass music I really done one thing in my favor. Now when we started work on the stage you see today, Roger was playing the fiddle, and Vernon was playing the bass, Joe Stuart was playing the guitar, and, ah, I was playing the mandolin and Brad on the banjo. And we had, ah, we had a good group right there. You . . . never know what, you might have a better group than you do when you have your own group there, if they don't get in and work hard. [laughter] But doing bluegrass you can go in any state, nearly, today, and if you want a bluegrass group to fill in and help you there why you can go looking around and you can round up a bunch that'll play a good 5-string banjo, play about as good as Brad or Don Reno, or Earl Scruggs or any of 'em. And, ah, course they don't play hardly as good a mandolin as, ah, one fellow I know [laughter] but they play a good fiddle and a good guitar. Boy, I've had, I've to work to stay ahead of 'em, I'm telling you. But that is right, laying all the joking aside, you can go in any place, New York and any place today and get a good bluegrass group.

Bill was in high spirits as he often was at Bean Blossom, playing for people he knew appreciated his music. He made dedications in the afternoon to the Hedrick brothers and to Vernon McQueen's mother, visiting from Kentucky that day.

It was a lively show that included singing by Melissa, and extra solos by Del. And, of course, Joe did comedy. Plugging the six o'clock show, the hootenanny, gave him a chance to pull the old gag about what happens when you cross "a nanny goat with a hoot owl." Bill said: "we're gonna try to get back on . . . that hootenanny thing that comes up here a little bit later on."

And, indeed, the final act of the six o'clock show was what Monroe called "the Blue Grass gang," a combination of the house band—Roger on fiddle, Jim on bass, Vernon on guitar—with Blue Grass Boys Joe and Del on guitar, and Brad on banjo. They did nine pieces. I came on stage for a couple of banjo duets with Brad, and Bill came out and did three pieces he rarely performed—"Get Up John" (using Gary Hedrick's specially retuned F4), "Put My Rubber Doll Away" and "Weary Traveler." Bessire closed that portion of the day with a reminder: don't forget to sign the guest book.

The evening show was even more relaxed and cordial, and the music continued hot. Brad chose "Blue Grass Breakdown" for his solo and Monroe responded to Brad's hot stuff with his own, once again ending his break by rapping his knuckles on the top of his mandolin—the first time he'd done it in my hearing on this tune. Local dedications continued with Bill speaking at length to thank Freddie and Jack, the Jamboree's favorite rockabillies, a source of amusement for all.

Silver Spur had arrived backstage before the show, and Bill invited him up. He stayed on stage to help Bill with the emcee work, and finally Bill suggested that they sing a duet together and Spur, always game, chose "Live and Let Live" as the piece to do. "I'll get the verse," Bill said, "and you catch me on the chorus." When the chorus came, Bill switched to a tenor part and Spur followed right along. Bill tried doing lead but Spur was right on his heels again. The rest of the band broke into laughter—and the audience, too. When they finished, Bill said tersely and jokingly, "You can't say that that's not harmony!"

Bill closed this rollicking show with his usual speech, adding to the "Good night, folks" after "Y'All Come": "We want to wish you all a merry Christmas and a happy new year, too."

Afterward, Bill, Bessie, and I sat down at the picnic table in the barn to speak about the future. They complimented me on—and thanked me for—the work I'd done this year and asked me to continue managing the Jamboree next year.

A wild trio with Spurs. Bessie Lee Mauldin, Bill Monroe, Joe Stuart, Denzel W. ("Silver Spur") Ragsdale. Last show of the year, 1963. (Courtesy of Jim Work)

I was flattered to be asked and thanked them, saying it had been a great experience. But, I explained, I could see that I was not going to have the same amount of time in the future to devote to the Jamboree as I'd given it this year. I was in the middle of my third year of graduate work at IU and still hadn't finished the master's thesis. I needed to push that to completion, and after that there would be qualifying exams for the PhD. Right now, I was struggling to keep up with four graduate seminars; a high grade average was required to stay in the program. So while I felt deeply about the music and didn't want to stop playing it, I couldn't spend every Sunday at the Jamboree. There was, finally, the fact that I had a wife and a new child who needed more of my time and attention.

What was their response? They expressed disappointment and understanding, and thanked me again. That was the last time I saw Bessie.

Last Report to Ralph
November–December 1963

THE NEXT TWO WEEKS were spent catching up on classes. But I also found time to pull together the past 4–1/2 months of Jamboree business records, preparing a final report for Ralph.

Friday the 22nd was the day scheduled for the New Lost City Ramblers' IUFC concert. That afternoon at Rone Music, I was checking out Gibson's new 12-string guitar, when Louis came out of the back room saying the radio had just reported that President Kennedy had been shot in Texas.

The Ramblers arrived later that afternoon. After consulting with the club executive, they decided to go ahead with the concert as a kind of memorial tribute. With new member Tracy Schwarz, the Ramblers had a better fiddler, and they were doing some bluegrass now, showing off Mike Seeger's fine mandolin playing. The attendees that night included Marvin Hedrick and Jim Peva, both of whom came away impressed with Mike Seeger as musician and historian. We had a bluegrass jam at the after-concert party. With memories of jamming with Mike in Berkeley three years ago, I was disappointed when the Ramblers made a polite appearance but did not join in.

That Sunday, I went over to Marvin's shop in Nashville to use his electric adding machine in preparing my Jamboree report. I was working away that Sunday when Marvin called from the house on the intercom—come over and see this on TV, someone just shot Oswald!

The next day, I wrote a four-page report with a four-page covering letter. I sent it airmail special delivery to Ralph in New York, hoping it would reach him before he left to go to California with Bill and the Blue Grass Boys. Money was needed for outstanding bills.[1]

Thanksgiving was a few days later. Our dinner guest was graduate student and friend Willie Benson, a bluegrass singer and guitarist newly arrived from Texas. That afternoon as we were getting ready to eat, we noticed a man walking around outside the house, looking in windows. When he came on the porch, Ann opened the door and asked him if he needed something. "No," he said, explaining in a heavily accented voice (he was from one of the Baltic countries) that he'd just purchased the house. "You're not going to evict us, are you?" she asked jokingly. "Yes," he said, smiling broadly.

We finished Thanksgiving in shock, leavened by a good deal of wine. On Monday, Ann went into the rental agency and complained about this rude notification. They told her he'd been warned not to speak to us, etc., and the upshot was that we ended up in a very nice apartment closer to campus. But we had to move in a hurry. It was the last week of classes; everything was in an uproar.

A few weeks after we moved, a Christmas card arrived from Bill Monroe. Printed on the front was a picture of Bill, smiling, mandolin in hand, with "Bill Monroe, Seasons' Greetings" and "Ralph C. Rinzler, Mgr., Ken Marvin, Agent, Box 30 W.S.M., Nashville, Tenn." beneath it. Handwritten on the back was a brief message:

> The very best of the season to both of you, and a heartfelt expression of thanks to you Neil. I had no idea of the potential involvements at Bean Blossom when I asked you to accept the job. Your report was a good indication. I can never thank you properly nor can Bill.
>
> Let me know if you want Watson for a small concert. Phone in N.Y. (212) AL5-1305 (collect).
>
> Best for now—Ralph.

Just before we moved, I had put all of the Jamboree papers at the very back of the lowest file drawer in my study desk. Later, I moved them into a big accordion folder. Some day, I thought, this will help me tell the story of my season at Bean Blossom. But, I thought, I won't write about this experience until Bill has gone to his reward; it's all too private and personal.

I might not have written about it at all had it not been for Judy Mc-Culloh, my classmate of the sixties and a lifelong friend. She'd been to Bean Blossom when I worked there, and regularly attended the festivals at Bean Blossom's Bill Monroe Memorial Music Park, selling books and renewing friendships. In her final years, she urged me to write about Bean Blossom. I have chosen to end my narrative here. But during my remaining years in Bloomington and beyond—I moved to Newfoundland, Canada, in 1968—my bluegrass business involvement continued.

After the Jamboree

1964–1967

AFTER THE 1963 SEASON at Bean Blossom when Ralph helped Monroe move into a new role as "Father of Blue Grass Music," we Jamboree regulars became activists in a movement to present bluegrass to the world. Our enthusiasm drew new people to the Jamboree. Berkeley friend Sandy Rothman returned with his Black Mountain Boys bandmate Jerry Garcia from Palo Alto to visit me in May 1964. We jammed a lot, and they kept busy taping: spending a day at Hedrick's, seeing and recording Bill at the Jamboree, and meeting Jim Work and me to catch the Osborne Brothers at Ruby's White Sands in Dayton, Ohio.

May was a busy month; Mayne and I both finished our MAs. That summer Mayne moved to Los Angeles to begin a PhD at UCLA. People expressed interest in his thesis, *Bluegrass Music and Musicians: An Introductory Study of a Musical Style in Its Cultural Context*, so he had about twenty-five copies duplicated. He sent me two. I loaned one to Marvin Hedrick and Jim Peva, who, along with Roger Smith and Jim's friend C. D. McClary, had just started The Brown County Music Corporation. They were negotiating with Monroe to lease and run the Jamboree in the coming year.[1]

I gave the other copy a close critical reading. On August 27th, I sent Mayne a four-page single-spaced typewritten letter that contained the kernel of my ideas about bluegrass history. During the following year, with Archie Green's help, these coalesced into my first scholarly article.

In October, Marvin and Jim Peva asked me to play banjo with the band in "The Evolution of Blue Grass Music," a show that their new Brown County Music Corporation was presenting at the Village Theater in Zionsville, a suburb on the north side of Indianapolis.

The first half of the show featured Jim and Marvin's scripted dialogue narrative with live musical illustrations. Drawing on Mayne's work and quoting the liner notes of Mitch Jaynes from the Dillards, they introduced the band in evolutionary steps. Beginning with old-time fiddle, other instruments and vocal arrangements led up to a full-fledged bluegrass band playing "Blue Grass Breakdown."

The second half of the show featured a performance by our Jamboree house band of last year—Roger, Vernon, Gary Hedrick, and me—with Russell Wesley on bass. Russell, a friend of C. D. McClary who'd been born in Kentucky and grew up in Idaho, illustrated old-time frailing banjo on the first half of the show. I had just begun working as a Graduate Assistant at the IU Archives of Traditional Music (ATM; formerly AFPM); I arranged to have the performance recorded for them.

A month later, Monroe showed up at the Jamboree with just one Blue Grass Boy, banjoist Don Lineberger. Bill filled out the band with local talent—Roger on fiddle, Birch on bass—and asked Marvin Hedrick to play guitar. Marvin hesitated until Roger and I insisted, practically pushing him onstage! He did fine and enjoyed it.

That fall, Judy McCulloh was back in Bloomington working on her dissertation and acting as associate director of the ATM. As my supervisor, she gave me an assignment: copy my growing collection of Bill Monroe show tapes for the Archive and prepare a listening version with a guide for visiting patrons. It was the first time I'd had an opportunity to re-listen to most of the recordings, and also my first chance to write in detail about Monroe's music.

At the start of the 1965 season, The Brown County Music Corporation, envisioning the Jamboree as a bluegrass headquarters, had leased it from Bill. That didn't work out and didn't last, but it was a harbinger of change; on Labor Day, Carlton Haney held the first multiday bluegrass festival in Fincastle, Virginia. Its "Story of Blue Grass" placed Monroe in the center as the fountainhead of this music.

I didn't make it to that first Haney festival, but many of my friends did, including Marvin Hedrick, Mayne Smith, and Sandy Rothman. I heard a lot about it and made plans to attend the second one in September 1966.

In June 1966, I became an employee of Indiana University, working at the Folklore Institute as a Research Associate. The American Folklore Society had just accepted my proposal to present a paper about bluegrass music history at their annual meeting in Boston that fall.

November 1964. The Blue Grass Quartet—Bill Monroe, Roger Smith, Birch
Monroe, and Marvin Hedrick, with Don Lineberger, behind, on banjo. (Neil
Rosenberg Collection)

In September, at Carlton Haney's second bluegrass festival I met many
like-minded people. Old friends were there, too, including Mayne, who'd
recently published "An Introduction to Bluegrass" in the *Journal of American
Folklore*, and Ralph, who had just produced *The High Lonesome Sound*, a
Decca album that reissued many of Bill Monroe's best recordings. Ralph
and I made archival recordings of the entire festival. I also met the edi-
tors of a new monthly magazine, *Bluegrass Unlimited*, and agreed to write
for them. A new friend, an IU graduate student from Japan named Toru
Mitsui, was with us in the crowd.

Just before Thanksgiving, I came to Boston to give my paper on bluegrass
history. We stayed at Jim Rooney's house in Cambridge with Bill and the
Blue Grass Boys, who were playing at Club 47 that weekend. We went to
see them there one night and Bill invited me up to guest on a tune with
the band, introducing me as being "from Bean Blossom." That got a laugh
from the crowd—most had never heard of it.

My first *Bluegrass Unlimited* piece came out early in 1967, not long before
the *Journal of American Folklore* published my Boston paper, "From Sound
to Style: The Emergence of Bluegrass."

At about the same time, Marvin Hedrick and Bill Monroe came to
our Bloomington home to ask for my approval of and participation in a

bluegrass festival at Bean Blossom in June. I gladly volunteered to help. Not wanting to be thought of as copying Carlton Haney, Bill didn't call his new event a "Festival." It was a "Celebration."

At the start of his first set there, Bill's new banjo player, Butch Robins, was nowhere to be found. Bill came on stage with the rest of the Blue Grass Boys—Roland White on guitar, James Monroe on bass, Byron Berline on fiddle—saw me sitting in the front row, and said "you got your banjo?" I nodded. "Get it and come up here and help me." I went backstage and hustled out the cabin door, putting on my picks and pulling out the capo. Bill chopped a chord in B, smiled at me, and said: "White House Blues."

Afterword

THAT WAS NOT THE LAST TIME I played with Bill, but from 1968 on, when my career took me to Canada, musical reunions brought us together only a few times.

Bluegrass remained in my life. Although I was far from the music's centers, I continued writing about its history. In 1969, I edited the first bluegrass historical anthology for Victor's *Vintage* album series. In 1974, The Country Music Foundation published my first book, *Bill Monroe and His Blue Grass Boys: An Illustrated Discography*. I began work on *Bluegrass: A History* (1985) while moonlighting as a bluegrass musician, cofounding a band in 1973 that is still active.

I was a professor of folklore at Memorial University of Newfoundland, offering annual folk music and ethnomusicology courses. My bluegrass experience was an asset in terms of understanding, writing, and teaching about music cultures. But I quickly learned that most of my students and academic colleagues didn't know bluegrass music, and many didn't care for it when they heard it. The challenge for me was to introduce this particular music system in terms of academic theories and ideas that would help explain its cultural significance.

Academic theories are, in essence, metaphors meant to help us understand lived reality. Discussing the book's title in the introduction to this memoir, I described myself as being part of a "generation of early activists . . . a nascent movement" and said that *generation* was just one metaphor for such phenomena. In 2005, Fred Bartenstein noted that "'generation' . . . has long been used in publications such as *Bluegrass Unlimited* and album liner notes to loosely categorize . . . musicians and their evolving styles."

Such descriptions, he lamented, have "lacked precision[;] collective data on the generations have not been systematically analyzed."[1]

Working from a data base of "biographical information collected on 680 professional musicians whose recordings have been nationally distributed and for whom sufficient data could be found," and drawing on scholarly conceptions of generations, Bartenstein and his collaborators arrived at a set of more precise temporal categories based on birth cohorts with shared experience.

In terms of age, almost all of the people I've described in this memoir as "a generation" would fit Bartenstein's second and third categories: "Pioneers" (b. 1901–1924) and "Builders" (b. 1925–1941). They were between the ages of 20 and 60 in 1961. Most fall into the latter category, which Bartenstein calls "the first generation to define themselves and become popularly known as bluegrass musicians."[2] I use "generation" somewhat differently than Bartenstein, describing a group that includes not just professional musicians but a constellation of fans and enthusiasts, drawn together by what Robert Cantwell called "believing in bluegrass."

Speaking of these believers in the introduction to *Bluegrass: A History*, I closed with a discussion of "the mythology of bluegrass" that grew when a separate bluegrass business structure emerged. Using metaphors familiar to folklorists and anthropologists I called this structure a "successful revival or revitalization movement" that had become an "establishment."[3]

In a review of Cantwell's *Bluegrass Breakdown*, Mayne Smith suggested another metaphor. "Monroe and most bluegrass musicians are profoundly affected by a kind of 'gentrification' of their audience."[4] I'd never seen that word applied to anything other than a neighborhood, but his argument made sense to me, and in 1992 I used it in a review essay on contemporary bluegrass recordings, saying: "I would extend Smith's idea somewhat; it is not just the audience that is gentrified, it is the music itself. Like working-class homes and neighborhoods refurbished by middle-class people, bluegrass strives to preserve the neat old features while adding tasteful new touches for comfort and style."[5]

Gentrification is a powerful metaphor that describes and interrogates cultural values. It's an objective-sounding container for subjective opinion, a weapon in the politics of capitalism, a fighting word used in arguments about tangible culture. But the questions of lifestyle and class it evokes can also be asked about intangible culture like music. The process of musical gentrification is both local and universal.

In 1993, I included it in my discussion of "revival," in "Starvation, Serendipity, and the Ambivalence of Bluegrass Revivalism," an essay that appeared in my book *Transforming Tradition: Folk Music Revivals Examined*. There, I discussed two articles, written in the late sixties at the start of the festival movement, by and for bluegrass advocates. I suggested that some accepted the change in the music wrought by their participation, and stayed involved, while others did not and left. I spoke of two kinds of change. One was romantic purism based on ideas of authenticity; the other was middle-class gentrification. That metaphor describes the social dynamics of the revival process. Since then, much has been written on music revivals—see the essays in Bithell and Hill's *Oxford Handbook of Music Revivals*. "Gentrification" does not appear in its index.

I detailed my ideas about bluegrass gentrification in "The Gentrification of American Bluegrass Music," a paper I read in March 1995 to the Tuesday Colloquium of the National Museum of American History at the Smithsonian Institution in Washington, D.C. That fall I presented a revised version, "Examining the Gentrification Metaphor" to the American Folklore Society. Neither was published.

I began this memoir with the intention of telling the story of my beginnings in the bluegrass music business. I wasn't thinking about the roles my fellow workers and I played in taking the music in new directions. *Gentrification* was not a word we knew.

The Opry Stars who gave shows at the Jamboree in the summer of 1963 had never encountered a park manager like me—a graduate student from California studying folklore. They were curious about my involvement in their music. I certainly wasn't thinking about management style at the time, I was just trying to help promote what I thought to be good music.

But my business orientation, such as it was, was far from typical of country music park managers. Newly arrived from California, my contacts were in the world of folk music. I not only gave the famously bad-tempered Grandpa Jones a bum check, I slighted, out of ignorance, other important people from the country music world. Not only that, Brown County businessmen didn't know who I was, and I didn't know them.

While working at Bean Blossom I made a point of letting my peers—music enthusiasts, mainly young, often students—know what was happening. Writing about the Jamboree in the IUFC newsletter, and performing at IU, helped draw a new crowd. One Sunday in late fall after spending an intermission going through the audience selling Opry history books,

Blue Grass Boy Joe Stuart reeled off the names of universities represented in the audience. We brought a new class of music consumer to this music.

This was a transformational moment. A diverse group of grassroots believers began working together for the first time at Bean Blossom in those years.

Making the Jamboree a "Bluegrass Headquarters" was part of the process. Marvin Hedrick, who coined the term, wanted to refurbish the neighborhood, bring in the music he'd grown up with. He came from a generation in Brown County that had worked hard to develop it as an upscale tourist destination. He'd grown up on a farm, ended up with his own successful business.

Jim Peva also recognized the cultural significance of the Jamboree and subsequent developments in Bean Blossom. At 87, he's still working to promote it.

Roger Smith devoted his life to playing bluegrass. He was a missionary. As he realized that people admired his musical gifts he responded by becoming a teacher.

None of us wanted to see the music change radically. We valued the creativity and innovation we saw in it. We watched with pride as youngsters embraced it and took it in new directions. We wanted others who shunned it (or simply didn't know about it) to learn about it as a valuable intellectual property—progressive cultural creativity worth encouraging and preserving.

Our music was like a valuable property in another sense, too; it was a country getaway—the cabin, the cottage, the camp, the ranch—we visited to play and relax when we could, just one shared facet in otherwise diverse and busy lives. This is why I think that, if you really feel you must have a metaphor to describe a musical preservation movement, "gentrification" works well.

RECORDINGS, NOTES, AND BIBLIOGRAPHY

Recordings

MY NARRATIVE IS BASED ON primary documents—artifacts of the events described. Tape recordings, like letters, business records, and photos, have proven particularly important. At the end of this appendix is a list of the tapes I used.

It's hard to imagine a time when recorded sound did not exist. At the beginning of the twentieth-century phonograph records were a new popular musical medium. From the late twenties into the early fifties, my parents built and listened to their own collection of records—something their parents had not done. Until midcentury, most recordings were like theirs—manufactured by companies from studio recordings.

The introduction of commercial tape recorders after WWII opened the door for amateur use. At Oberlin College in 1957, I met classmates who owned reel-to-reel tape recorders. In 1959, I bought a Wollensak T-1500 recorder. At first, I rarely used its microphone, instead obtaining recordings for entertainment and education by copying records and trading tapes. The recorder and a small collection of tapes came with me when we moved to Indiana in 1961.

In July 1962, using a new microphone and mike stand, I began recording at the Jamboree. My tape collection grew. As I got into studying folklore and ethnomusicology at IU, I realized that my tapes needed organization. I began numbering them, giving the old ones roman numerals in a "Blue-grass Anthology" series—"BGA I," etc.—and giving my new tapes Arabic numbers in a series I now identify with the prefix "NVR #001," etc. Almost all recordings referenced in this book use those numbers.

The collection grew to over 300 tapes. In 2002, I donated it to the American Folklife Collection at the Library of Congress. The AFC provided me with digitized copies of the recordings from Bean Blossom and Mocking Bird Hill.

These copies of the shows were unedited—each track was the uninterrupted length of a tape side. During my early years of collecting, I was always pressed to find usable tape for new recordings, and consequently the sequence of shows or parts of shows in my tape collection was not straightforward.

Using the original tables of contents, I worked with Brooklyn-based sound engineer Brian Miksis, who took the AFC's digital copies and edited them in sequence, show by show, placing each spoken segment and musical performance on a separate track.

In 2013, I began listening to these edited shows. Following their chronological order (now accessible on computer), I created new tables of contents and then transcribed all of the speech between the musical segments.

I had, of course, listened to these tapes right after I first recorded them, when I made tables of contents. Occasionally, I had a chance to re-listen to a tape when I copied it for a tape-trading friend. But that was rare; I was working full-time. I was glad to have a chance to rehear some in 1964, when I created the listening collection of my Monroe shows for IU's Archives of Traditional Music.

In the 1970s, as Bean Blossom became a famous musical destination and the bluegrass music business grew, a new record company, the Rounder Collective, contacted me. Between 1973 and 1975, I worked with them on a project to publish my recordings from Bean Blossom.

Somehow I found time to go through tapes in my collection, listening and making notes on the tables of contents. Then I got busy—sabbatical, books, etc.—and nothing was released.

In the 1980s, I again listened to parts of the collection, researching my book, *Bluegrass: A History*.

In January 1993, Ralph Rinzler called me. He was working at Smithsonian/Folkways to produce albums of live recordings by the two men he'd managed in the early sixties, Doc Watson and Bill Monroe, both of whom had gone on to great success. He was drawing from the collections of people like me who'd set up recorders with mikes onstage to record Bill in shows and concerts. He asked what I could send him.

I wanted to go back and listen carefully to those tapes but there was no time! I was teaching full-time, running a weekly radio show, writing a monthly magazine column, and finishing work on a new book. When Ralph's CDs were published later that year I heard for the first time that he was seriously ill. In a letter of condolence, I wrote:

> When we last spoke together at the beginning of the year you were working on the Bill Monroe and Bill & Doc albums. I'm sorry I wasn't able to contribute to them but it looks to me like you got along just fine without my input. I've seen both (on display at the AFS) and review copies are on their way to me now. I've already read a lot of positive things about them on the bluegrass e-mail, and am looking forward to hearing them soon.
>
> This summer I did take the time to rent a digital recorder and dub a bunch of my Bean Blossom tapes onto that format. What memories it brought back! Spending all that time hearing Bill (and so many other good musicians) at Bean Blossom was one of the high points of my musical life. I don't think I can, ultimately, explain why Bill is so special to anyone who hasn't had the experience of hearing him in that setting. I'll always be grateful to you for giving me an opportunity to become an insider at Bean Blossom back in 1963. And I have many fond memories of all the crazy things that went on that summer, including our travels with Bessie and Del Wood.[1]

Now, over a half-century later, I've finally had a chance to compare the fond memories of crazy things with the aural record. Here's the list of the tapes I listened to and the chapters where I discussed them:

NVR #249: Shehans and home jam, August 1961, cf. "Letters to Home" (pp. 35–37).

NVR #001: Monroe, September 1961, cf. "Monroe Again" (pp. 57–58); October 1961, cf. "Stepping Up" (pp. 61–67).

NVR #008-010: Barrier Brothers and Stringbean, July and August 1962, cf. "Back to the Jamboree" (pp. 98–100).

NVR #010: Flatt & Scruggs, September 1962, cf. "Mocking Bird Hill" (pp. 113–14).

NVR #056: Jim & Jesse, September 1962, cf. "Mocking Bird Hill" (pp. 115–17).

NVR #064-065: Pigeon Hill Boys, October 1962, cf. "Folk and Country" (p. 119).

NVR #039 and 054: Roger Smith et al. and Barrier Brothers, October 1962, cf. "Folk and Country" (pp. 119–20).

NVR #054-055: Harry Weger and Charlie Monroe, October 1962, cf. "Folk and Country" (pp. 120–21).

NVR #047: Monroe, October 1962, cf. "Folk and Country" (pp. 121–22).

NVR #079: Monroe, Opry, March 1963, cf. "On the Road" (pp. 135–37).

NVR #048-049: Monroe, April 1963, cf. "Spring Pickin'" (pp. 141–45).

NVR #050-051: Reno & Smiley, April 1963, cf. "Reno & Smiley" (pp. 146–49).

BGA XXII and NVR #052: Stoneman Family, May 1963, cf. "Stonemans, Banjo Contest" (pp. 150–53).

NVR #052-053: Monroe, June 1963, cf. "Meeting Ralph Rinzler" (pp. 159–64).

NVR #066: Monroe, June 1963, cf. "Ralph Fires Birch" (pp. 168–70).

NVR #062-063: Monroe, August 1963, cf. "Mandolin Sunday" (pp. 196–201).

[no numbers, 3 reels]: Redwood Canyon Ramblers, August 1963, cf. "Berkeley Bluegrass" (pp. 203–4).

NVR #058-057: Monroe, September 1963, cf. "Back to the Barn" (pp. 216–17).

NVR #067-068: Monroe, October 1963, cf. "Monroe Day" (pp. 220–23).

NVR #069: Osborne Brothers, October 1963, cf. "Bluegrass HQ" (pp. 225–26).

NVR #070-071: Jim & Jesse, November 1963, cf. "Bluegrass HQ" (pp. 227–28).

NVR #087-088: Monroe, November 1963, cf. "Bean Blossom Hop" (pp. 229–31).

Notes

Abbreviations

FM	Franklin Miller III
JD	John Duffey
JP	Jim Peva
JW	Jim Work
MH	Marvin Hedrick
MJR	Mitzi and Jess Rosenberg
MS	Mike Seeger
NR	Neil Rosenberg
RR	Ralph Rinzler
SH	Scott Hambly
SP	Sandy Paton
WS	Walt Spencer

Foreword

1. Adler, *Bean Blossom*, 12 and 48.

2. Marvin Hedrick was the pioneer recordist at Bean Blossom, an important mentor to Neil Rosenberg, and a close friend of Bill Monroe. In 2015, Gary and David Hedrick donated their father's original open-reel tapes to my institution, the Center for Popular Music at Middle Tennessee State University. Thanks to a grant from the Grammy Foundation, we digitized and cataloged the entire collection and generated a dedicated website with photographs and sound samples. The site can be reached via mtsu.edu/popmusic.

Prologue

1. Goldsmith, *Bluegrass Reader*, 132.

2. Machado, *Hear Me Howling!* 42–43; Wald, "Jesse Fuller Profile." Neither

mention a key turning point in Fuller's career, when he won a talent contest that led to his appearance on a popular late-night TV show, Don Sherwood's "San Francisco Tonight."

3. See Malone, *True Vine*, 40, 83–84.

4. Rosenberg, *Bluegrass*, 155–158.

5. The record, *Gold Leaf 106*, was reissued on Rounder.

6. Johnston, website.

7. Rosenberg, "Weekend Folk Festival."

8. JD to NR, June 6, 1961.

Meeting Monroe

1. The full quote comes from a letter sent by Francis James Child of Harvard to European ballad scholar Svend Grundtvig in Copenhagen, August 25, 1872: "The immense collections of Broadside ballads, the Roxburghe and Pepys . . . doubtless contain some ballads which we should at once declare to possess the popular character, and yet on the whole they are veritable dung-hills, in which, only after a great deal of sickening grubbing, one finds a very moderate jewel." Hustvedt, *Ballad Books and Ballad Men*, 254.

2. Roger Siminoff, "Worst-Case Repair," in Ewing, *Bill Monroe Reader*, 180–182.

3. NR to MJR, "July 1961" penciled in by my mother.

4. Ibid.

House Band

1. Composed by Felice and Boudleaux Bryant.

Meeting the Audience

1. Rosenberg, "Picking Myself Apart."

2. Rosenberg, *Bluegrass*, 157.

Playing the Five

1. Scruggs, *Earl Scruggs*, 22.

Meeting the Regulars

1. NR to MJR, August 25, 1961.

2. Pearson, "Life with Dale Bessire."

3. I draw also from the interviews conducted in 2012 by David Hedrick; links were accessed from Roger Smith's obituary at Lawless, website.

4. My narrative is based on Bryant's son Jerry's extensive biography of his father, "The Kentucky Rambler," posted on his website; see Wilson. It draws extensively from the research of Norman Carlson.

5. Bartenstein, *Bluegrass Hall of Fame*, 160.

Monroe Again

1. JD to NR, September 20, 1961. See discussion in Rosenberg, *Bluegrass*, 176.

Autumn Work

1. NR to MJR, October 5, 1961, by my mother. "Next Saturday" would have been October 7.

Stepping Up

1. Rosenberg, *Bluegrass*, 236.

White House Blues

1. Wilgus, *Anglo-American Folksong*, 235.

End of the Season

1. SH to NR, November 23, 1961.

2. NR to SH, November 26, 1961.

3. SH to NR, November 23, 1961. Soon after the concert, a package arrived from Mayne and Scott containing not only the poster but also a tape of the show.

Cannonball Blues

1. Rosenberg, *Bluegrass*, 135–136.

2. See Malone, *Bill Clifton*.

3. McIntyre, *Country Gentlemen*, 9.

Meeting Marvin Hedrick

1. See photo in Fleischhauer and Rosenberg, *Bluegrass Odyssey*, 56.

2. Adler, *Bean Blossom*, 26–27.

College Kids

1. NR to MJR, April 30, 1962. "Sheehan" was Shorty Shehan's stage name. See Adler, *Bean Blossom*, p. 196, note 22.

Back to the Jamboree

1. NR to MJR, September 2, 1962.
2. JD to NR, August 28, 1962.

Folk in Bloomington

1. NR to SP, August 21, 1962 (from draft).
2. SP to NR, September 16, 1962.
3. NR to MS, August 21, 1962 (from draft).
4. NR to MJR, October 2, 1962.

Mocking Bird Hill

1. NR to SH, October 1, 1962.
2. Ibid.
3. FM to NR, October 20, 1962.

Folk and Country

1. MS to NR, September 25, 1962.
2. JP to NR, November 8, 1962.

College Folk, Bluegrass, Banjo Necks

1. FM to NR, October 20, 1962.
2. Antioch College *Record*, 6. Five "folk" events were listed for Saturday, November 17: "Folk workshops" at 10 a.m. and noon; "Square Dance, Gym" at 1:30 p.m.; "Folk Dance Workshop, Gym" at 4:00; "Folk Jamboree, Kelly Hall" at 7:30 p.m.; and "Community Folk Dance, Mills Lawn," at 8:00 p.m. Thanks to Antioch historian Scott Sanders for this information.
3. Hickerson, Foreword, ix.

On the Road

1. Smith, "Bluegrass as a Musical Style."
2. NR to MJR, January 27, 1963.
3. JD to NR, undated but filed prior to letter of March 14, 1963.
4. Ewing, *Bill Monroe Reader*, 26.
5. JD to NR, March 14, 1963.

Spring Pickin'

1. Spencer, "Folk Music Is Everywhere."
2. JP to NR, April 18, 1963.

3. Spencer listed the musicians playing at the Opry shows at the Indianapolis Coliseum that day: "Hank Snow, Webb Pierce, Red Sovine, Minnie Pearl, etc." Bill's final sentence—a sly southern reference to moonshine—seems like intended humor as I hear it today, but nobody laughed at it.

Stonemans, Banjo Contest

1. Tribe, *The Stonemans*, 161.

Meeting Ralph Rinzler

1. JW to NR, ca. June 18, 1963.

Ralph Fires Birch

1. Von Schmidt and Rooney, *Baby Let Me Follow*, 159, 162.

A Business Model

1. NR to RR, June 25, 1963.

Two Country Sundays

1. NR to WS, July 5, 1963.
2. Cooper website.

Conversations with Ralph

1. NR to RR, July 15, 1963.

Week 6 and the Letter

1. NR to RR, July 29, 1963. I also mentioned some earlier business we'd been discussing: booking Baez at IU and Purdue.

Mandolin Sunday

1. Cooper, "Jean Shepard," 481.
2. FM to NR, November 18, 1963.

Marvin Takes Over

1. MH to RR, August 22, 1963.
2. MH to NR, August 31, 1963.
3. MH to RR, September 9, 1963.

Back to the Barn

1. Gagné, "Ralph Rinzler," 28.
2. Babcock, Video interview.
3. The gentleman from Texas was Willie Benson, guitarist, singer, and newly arrived IU grad student.
4. The boy from California was Sandy Rothman, who'd been in Bloomington since arriving from Berkeley with Mayne Smith a few weeks earlier.

Monroe Day

1. Adler, *Bean Blossom*, 13–14.

Last Report to Ralph

1. NR to RR, November 25, 1963, includes entire report.

After the Jamboree

1. Adler, *Bean Blossom*, 82–84.

Afterword

1. Bartenstein, *Generations*, 21.
2. Ibid, 31.
3. Rosenberg, *Bluegrass*, 13–14.
4. Smith, *Review*, 33.
5. Rosenberg, "From the Sound," 468–469.

Recordings

1. NR to RR, November 30, 1993. Rinzler died July 2, 1994.

Bibliography

Adler, Thomas A. *Bean Blossom: The Brown County Jamboree and Bill Monroe's Bluegrass Festivals*. Urbana: University of Illinois Press, 2011.

Antioch College *Record*. November 16, 1962.

Babcock, Blair. Video interview of Peter Aceves Narváez. St. John's, Newfoundland, August 2009. Posted on Facebook, 2013.

Bartenstein, Fred, "Bluegrass Generations: An Historical Perspective." *International Country Music Journal* (2014): 21–51.

———, Gary Reid, and Others. *The Bluegrass Hall of Fame, Inductee Biographies*. Louisville: Holland Brown, 2014.

Bithell, Caroline, and Juniper Hill, ed. *The Oxford Handbook of Music Revival*. Oxford: Oxford University Press, 2014.

Cantwell, Robert. *Bluegrass Breakdown*. Urbana: University of Illinois Press, 1984.

Cooper, Daniel. "Jean Shepard," in Paul Kingsbury, ed. *The Encyclopedia of Country Music*. New York: Oxford, 1998. 481–482.

Cooper, Peter. "Jimmy C. Newman, Cajun Country Pioneer, Dies at 86." http://www.tennessean.com/story/entertainment/music/2014/06/22/jimmy-c-newman-obituary/11232265/, accessed December 4, 2014.

Ewing, Tom, ed. *The Bill Monroe Reader*. Urbana: University of Illinois Press, 2000.

Fleischhauer, Carl, and Neil V. Rosenberg. *Bluegrass Odyssey*. Urbana: University of Illinois Press, 2001.

Gagné, Richard. "Ralph Rinzler, Folklorist: Professional Biography." *Folklore Forum* 27.1 (1996): 20–49.

Goldsmith, Thomas, ed. *The Bluegrass Reader*. Urbana: University of Illinois Press, 2004.

Hickerson, Joseph C. Foreword in Guthrie T. Meade with Dick Spottswood and Douglas S. Meade, *Country Music Sources: A Biblio-Discography of Com-*

mercially Recorded Traditional Music. Chapel Hill: Southern Folklife Collection, UNC, 2002. ix–x.

Hustvedt, Sigurd Bernhard. *Ballad Books and Ballad Men.* Cambridge: Harvard University Press, 1930.

Johnston, Richard. "Obituary: Guitar Dealer Jon Lundberg." http://www.fret boardjournal.com/features/online/obituary-guitar-dealer-jon-lundberg, accessed November 4, 2015.

Lawless, John, with Richard Thompson. "Roger Smith Passes." http://bluegrass today.com/roger-smith-passes/, accessed May 23, 2013.

Machado, Adam. Text, Arhoolie CD/Book 518, *Hear Me Howling!* n.p. Arhoolie, n.d. (second printing 2011).

Malone, Bill C. *Bill Clifton: America's Bluegrass Ambassador to the World.* Urbana: University of Illinois Press, 2016.

———. *Music from the True Vine: Mike Seeger's Life and Musical Journey.* Chapel Hill: University of North Carolina Press, 2011.

McIntyre, Les. Notes, *The Country Gentlemen on the Road (and More).* Smithsonian Folkways SFW CD 40133, 2001.

Pearson, Julia. "Life with Dale Bessire." *Our Brown County.* http://www.our browncounty.com/0912s3.htm, accessed November 24, 2014.

Rosenberg, Neil V. *Bluegrass: A History.* Urbana: University of Illinois Press, 2005.

———. "From the Sound Recordings Review Editor: Bluegrass Today." *Journal of American Folklore* 105 (1992): 459–470.

———. "Picking Myself Apart: A Hoosier Memoir." *Journal of American Folklore* 108 (1995): 277–286.

———. "Weekend Folk Festival." *Oberlin [College] Review* (May 12, 1961): 2, 4.

———, ed. *Transforming Tradition: Folk Music Revivals Examined.* Urbana: University of Illinois Press, 1993.

Rounder Collective (Ken Irwin, Marian Leighton, Bill Nowlin) and Dick Spottswood. Notes, *The Early Days of Bluegrass, Volume 2.* Rounder 1014, 1975.

Scruggs, Earl. *Earl Scruggs and the 5-String Banjo.* New York: Peer International, 1968.

Smith, L. Mayne. "Bluegrass as a Musical Style." *Autoharp: Organ of the Folksong Club of the University of Illinois* III.3 (February 8, 1963): n.p.

———, Review of *Bluegrass Breakdown* by Robert Cantwell. *JEMF Quarterly* 20 (1984): 3–38.

Spencer, Walter. "Folk Music Is Everywhere." *Indianapolis Sunday Times,* April 14, 1963. 31.

Tribe, Ivan M. *The Stonemans: An Appalachian Family and the Music that Shaped Their Lives.* Urbana: University of Illinois Press, 1993.

Von Schmidt, Eric, and Jim Rooney. *Baby Let Me Follow You Down.* Garden City, N.Y.: Anchor, 1979.

Wald, Elijah. "Jesse Fuller Profile" [originally published in *Acoustic Guitar*]. http://www.elijahwald.com/bluarch.html, accessed March 25, 2013.

Wilgus, D. K. *Anglo-American Folksong Scholarship since 1898*. New Brunswick, N.J.: Rutgers University Press, 1959.

Wilson, Jerry. Wilson website. http://wilstar.com/ky-ramb, accessed January 22, 2010.

Credits

General Index

Hedrick, Marvin, xi, 135, 140, 142, 171, 182, 191, 192, 222, 233, 235, 249n2; guitar style, 84; Jamboree manager, 196, 206, 235, 242; Jamboree sound system, 182–83, 196; jam sessions, 38, 71, 83–86; performer, 236; tape recordings, 85–87, 196, 249
Hee Haw (TV program), 151
Helms, Bobby, xi, 173, 176, 178–79, 193
Hensley, Tom, 47, 86, 89, 90, 92, 97, 132, 179
Hensley, Walter, 6, 78, 117
Hickerson, Joe, xi, 10–11, 48, 97, 124–25, 132, 159, 161, 175
Hickory Records, 226
High Lonesome Sound, 237
Hildebrand, Greg, 125, 132
Hillman, Chris, 160
Hoffman, Frank A., 48–49, 55–57, 61, 68, 72; photographer, 62
Holly, Buddy, 45, 134, 184
Hoosier Folklore Society, 226
Hoppers, Lonnie, 121
Howard, Harlan, 188
Hughes, Randy, 134
Hyden, KY, 225

Indiana Motor Truck Association, 106
Indianapolis, IN, 26, 37, 40, 140, 141. *See also* WGEE (radio station: Indianapolis, IN)
Indianapolis Star, 19
Indianapolis Times, 139, 182
Indiana University: folk music scene, 6, 11, 35, 48, 124, 159
Indiana University Archives of Folk and Primitive Music, 92–93
Indiana University Archives of Traditional Music, 236, 246
Indiana University Folksong Club (IUFC), 124, 126, 138, 166–67, 177, 184; concerts, 132, 171, 229, 233
Introduction to Bluegrass, 237
IUFC. *See* Indiana University Folk Club
IUFC Newsletter, 138, 224, 241

Jackson, Stonewall, 208
Jacobsen, Erik "Jake," 90, 91, 124
Jaynes, Mitch, 236
J. D. Crowe and the New South (Rounder 0044, 1975), x
Jefferson, Thomas, 30
Jim & Jesse, 11, 32, 58, 115–18, 120, 226–28
Jim Denny Artist Bureau, 34, 173
Jimmie Skinner Music, 4
Johnson, Hack, 87
Johnson County Ramblers, 44
jokes, 24, 70, 133; parrot, 133, 138, 226
Jones, George, 57, 151
Jones, Grandpa, 102, 184–85, 190–92, 241
Journal of American Folklore, 73, 237

Keil, Charlie, 140
Keith, Leslie, 41
Keith, William Bradford "Bill"/"Brad," 135–37, 140, 142, 159, 219, 227; banjo style, 141, 144, 160, 198, 205, 221
Keithly, Jocko, 63, 68–69
Keith tuners. *See under* banjo
Kelley Brothers, 85
Kennedy, John: assassination, 233
Kentucky Colonels, 203
Kentucky Ramblers, 44
King, Claude, 147
Kingston Trio, 186
Knob Lick Upper Ten Thousand, 124, 131
KPFA-FM (radio station: Berkeley, CA), 2, 5, 8
Kuykendall, Pete, 74, 83

Land, Mitchell, 37
Lead Belly. *See* Ledbetter, Huddie "Lead Belly"
LeBlanc, Shorty, 185
Ledbetter, Huddie "Lead Belly," 2
Lee, Bernard, 84, 86
Leinenweber, Charlie, 11, 15–16
Liberty Records, 34, 145
Lilly Brothers, 16, 32
Lindley, David, 160
Lineberger, Don, 236–37

Scruggs, Louise, 113
Scruggs tuners. *See under* banjo
Seeger, Mike, 4, 8–9, 78, 80, 83, 105, 119, 219, 233; producer, 6, 15, 58, 78, 150
Seeger, Peggy, 1
Seeger, Pete, 1, 30, 53
Sharp, Cecil, 73
Sharrett, Ritchie, 5
Sheehan, Shorty. *See* Shehan, Shorty
Shehan, Juanita, 23, 35, 72
Shehan, Shorty, 25, 35, 45, 140, 251n2; Blue Grass Boy, 16, 23, 25, 38–40, 56, 72, 176
Shehan, Shorty & Juanita, xi, 16–18, 39, 72, 104; performances, 23–25, 36, 54, 92, 98, 142–43, 185, 198–99; recording, 35, 37, 76, 104–5; stories about other performers, 38, 41, 75, 176, 179, 184
Shelton, Allen, 116
Shelton, B. F., 89
Shelton, Robert, 80
Shenandoah Valley Trio, 53–54, 56, 61, 62, 170
Shepard, Jean, 195–96, 199
show cards (posters), 45, 93, 114, 188
Shubb, Rick, 80, 203
Siegel, Pete, 165
Silver Spur. *See* Ragsdale, Denzel "Silver Spur"
Silverstein, Harry, 164
Sing Out!, 48, 89, 133, 162
Smiley, Red, 102, 114
Smith, Arthur "Fiddlin' Arthur," 221
Smith, Bobby, 16, 54, 56–57, 61, 62, 64
Smith, Happy, 43
Smith, Harry, 73–74, 76, 150
Smith, Mayne, 30, 120, 138, 155, 159, 167, 202, 236; academics, 90, 132, 235, 237, 240; band activity, 5, 8, 80, 97–98, 106, 124, 132, 135, 203–4; banjo player, 2, 4, 30; Dobro player, 100–101, 120–21; graduate work, 235
Smith, Roger, xi, 40–43, 119, 143, 194, 196, 207, 222, 235, 242; banjo player, 42, 70–71, 141, 214; Blue Grass Boy, 43, 159, 170, 230, 236, 237; fiddler, 100–

101, 119–22, 147–48, 196, 207, 221, 236; music teacher, 86, 183, 242
Smithsonian/Folkways Records, 246
Smoak, Jim, 87
Songs from the Depression, 105
sound systems, 183
Specht, Phil, 5
Spencer, Walt, 139, 182, 253n3
square dancing, 69, 197
Stanley, Ralph: banjo style, 2, 90, 91
Stanley Brothers, x, 7, 15, 24, 58, 85, 90, 111, 147; repertoire, 89
Starday Records, 6, 7, 40, 77–79, 80, 100, 115, 140, 150–53
Stoneman, Donna, 151–53
Stoneman, George V. "Pop," 150–52
Stoneman, Jim, 151
Stoneman, Roni, 151
Stoneman, Scott, 152–53
Stoneman, Van, 152
Stoneman Family, 150–53, 164
Story, Carl, 44
Story, Dwain, 124
Stover, Don, 16, 32, 153
Stringbean, 99, 100, 113, 144
Stripling, Chick, 90
Stroud, Toby, 87
Stuart, Joe, 85–87, 195, 197, 200, 229, 230, 242
Sunset Park (Oxford, PA), 6, 45
Sutherland, David, 116

Tanner, Gid, & the Skillet Lickers, 205
tape recording, 85–87, 245–47
tape recordings, trading, 32, 72, 83, 115
Taylor, Earl, & the Stoney Mountain Boys, 6, 58, 78
Taylor, Red, 144
Terry, Gordon, 39–40, 87, 176, 178–81
Terry, Sonny, & Brownie McGhee, 1
Terrytown (Loretto, TN), 180
Thibodeaux, Rufus, 185
Thomas, John, 2
Thompson, Bobby, 32, 54, 115–16
Todd, Bob, 174, 178, 182, 184

Song Title Index

NEIL V. ROSENBERG is Professor Emeritus of Folklore at Memorial University of Newfoundland. He is the author of *Bluegrass: A History* and coauthor of *Bluegrass Odyssey* and *The Music of Bill Monroe*.

MUSIC IN AMERICAN LIFE

Record Makers and Breakers: Voices of the Independent Rock 'n' Roll Pioneers
John Broven
Music of the First Nations: Tradition and Innovation in Native North America
Edited by Tara Browner
Cafe Society: The Wrong Place for the Right People   *Barney Josephson,*
with Terry Trilling-Josephson
George Gershwin: An Intimate Portrait   *Walter Rimler*
Life Flows On in Endless Song: Folk Songs and American History
Robert V. Wells
I Feel a Song Coming On: The Life of Jimmy McHugh   *Alyn Shipton*
King of the Queen City: The Story of King Records   *Jon Hartley Fox*
Long Lost Blues: Popular Blues in America, 1850–1920   *Peter C. Muir*
Hard Luck Blues: Roots Music Photographs from the Great Depression
Rich Remsberg
Restless Giant: The Life and Times of Jean Aberbach and Hill and
Range Songs   *Bar Biszick-Lockwood*
Champagne Charlie and Pretty Jemima: Variety Theater in the
Nineteenth Century   *Gillian M. Rodger*
Sacred Steel: Inside an African American Steel Guitar Tradition
Robert L. Stone
Gone to the Country: The New Lost City Ramblers and the Folk Music Revival
Ray Allen
The Makers of the Sacred Harp   *David Warren Steel with Richard H. Hulan*
Woody Guthrie, American Radical   *Will Kaufman*
George Szell: A Life of Music   *Michael Charry*
Bean Blossom: The Brown County Jamboree and Bill Monroe's
Bluegrass Festivals   *Thomas A. Adler*
Crowe on the Banjo: The Music Life of J. D. Crowe   *Marty Godbey*
Twentieth Century Drifter: The Life of Marty Robbins   *Diane Diekman*
Henry Mancini: Reinventing Film Music   *John Caps*
The Beautiful Music All Around Us: Field Recordings and the
American Experience   *Stephen Wade*
Then Sings My Soul: The Culture of Southern Gospel Music
Douglas Harrison
The Accordion in the Americas: Klezmer, Polka, Tango, Zydeco, and More!
Edited by Helena Simonett
Bluegrass Bluesman: A Memoir   *Josh Graves, edited by Fred Bartenstein*
One Woman in a Hundred: Edna Phillips and the Philadelphia Orchestra
Mary Sue Welsh
The Great Orchestrator: Arthur Judson and American Arts Management
James M. Doering

The University of Illinois Press
is a founding member of the
Association of American University Presses.

Text designed by Jim Proefrock
Composed in 10.5/13.5 Adobe Caslon Pro
with Avenir display
at the University of Illinois Press
Cover designed by Faceout, Inc.
Cover illustration: October 15, 1961. Benny
Martin's Caddy parked at the back of the
Brown County Jamboree barn. (Courtesy of
Ann Milousoroff)
Manufactured by Sheridan Books, Inc.

University of Illinois Press
1325 South Oak Street
Champaign, IL 61820-6903
www.press.uillinois.edu